JOHNSON, WRITING, AND MEMORY

Johnson, Writing, and Memory demonstrates the importance of memory in Samuel Johnson's œuvre. Greg Clingham argues that this is a notion of memory that is derived from the process of historical and creative writing, and is found to be embodied in works of literature and other cultural forms. He examines Johnson's writing, including his biographical writing, as it intersects with eighteenth-century thought on literature, history, fiction, and law, and in its subsequent compatibility with, and resistance to, modern theory. Clingham's widely researched study provides an account of Johnson's intellectual positions that incorporates the challenges they pose to recent critical theory, and argues for Johnson's inclusion in a new theorization of terms such as "authority," "nature," and "memory." Clingham does this work of intellectual abstraction while remaining focused in the concrete realities of Johnson's writing itself, offering a theoretically nuanced and original account of Johnson's work.

GREG CLINGHAM is Professor of English and Director of the University Press at Bucknell University. He has written and co-written several books, including *Questioning History: The Postmodern Turn to the Eighteenth Century* (1998), *Making History: Textuality and the Forms of Eighteenth-Century Culture* (1998), *The Cambridge Companion to Samuel Johnson* (Cambridge, 1997), and *Literary Transmission and Authority: Dryden and Other Writers* (Cambridge, 1993).

JOHNSON, WRITING, AND MEMORY

GREG CLINGHAM
Bucknell University

CAMBRIDGE
UNIVERSITY PRESS

PUBLISHED BY THE PRESS SYNDICATE OF THE UNIVERSITY OF CAMBRIDGE
The Pitt Building, Trumpington Street, Cambridge, United Kingdom

CAMBRIDGE UNIVERSITY PRESS
The Edinburgh Building, Cambridge CB2 2RU, UK
40 West 20th Street, New York, NY 10011-4211, USA
477 Williamstown Road, Port Melbourne, VIC 3207, Australia
Ruiz de Alarcón 13, 28014 Madrid, Spain
Dock House, The Waterfront, Cape Town 8001, South Africa

http://www.cambridge.org

© Greg Clingham 2002

This book is in copyright. Subject to statutory exception
and to the provisions of relevant collective licensing agreements,
no reproduction of any part may take place without
the written permission of Cambridge University Press.

First published 2002

Printed in the United Kingdom at the University Press, Cambridge

Typeface Baskerville Monotype 11/12.5 pt   *System* LaTeX 2$_\varepsilon$ [TB]

A catalogue record for this book is available from the British Library

ISBN 0 521 81611 4 hardback

*For my mother, Aileen Zimmermann;
my wife, Merrill David;
and my daughters –
Eden Jaia Clingham-David and Brontë Francesca Clingham-David*

Contents

Acknowledgments		*page* viii
List of abbreviations		x
	Introduction: Johnson and authority	1
1	Johnson and memory	14
2	Johnson and nature	36
3	Law, narrative, and memory	60
4	Narrative, history, and memory in the *Lives of the Poets*	89
5	Translation and memory in the *Lives of the Poets*	122
6	Historiographical implications	158
Notes		168
Bibliography		202
Index		216

Acknowledgments

This book has been long – perhaps too long – in the making and many people have influenced its evolution and composition. For conversation, advice, criticism, and support I am grateful to Paul Alkon, Michael Chappell, Merrill David, John Drozd, Howard Erskine-Hill, the late John Fletcher-Harris, Clement Hawes, David Hopkins, Kathleen Nulton Kemmerer, Paul J. Korshin, the late Christopher Macgregor, the late H. A. Mason, John Mason, Tom Mason, Earl Miner, John Newton, Fred Parker, Michael Payne, Claude Rawson, Cedric Reverand, Marc Ricciardi, Christopher Ricks, Philip Sicker, Philip Smallwood, Simon Varey, and Howard Weinbrot. Stephen Fix, J. Paul Hunter, Clifford Siskin, and John Sitter – initially anonymous readers on a review panel – read an earlier, much longer version of this book, and to them I am indebted for their vote of confidence as well as for their collective eagle eye which drew my attention to various aspects of the manuscript, both small and large, that needed attention – a process of honing and improvement that was loudly echoed by the critical rigor and boldness of the still-anonymous readers for the Press.

Above all, I would like to thank my friend Phil Smallwood for the great generosity of spirit and critical intelligence with which he has read my work over the last several years.

The editors at Cambridge University Press have shown extraordinary patience, tact, and acumen during long periods while this work was in progress: I am grateful to Kevin Taylor, Josie Dixon, and especially to Linda Bree, who kept my courage to the sticking place, and who herself courageously and consistently stayed with this project when all seemed lost.

As my sense of the compelling and rewarding nature of Johnson's writing deepened and changed over time, I found myself formulating and reformulating many of my ideas in response to the demands of a modern interdisciplinary curriculum, and the interests – and resistance – of my students, and in part it is with their fresh, urgent, and mostly unformulated perspectives in mind that I have finally brought this book to a close to make its own way in the world.

My work on Johnson, Boswell, and related matters has benefited from the institutional support of Fordham University, Bucknell University, and the National Endowment for the Humanities. While working on this book I was appointed to the NEH Chair in the Humanities at Bucknell, an honor which not only recognized my past work but also gave me generous new opportunities for research. I owe a particular debt of gratitude to Dan Little, the former Vice President for Academic Affairs, Genie Gerdes, the Dean of Arts and Sciences, and to successive English Department Chairs (Michael Payne, Dennis Baumwoll, and John Rickard) at Bucknell University for continuing financial support, course releases, and a full sabbatical during which I completed this book. Their goodwill and enlightened perspectives have allowed me to work in the fancied yet quite real hope that the liberal arts ideal of the scholar–teacher is at least partially realizable.

For assistance in a wide range of bibliographical matters I wish to thank the staff of the Cambridge University Library, the Pierpont Morgan Library, The Victoria and Albert Museum Library, the Berg Collection of the New York Public Library (especially the late Lola Szladits), the Johnson Museum Trust, the Duane Library at Fordham University, and the Bertrand Library at Bucknell University.

For permission to rework previous publications I wish to thank *The Age of Johnson, Modern Language Studies, English,* and Cambridge University Press.

Finally, it is with the sweetest pleasure and a full sense of my tremendous good fortune that I recall the love and support I have enjoyed from my family during the years on which I worked at this particular project. The origins of this book predate the birth of my daughters, Jaia and Frankie, and little did they know, poor dears, that by their second birthday they would be distinguishing between Sam Johnson and his seventeenth-century namesake! Their involvement, all, has humanized *Johnson, Writing, and Memory* for me in incalculable and precious ways.

Abbreviations

JOHNSON

The Yale Edition of the Works of Samuel Johnson, ed. Allen T. Hazen et al. (New Haven: Yale University Press, 1958–)

DPA	*Diaries, Prayers, and Annals*, ed. E. L. McAdam, Jr. with Donald and Mary Hyde (1958).
Idler	*The Idler and The Adventurer*, ed. W. J. Bate, John M. Bullitt, and L. F. Powell (1963).
Adventurer	*The Idler and the Adventurer*, ed. W. J. Bate, John M. Bullitt, and L. F. Powell (1963).
Rambler III–V	*The Rambler*, ed. W. J. Bate and Albrecht B. Strauss, 3 vols. (1969).
Shakespeare	*Johnson on Shakespeare*, ed. Arthur Sherbo, with introduction by Bertrand H. Bronson, 2 vols. (1968).
Sermons	*Sermons*, ed. Jean Hagstrum and James Gray (1978).
Journey	*A Journey to the Western Islands of Scotland*, ed. Mary Lascelles (1971).
Political Writings	*Political Writings*, ed. Donald J. Greene (1977).
Rasselas	*Rasselas and Other Tales*, ed. Gwin J. Kolb (1990).
Critical Heritage	*Johnson: The Critical Heritage*, ed. James T. Boulton (London: Routledge and Kegan Paul, 1971).
Dictionary	*A Dictionary of the English Language*, 1st edn (1755) and 4th edn (1773), ed. Anne McDermott. CD-ROM (Cambridge University Press, 1996).
EB	*The Early Biographies of Samuel Johnson*, ed. OM Brack, Jr, and Robert E. Kelley (Iowa City: University of Iowa Press, 1974).

Letters	*The Letters of Samuel Johnson*. The Hyde Edition, ed. Bruce Redford, 5 vols. (Princeton University Press, 1992–94).
Lives	*Lives of the English Poets*, ed. G. B. Hill, 3 vols. (Oxford: Clarendon Press, 1905).
JM	*Johnsonian Miscellanies*, ed. G. B. Hill, 2 vols. (Oxford: Clarendon Press, 1897).
Poems	*The Poems of Samuel Johnson*, ed. David Nichol Smith and Edward L. McAdam, 2nd edn (Oxford: Clarendon Press, 1974).
P&D	*Johnson's Prefaces and Dedications*, ed. Allen T. Hazen (1937; Port Washington, NY: Kennikat Press, 1973).
SJ	*Samuel Johnson: The Oxford Authors*, ed. Donald Greene (Oxford and New York: Oxford University Press, 1984).

BOSWELL

Life	*The Life of Samuel Johnson, LL.D., with a Journal of a Tour to the Hebrides*, ed. G. B. Hill, rev. L. F. Powell, 6 vols. (Oxford: Clarendon Press, 1934–64).
Journal	*Boswell's Journal of a Tour to the Hebrides with Samuel Johnson 1773*, ed. Frederick A. Pottle and Charles H. Bennett (New York: McGraw-Hill, 1961).
Hawkins	Sir John Hawkins, *The Life of Samuel Johnson, LL.D.* 2nd edn (London, 1787).

DRYDEN

Dryden: *Poems*	*The Poems of John Dryden*, ed. James Kinsley, 4 vols. (Oxford: Clarendon Press, 1970).
Watson	*John Dryden: Of Dramatic Poesy and Other Critical Essays*, ed. George Watson, 2 vols. (London: Dent, 1962).

POPE

TE 1–10	*The Twickenham Edition of the Works of Alexander Pope*. General Editor: John Butt, 10 vols. (London: Methuen, 1951–67).

GENERAL

AJ	*The Age of Johnson: A Scholarly Annual*
BJECS	*British Journal for Eighteenth-Century Studies*
Companion	*The Cambridge Companion to Samuel Johnson*, ed. Greg Clingham (Cambridge University Press, 1997, 1999).
CQ	*The Cambridge Quarterly*
ECL	*Eighteenth-Century Life*
ECS	*Eighteenth-Century Studies*
ECTI	*Eighteenth Century: Theory and Interpretation*
ELH	*English Literary History*
JEGP	*Journal of English and Germanic Philology*
JHI	*Journal of the History of Ideas*
MLR	*Modern Language Review*
MP	*Modern Philology*
NQ	*Notes and Queries*
PMLA	*Publications of the Modern Language Association of America*
PQ	*Philological Quarterly*
RES	*Review of English Studies*
SECC	*Studies in Eighteenth-Century Culture*
SLI	*Studies in the Literary Imagination*
TLS	*Times Literary Supplement*

INTRODUCTION

Johnson and authority

The question of authority is a subject of almost all criticism devoted to the life and writing of Samuel Johnson. This book attempts to identify a specific kind of Johnsonian authority arising from a structure of memory governing most if not all of Johnson's writing, most clearly exemplified in the *Lives of the Poets*. In biography, authority and memory are functions of Johnson's narrative, especially in the various ways in which his engagement of the lives and writings of specific writers enables his reflection on history, literary history, and time. Within a complex nexus of different moral, political, linguistic, and historical discourses, the *Lives*, I will argue, constitutes (in the words of Pierre Nora) *les lieux de mémoire*,[1] a sophisticated attitude toward time and historiography that newly contextualizes Johnson within eighteenth-century and modern discourses about fiction and history.

William Hamilton's much-quoted words on the death of Johnson – "He has made a chasm, which not only nothing can fill up, but which nothing has a tendency to fill up"[2] – is only one of the earliest expressions of the kind of unique and natural power that Johnson represented for his contemporaries, that commentators have grappled with ever since. This power was invariably seen as intellectual and moral. Drawing upon images of Milton's paradise and Johnson's own Happy Valley, Hester Thrale, for example, described Johnson's mind as "indeed expanded beyond the common limits of human nature, and stored with such variety of knowledge, that I used to think it resembled a royal pleasure-ground, where every plant, of every name and nation, flourished in the full perfection of their powers, and where, though lofty woods and falling cataracts first caught the eye, and fixed the earliest attention of beholders, yet neither the trim parterre nor the pleasing shrubbery, nor even the antiquated ever-greens, were denied a place in some fit corner of this happy valley."[3] And for Boswell, Johnson's intellectual power resided not only in the range and comprehensiveness of his knowledge but, specifically, in his powers of language, both written and spoken, and in the moral caste of his sentiments: "his superiority over other learned men consisted chiefly in what may be called the art of thinking, the art of using his mind; a certain continual power of seizing the useful substance of all that he knew, and exhibiting it in a clear and forcible manner; so that knowledge, which we often see to be no better than lumber in men of dull understanding, was, in him, true, evident, and actual wisdom."[4]

It is remarkable how many of Boswell's terms form the basis of Johnson's reputation and authoritative status among scholars of the twentieth century: the extensive and varied knowledge; the powerful and incisive intellect; the readiness, clarity, and aptness of expression; the moral nature of his thinking; the knowledge of real life; the wisdom arising from all the above. This bold, realistic, and seemingly self-articulated image of Johnson was once thought to be mainly the work of Boswell's biography, but it has become increasingly clear of late that the image of the cultural icon, representative of the "Age of Johnson," was due to a broad cultural and journalistic activity extending from the 1780s through the nineteenth century.[5] Indeed, Boswell's critical terms of evaluation have shaped the great opinion-forming scholarly studies of Johnson's writing during the twentieth century;[6] and at the end of the twentieth century Harold Bloom finds recourse to precisely the same terms as Boswell does in designating his sense of the importance of Johnson's "cognitive power, learning, and wisdom, [and] . . . the splendor of his literary personality"[7] in literary history. Bertrand Bronson's notion of the two traditions within which Johnson was formerly thought to have come down to us – the popular (privileging his conversation as a means of knowing the "man") and the academic (privileging the works as means of doing the same thing)[8] – has been untenable for a long time because it concedes too much to the weaker side of Boswell's biographical enterprise, the myth-making, as a guide to what can be critically thought and known about Johnson at all.

Although a man of compelling interest for the religious tensions that characterized a life of spiritual exemplariness, it is clear that Johnson's authority has consistently been implicated in his life of writing. Johnson has been seen to embody the quintessential qualities of modern authorship.[9] Hart, however, would have the inauguration of an "Age of Johnson," and the continuing scholastic habit of privileging Johnson's character (as a *sui generis* rather than contingent entity) over his writing, as a sign of the *inevitable* supremacy of Boswell's writing over Johnson's in memorializing

Johnson and fostering his proper authority. But, while Johnson's character is a legitimate and real subject of interest in literary criticism or biography, it is salutary to remember that it is Johnson's writing – specifically, his being a great author – which occasions Boswell's interest *in* Johnson's life and personality in the first place. Before he meets Johnson in 1763, Boswell explains: "I had for several years read his works with delight and instruction, and had the highest reverence for their author, which had grown up in my fancy into a kind of mysterious veneration,"[10] and the *Life of Johnson* is peppered with remarks to the effect that "I profess myself to have ever entertained a profound veneration for the astonishing force and vivacity of mind which *The Rambler* exhibits" (1, 213).

For Boswell, Johnson's writings in general display a continuing struggle and reconciliation between nature and grace, and he consequently constructs a portrait of Johnson as a Christian hero who passes through fear, doubt, and the dark night of the soul to emerge at the end (of the *Life of Johnson*) in repentance and tranquility. For Walter Jackson Bate, for example, Johnson's writings in general enact the psychological and moral drama of the melancholic and guilty self, in opposition with itself, and consequently *he* constructs a character for Johnson that emphasizes heroic and exemplary self-scrutiny, honesty, and self-transcendence.[11] It seems that the *kind* of author one takes Johnson to be continues to shape the kind of authority one sees Johnson as representing or as having possessed. The idea of authorship has now been thoroughly historicized, and shown by many scholars to pertain to both sociological and linguistic, as well as to ontological characteristics within a larger historical, economic and social matrix of influences in the seventeenth and eighteenth centuries.[12] Alvin Kernan squarely identifies Johnson's authority and professional identity with authorship and with the proliferation of print technology, though Kernan (like other critics) believes that it was Boswell who made Johnson into the "literary type that he is, the towering and highly charged image of the first writer in the industrial, democratic, rationalistic age of print."[13] Yet, Johnson's authorial agency and autonomy have been problematized by various studies emphasizing the rhetorical and politically compromised nature of his authority.

In 1983 John Barrell argued that Johnson's very notion of language was conditioned (and, by implication, severely limited) by his adherence to a specific conservative politics and his belonging to a particular social class, so that, as he worked on the *Dictionary*, or engaged in political debate, or offered literary judgments, he operated on the principle of an analogy between proper government and proper language. The maintenance, therefore, of "just" or "polite" language and letters in English society entailed a series of rhetorical ploys on Johnson's part to ensure that only certain voices and perspectives were heard and seen, and these were the values and texts that Johnson's considerable authority helped naturalize and canonize.[14] Those rhetorical ploys have attracted much attention. For Tim Fulford, Martin Wechselblatt, and Fredric Bogel, Johnson's rhetoric (rather than his "writing") is the basis of his authority. Fulford, working within a broadly Foucaultian framework, believes that it is called out in relation to his threatened sense of power, such as occurs when he is faced with the variety and imaginativeness of the works of Shakespeare or Milton, or with the sublimity of the Scottish landscape, or with the authenticity of the Ossianic oral culture – or with the independence of women. In each of these cases, we are told, Johnson wields his descriptive language as a weapon, so as to control the otherness of his subject matter, rhetorically enforcing his own "power as master of order and right in language" and "reproduc[ing] the actual social and property relations of contemporary Britain."[15] Johnson's "authority," in other words, is unfounded, or at least "usurped" or "appropriated" – certainly, a lesser thing than we have hitherto thought.

Bogel and Wechselblatt approach the question of Johnson's authority from what might be described as a Habermasian point of view, emphasizing the performative and public aspect of self and authority, and their place in the broader network of social discourses.[16] While their different accounts of Johnson's rhetorical construction of authorial identity are more engaged than Fulford's, they exemplify a common theoretical resistance to Johnson's practice that limits their usefulness, but which, at the same time, goes to the heart of my interest in Johnson's writing. For both critics, authority is ambiguous in that it is both attributive and performative. Johnson is repeatedly described as "performing authority." The observation that Johnson himself was ambiguous about the mingling of the real and the fictive implied by performativity resonates with the received understanding of Johnson's sensitivity about the relations between what he called truth and fiction.

It seems, however, that Bogel and Wechselblatt are themselves ambivalent in ways that are not Johnson's. Although their terms are postmodern, they also betray a binary understanding when it comes to the components of the different terms comprising Johnson's rhetoric. Johnson's definitions of "authoritative" in the *Dictionary*, as well as his actual "performances," are invariably seen as conflicted. Johnson's first two definitions of "authoritative" are "having due authority" and "having an air of authority," "express[ing]," according to Wechselblatt, "an antithesis between the term's constative and performative meanings, as though that antithesis were, for Johnson, endemic to conceptualizing an authoritative action" (24). This leads to the conclusion that for Johnson authority "is alternately the actual signature of authority ... and merely its discursive representation, a positive application without prior origin in an a priori general principle," leading to a contradictoriness in his thinking, because "any self-assertion implies an absolute constative claim of authority, which then inevitably invites exposure as a mere performative" (25). For Bogel, similarly, Johnson "discloses the *inherently* dramatic or histrionic character of authority, and thus the space between the attributive and rhetorical aspects of authority" (*Dream of My Brother*, 62). Johnson's repeated display of imperfection and limitation is the repeated signaling of that which *compromises* full authority; display itself is deemed to be rhetorical, and thus conditioning a *mere* assumption of authority (ibid., 60–61).

However, these accounts of Johnson's performativity, which I have had to summarize at length, implicitly disclose a dichotomy between performance and possession that entirely undermines the critiques themselves. Why should Johnson's performance of authority (if one chooses to use such language) be described as "mere," and why is the "merely performative" *opposed* to the "real" possession and display of authority? What theoretical paradigm insists on this nominal division between a rhetorical *assumption* of authority (the "air of authority") and the actual *possession* of authority ("having due authority"), when the cultural materialism within which Bogel and Wechselblatt work presupposes the material and rhetorical nature of *all* forms of publically and personally constructed identities? The fact that the public sphere is (partly) rhetorical does not necessarily diminish its reality – it *is* always the public sphere – nor does it necessarily undermine a subject's capacity for action, since those are the *already* encoded and accepted contextual terms within which meaning is produced.

If one accepts Johnson's world as being thus linguistically and rhetorically constructed, then he appears to be more rather than less attuned to its dynamic than he has been described as being. Within such a world, Johnson's authority operates somewhat as subjects communicate in Stanley Fish's "interpretive communities," where "communication occurs within situations and ... to be in a situation is *already* to be in possession of (or to be possessed by) a structure of assumptions, of practices understood to be relevant in relation to purposes and goals that are already in place."¹⁷ This proposition is not so alien when applied to Johnson as the reader might think. When Boswell solicited Johnson's opinion on the ethics of legal rhetoric – specifically, on whether or not, and on what grounds, an advocate is justified in arguing a case he does not believe in or knows to be bad – Johnson's response addresses the morality of the issue as an *effect* of its rhetoric or textuality:

> Sir, you do not know it [the cause] to be good or bad till the Judge determines it. I have said that you are to state facts fairly; so that your thinking, or what you call knowing, a cause to be bad, must be from reasoning, must be from your supposing your arguments to be weak and inconclusive. But, Sir, that is not enough. An argument which does not convince yourself, may convince the Judge to whom you urge it; and if it does convince him, why, then, Sir, you are wrong, and he is right. (*Life*, II, 47)

In offering his advice, Johnson's rhetorical purposes are several. One purpose is to set up an appropriate contextual field within which the legal and moral questions are to be determined: hence the Judge is made the test and terminus of both legal argument *and* (surprisingly) moral responsibility. A second purpose is to exonerate the individual will from the inevitable taint of moral transgression so he can function effectively: hence Johnson's emphatic denial of Boswell's suggestion that an advocate's rhetoric is a form of "dissimulation" "by effecting a warmth when you have no warmth." Johnson responds to this idea by invoking the specifically rhetorical and textual nature of the advocate's argument: "Everybody knows you are paid for affecting warmth for your client; and it is, therefore, properly no dissimulation ... Sir, a man will no more carry the artifice of the bar into the common intercourse of society, than a man who is paid for tumbling on his hands will continue to tumble upon his hands when he should walk on his feet" (*Life*, II, 47–48)

This introduces a third function of Johnson's rhetoric, which is to naturalize the artifice of legal discourse. Advocacy for Johnson has a controversial and political dimension. Illustrating this aspect in his definition of "advocate," Johnson quotes Temple on the necessary connection between successful politics and good advocacy: "Of the several forms of government that have been, or are, in the world, that cause seems commonly the better, that has the better *advocate*, or is advantaged by fresher experience." To Boswell, Johnson's suggestion is that legal rhetoric is not only *not* culpable or dishonest, since it is the formal and appropriate mode of discourse for those at the bar, but, *within this context*, the advocate's very authority – and, therefore, the truth of his argument – depends on his artifice. Rhetorical efficacy – which, as Johnson reminds Boswell, is to be determined by the judge[18] – will reflect, indeed, create, the advocate's particular authority. That legal rhetoric is artificially produced or "performed" does not diminish the reality or the authenticity of the advocate's authority, because it meets the implicit terms and requirements of the specific social context, and because the legal apparatus determines what is and is not true. Resistant as we might be to such an idea – and to the suggestion that Johnson is complicit in such rhetorical strategies – Johnson himself seems to understand the notion of "truth" in this legal context much as it is described by Robert Weisberg: "Truth is not the property of an event; rather, it is the property of an account of an event."[19] Naturally, this does not mean that Johnson believed that there was no truth to be found in Boswell's dispute; just that it was to be found – that is, determined – via the performative rhetoric of the advocate. As with the advocate, so with the writer.[20]

It may be, then, that "the space between the attributive and rhetorical aspects of authority," to quote Bogel, *is* where Johnson locates authority, but his is not therefore two different kinds of authority, indicative of conflicting and mutually exclusive interpretive protocols, making for one more and one less real or present or potent than the other. His is *one* authority, reflecting one kind of reading and reasoning – albeit predicated on a broad understanding of cultural and linguistic difference, and which might take different forms. This is an authority whose nature is obviously complex, even hybrid, and indicating a mode of apprehending the world which holds together, in highly distinctive and meaningful ways, such different entities as truth and fiction, substance and performance, and history and memory. These propositions clearly need to be further discussed in the course of this book, for the notion of a rhetorically sophisticated Johnson who sees textuality as a part of (rather than opposed to) historical truth, finds little credibility today, even though the basic idea is common currency in historiography, the social sciences, and literary theory. Postcolonial and new historical contingents in eighteenth-century studies have found it nearly impossible to imagine a meaningful dialogue between Johnson, other eighteenth-century figures (whether canonical or otherwise) who have been theorized, and our present critical interests. Although Johnson has recently been the subject of several explicitly theoretical studies,[21] he continues to be identified by all and sundry as the *locus* of Enlightenment hegemony and an illiberal authoritativeness.[22]

Yet not only is authority for Johnson at once performative and real, it is part of the argument of this book that performativity and its attendant authority go to the root of his concepts of law, language, history, and memory. The foundation of the law for Johnson *was* language, on which his very sense of reality and of truth were based. The nexus between these fundamental aspects of his thought are suggested by the Preface to the *Dictionary*, which, though subscribing on one level to a positivistic lexicographical project of "fixing" the language, is remarkable for giving equal if not more weight to its historical and differential nature:

> I am not so lost in lexicography, as to forget that *words are the daughters of earth, and that sons are the things of heaven*. Language is only the instrument of science, and words are but the signs of ideas: I wish, however, that the instrument might be less apt to decay, and that signs might be permanent, like the things which they denote. (*SJ*, 310)

The conjunction in this passage of traditionally conceptualized sexual difference and historical linguistics seems to confirm a binary conception of knowledge. Like Locke, who is invoked here, Johnson seems to be saying that the content of knowledge is "Things as they are," and that the admission of language into that equation is a necessary inconvenience enforced by nature and custom. Not only did Locke explain the function of rhetoric as "nothing else but to insinuate wrong Ideas, move the Passions, and thereby mislead the Judgment; and so indeed are perfect cheat," but gendered such "Eloquence" as being "like the fair Sex, [it] has too prevailing Beauties in it, to suffer it self to be spoken against. And 'tis vain to find fault with those Arts of Deceiving, wherein Men find Pleasure to be Deceived."[23]

Yet Johnson clearly appropriates Locke's trope of figurative language as pleasurable and dangerous woman in order to revise his epistemology and idea of language. However much Johnson might *wish* for coincidence between words and things, for the unmediated presence of the things of the world, he knows that language does not function thus. Johnson's main point about "things" is that they are inaccessible to meaning without "words," and hence (with Locke) outside of their social context. While "things" might be identified as male and associated with "truth," truth actually cannot come into existence without the work of the female, "words." "Things" might be the signified object of discourse, but language, *what* signifies, turns out to be their origin. Rather than words being subordinate to ideas and things,[24] words are indispensable. The patriarchal conception of language (which subordinates it to science) is invoked here by the images and then revised, for Johnson is clear that "language is ... the instrument of science." That is, science (by which he means knowledge) cannot come into being without language, even though it might subsequently stand as if independent of language.

Johnson's point is conveyed by the tropological shape of his narrative of temporal (and social) change which seems to (but does not actually) gainsay his more explicit statement about the desirability of permanence:

> [I]t must be remembered, that while our language is yet living, and variable by the caprice of every one that speaks it, these words are hourly shifting their relations, and can no more be ascertained in a dictionary, than a grove, in the agitation of a storm, can be accurately delineated from its picture in the water. (*SJ*, 316)

The metaphoric shape of Johnson's sentence is highly rhetorical in accomplishing several overlapping aims at once. It draws a parallel between the realms of nature and language, and between art and dictionary-making, thereby dignifying lexicography and also excusing and explaining its limits. Moreover, the tone of the whole sentence exceeds its explicit statements, thus registering its own emotional resignation to general and natural forces, in spite of the opposition of the personal will. Finally, the poetic caste of the sentence is memorable and exemplary, and continues an important argument of the *Dictionary* as a whole. By exemplifying the operation of words within a specific context, as against the decontextualized space of definition, this passage performs like Johnson's quotations in the *Dictionary* to illustrate the definitions of individual words, of which he says: "The solution of all difficulties, and supply of all defects, must be sought in the examples subjoined to the various senses of each word, and ranged according to the time of their authors" (*SJ*, 318). Paradoxically, therefore, while language may be changing all the time, literature (as symbolized by and manifested in the quotations in the *Dictionary*) is a place in which "words" and "things" come into approximate relationship with each other, and make for a kind of permanence and accessibility, within historical change. The works on which Johnson draws for his quotations – literary as well as philosophical and theological works of the Renaissance, the Restoration, and the eighteenth century, including the King James version of the Bible – are among those that go towards comprising his canon.

It is generally agreed that Johnson's sense of his own literary authority, and his evolving understanding of and advocacy for a specifically English literary culture, are deeply woven into his endeavours at canon-formation, starting as early as *London* and culminating in the *Lives of the Poets*.[25] "Canon-making," Alvin Kernan remarks, "may be considered the central activity of letters, the principal way that a text-centred institution formally objectifies its reality, defines itself, and gives an aura to its primary writings" (*Impact of Print*, 158–59). However, the process of cultural memory implicit in canon-formation does not exhaust the historiographical dimension of Johnson's various literary enterprises, which rest, so I will be arguing, upon specific and conscious appropriations of memory, textuality, narrative, and law.

The definitions of "authority" in the *Dictionary* suggest in brief how Johnson's authority – or the particular kind of authority I wish to argue for – evolves out of the elements mentioned above. Six different yet related definitions are offered for the noun "authority," together with their different exemplary quotations, covering law, power, evidence, and testimony. A quotation from Sir William Temple for the first meaning ("legal power") suggests the relationship between these general phenomena: "Power arising from strength, is always in those that are governed, who are many; but authority arising from opinion, is in those that govern, who are few." While "opinion" is usually used by Johnson as a form of pseudo-knowledge (his *Dictionary* defines it as "perswasion of the mind, without proof or certain knowledge") it is clear that in the Temple quotation Johnson sees it as associated with authority as legal power. Reading the quotation against the mini-narrative constituted by the several quotations for "authority," "authority" seems to be what arises from the transformation of power through knowledge ("opinion"). Such a narrative of transformation informs many of Johnson's texts about knowledge, as it does in "Rambler" 92. Discussing there the relativity of the idea of literary beauty, Johnson defines the task of criticism as to "improve opinion into knowledge," and then proceeds to enact that procedure by "example and authority" in the body of the essay (IV, 121–22).

Many as the forms of knowledge are in Johnson's writing – corresponding, at least, to the different genres in which he wrote – the mnemonic–historical writing that is the primary subject of this book rests on three main propositions, to which I return repeatedly. The first is a matter of general principle, as expressed in "Rambler" 41, to the effect that "Memory is the purveyor of reason ... indeed, the faculty ... which may be said to place us in the class of moral agents" (III, 223). The second is an observation about methodology, to the effect that "men more frequently require to be reminded than informed."[26] Both of these propositions are encompassed by a general philosophical notion that "Memory is, among the faculties of the human mind, that of which we make the most frequent use, or rather that of which the agency is incessant or perpetual. Memory is the primary and fundamental power, without which there could be no other intellectual operation."[27] As epistemology, this last insight has something in common with the views of Locke and Hume, but my interest is not primarily in Johnson as a formal philosopher of mind (like Ryle or Quine) or as a literary theorist (like Derrida, de Man, or Hartman) – insofar as he might be these things – but as an imaginative writer who draws intelligently on the engrammatological tradition of Aristotle, Augustine, and Locke to produce highly memorable writing.

The above-mentioned interlinked principles underpin Johnson's handling of most aspects of historical experience. They make themselves felt in all his writings. I draw on many of his texts, and a wide range of contextual material, in order to suggest how memory within the Augustinian–Lockean tradition – and as defined in critical, legal, and narrative terms – functions as an organizing principle of Johnson's apprehension of time, human consciousness, and history. This structure of memory, and what might be called the associated hermeneutics of the "present," contribute to the formation of Johnson's sense of general nature, a flexibly conceived and applied critical standard by which he reads all manner of literature (chapters 1–3). A recurring motif in these chapters is the question of how the past is situated in Johnson's thought in relation to the present, and what the present *is* in terms of human experience. What are the contents of the present and how is it produced? What place does the present have in Johnson's biographical and historical enterprise? Why does it so often seem to occur in conjunction with Johnson's warmth of response to nature as a critical standard? What is the role of language, and especially of writing, in the production of *les lieux de mémoire*, which also seem repeatedly to arise in connection with the present?

Chapter 4 discovers these questions to be integral to the structure of memory in the *Lives of the Poets*, as exemplified mainly by the lives of Milton and Butler, the last two great epic writers in English for Johnson, though of contrasting kinds. My discussion in this chapter develops Johnson's notion of authorship as evolving out of the work by which a writer transforms, through the linguistic embodiment of memory, the materials of experience (both personal and historical) into something memorable. Literary character is part of Johnson's concept of authorship, and, as part of an author's memorability, this chapter traces some of the continuities and discontinuities between his concept of character and the developing realistic character of novelistic fiction. As before, the comparative and relational nature of Johnson's own writing (transcending the nominal generic boundaries between biography, criticism, and fiction) is important to the manner in which the literary characters of writers are felt to reveal (or not to reveal) themselves, and the fictive shape and meaning given to their lives as a whole by Johnson's narrative.

Chapter 5 argues for the translational quality of the *Lives* as a key aspect of their commemorative and engrammatological nature. The center of my attention here is the comparative lives of Dryden and Pope, the two great poets of Augustan culture whose epic status was achieved in translations, and whose intellectual idiom Johnson is often thought to share. Johnson's treatment of the lives and works of these two poets establishes two very different kinds of poetic engagement with the world and with language – crystalized by the contrasting notions of Dryden's comprehensiveness and Pope's artifice. Since Johnson saw their translations as constituting their most characteristic work, I use his readings of their respective translations of Homer's *Iliad* in order to clarify his sense of their relation to history and to memory, and also to articulate my sense of the *Lives* contribution to literary history.

That literary history is the subject of the sixth and final chapter, and I here argue for the existence of several different historical discourses in the *Lives*. One of those discourses (the most frequently remarked on) follows a teleological logic that sees literature progressing, and associates the formation of an English canon and national consciousness with the development of an Augustan poetics. Another, more interesting discourse finds the logic of progress to be disrupted or reversed by writers of nature – such as Shakespeare and Dryden – who are incorporated into the *Lives* as critical touchstones. Contrary to a widespread assumption, Pope does not represent a natural or teleological culmination for Johnson, but rather a success whose very refinement undercuts its own ideals – "to attempt any further improvement of versification will be dangerous"[28] – opening (somewhat as it does for Wordsworth in the 1798 and 1801 Prefaces) a linguistic and cultural gap for Johnson between history and his present. Thus I conclude that, while the narrative of memory in the *Lives* gives us access to a remembered and fictively imagined past, it cannot be equated with history. Rather, as deliberately constructed *lieux de mémoire*, the *Lives* stand between memory and history, drawing on both, having opened up a space for new relationships with language, and thereby with the past and the present. They thus resonate with the archaeological historicization of literate discourse that Foucault sees as distinguishing the late eighteenth century,[29] and ought to find their place in the broad historicization of all forms of eighteenth-century literature and culture that marks the most recent phase of scholarship.

Johnson, Writing, and Memory, however, does not intend to turn Johnson into a Foucaultian, Derridean, or a postcolonial critic, but rather to demonstrate the many productive ways in which his thinking and writing engage with our present historical and theoretical concerns. We should no longer permit ourselves to assume that we have the measure of Samuel Johnson, or that he simply exemplifies the absolutist or monolithic aspects of the Enlightenment – a constant embarrassment to our postmodern sympathies – and that he is therefore dispensable. Of course, Johnson's "engagement" is seldom anything so anaemic as to merely echo contemporary positions, so we should not expect an easy coincidence between Johnson's views and our views. We should expect Johnson's engagement with us to work more in terms of difference. We might, therefore, become more sensitive to the critical implications of his resistance to us; and by recognizing and exploring the dialectical tension between his positions and our own, we could historicize our own readings of and theoretical resistance to Johnson. Among other things, such an act of self-criticism on our part would recognize the strategic, even poetic function of limits in Johnson's thinking, for the limits of human consciousness, of history, and of work form certain boundary lines for Johnson, marking the horizons towards which his strongest thinking looks.[30] The paradox of limits is captured in Johnson's small but significant addition to Goldsmith's *The Traveller*: "How small, of all that human hearts endure, / That part which laws or kings can cause or cure" (lines 429–30).[31] Those limits mark the moral dimension of Johnson's thought, but also the legal framework. For, as James Boyd White remarks, the law in all of its historical and linguistic particularity is a means of making meaning within a world in which there are no moral absolutes, and of "creating a rhetorical community over time."[32]

CHAPTER I

Johnson and memory

By all accounts Johnson had an extraordinary memory. Boswell remarks on his "almost incredible" powers of memory as a small child, and Edmund Hector observed that as early as his school days Johnson's "memory [was] so tenacious, that whatever he read or heard he never forgot."[1] All of Johnson's contemporary biographers have stories about this strength of memory, and the precise terms of their commemoration deserve notice. The most commonly remarked on feature is Johnson's ability to retain in his mind over a period of time almost anything he had once heard or read.[2] This form of memory corresponds to Johnson's first definition in the *Dictionary*: "the power of retaining or recollecting things past; retention; reminiscence; recollection." The quotation from Locke offered to illustrate this definition, however, immediately problematizes the notion of memory as mere retention. As part of a larger argument about personal identity, to which I turn below, Locke's quotation proposes that "Memory is the power to revive again in our minds those ideas which after imprinting have disappeared, or have been laid out of sight." This introduces the paradoxical notion that the memory is able to retain ideas which are actually *absent* from the mind – either because they have "disappeared" or "been laid out of sight." Memory, from this perspective, seems to be a sophisticated engrammatological technology, an ironic, multiple, even duplicitous "power," "imprinting" that which is recollected, inventing that which is retained, and introducing a relationship of significant difference between Johnson's apparently interchangeable terms in this first definition of memory: retention, reminiscence, and recollection.

Johnson's early biographers echo this more complex, linguistically constructed understanding of memory as a power – perhaps *the* power – governing his intellectual life. For example, William Shaw observes that Johnson's "memory retained with exactness whatever his judgment had matured," considering memory as the product of knowledge rather than merely a faculty for retaining or recollecting information.[3] William Cooke, likewise, equates Johnson's memory with knowledge, but also describes it as an *instrument* of argumentation and insight. Describing the "amazing powers of [Johnson's] *memory*," Cooke remarks: "The great stores of learning which he laid in, in his youth, were not of that cumbrous and inactive quality, which we meet with in many who are called *great scholars*; for he could, at all times, draw bills upon this capital with the greatest security of being paid."[4] Cooke's formulation takes the form of a narrative in which memory is the unifying principle in Johnson's intellectual life: the study of his early years bear fruit in his later years, when he is able to draw on – that is, recollect – that learning in a display of mature authority. Such memory, according to Cooke, underwrote Johnson's argumentative supremacy: "When quotations were made against him in conversation, he either, by applying to the context, gave a different turn to the passage, or quoted from other parts of the same author, that which was more favourable to his own opinion" (*EB*, 130). Thus memory operates in Johnson's thinking very much in accordance with his third definition of the term in the *Dictionary*, "Time of knowledge," associated in the illustrative Milton quotation with "how first this world, and face of things, began" – that is, to a time "before thy memory."

Cooke's concatenation of ideas evidently resonated for Boswell because his account of Johnson's intellectual powers echoes Cooke's particular terms, though now as part of a more dramatic exploration of Johnson's life. For Boswell, Johnson's "superiority over other learned men consisted chiefly in what may be called the art of thinking, the art of using his mind; a certain continual power of seizing the useful substance of all that he knew, and exhibiting it in a clear and forcible manner; so that knowledge, which we often see to be no better than lumber in men of dull understanding, was, in him, true, evident, and actual wisdom" (*Life*, IV, 427–28). Seizing the useful substance of all that he knew took many forms for Johnson, all of which commanded extensive linguistic and recollective powers. Johnson not only has a good memory, in the passive pseudo-scientific sense of the word, but it is an active, constitutive, and self-reflexive principle that characterizes his best thinking. There are moments in which Johnson's thought becomes explicitly recollective and commemorative, such as the remarkable conclusion to the "Life of Smith," where Johnson's memory of Gilbert Walmsley acknowledges and overrides their political differences ("He was a Whig, with all the virulence and malevolence of his party; yet difference of opinion did not keep us apart") in order to record his learning and experience, and their companionship – and where the memory of Walmsley, in turn, enables the memory of Garrick, whose recent death "has eclipsed the gaiety of nations and impoverished the publick stock of harmless pleasure."[5] This mini-character of Walmsley suggests how whole works, such as the elegy on the death of Dr. Robert Levet and the *Lives of the Poets*, take a commemorative form. Memory as "memorial," "monumental record," and "exemption from oblivion" are among Johnson's definitions for the term in the *Dictionary*, and govern his sense of the work of writing.

Fundamental to acts of commemoration in Johnson's writing is a structure of thought and feeling that engages with fundamental questions of consciousness, time, and language. His wide-ranging interests in literature, history, and the human sciences repeatedly return the reader to questions of memory. As Johnson's use of Locke's quotation suggests, memory is the hinge of difference, and is at the cutting edge of his engagements with the otherness of historical experience, including the many lives of others he encountered in his biographies great and small. Difference is a key term in Johnson's writing: it might be said to condition his whole understanding of the relationships between the human mind and the natural world, between words and things, and to complicate his notions of presence and truth.

For Johnson, the mind's relations with the world and the self are inherently discrepant. It is perhaps only a slight oversimplification to say that all of his writing is conditioned by an understanding – developed from Locke's epistemology – that the mind, the heart, the world, and language all exist in distinct, though interrelated, dimensions. One does not have to read far in Johnson's writing to appreciate that it is not within the ordinary terms of human existence for these different dimensions to come together, that "[t]o take a view at once distinct and comprehensive of human life, with all its intricacies of combination, and varieties of connexion, is beyond the power of mortal intelligences." Like Montaigne and Hume, Johnson felt that the consequence of such rational limitation was to privilege experience – "we snatch a glimpse, we discern a point, and regulate the rest by passion, and by fancy."[6] Yet, Johnson's project is very different from that of Montaigne and Hume, for it is very prescient of some of the basic insights of psychoanalysis, in that the differential nexus of these experiential dimensions form the very site of human consciousness. Consciousness, and how and with what objects it is to be filled, is one of Johnson's great subjects, not only in the essays, but also in the political writings – where restlessness of mind is often seen to threaten political order – the biographies, and even in his lexicographical work. That "the natural flights of the human mind are not from pleasure to pleasure, but from hope to hope"[7] points to a residual state of mind, which, as in almost every scene of *Rasselas*, either leaves the mind empty without action ("That I want nothing... or that I know not what I want, is the cause of my complaint"), or the person active without thought ("He busied himself so intensely in visionary bustle, that he forgot his real solitude").[8]

Fundamental to Johnson's sense of the discrepancy of experiential phenomena is his understanding of the limits and the energies of the mind operating in dialogical relationship with one another. Human consciousness seems to be caught uneasily in a net of conflicting and overlapping claims; between that which we cannot fully know or grasp and that which we necessarily need to imagine and desire. As Johnson notes in "Rambler" 2, "as his powers are limited, he must use means for the attainment of his ends, and intend first what he performs last" (*Rambler*, III, 10). Johnson's sense of the mind's energies – frequently felt as operating in *excess* of rational structures and external objects – leads to two apparently contradictory observations about the nature of consciousness, whose combination actually produces some of Johnson's most powerful thinking. The first is that the excess of the mind – its ability to "contrive in minutes what we execute in years"[9] – is actually a sign of its spiritual and creative nature. The second is that the same excess of mind has the effect of undercutting a person's capacity for moral action and knowledge, because it takes the mind out of the present moment, and dulls the felt reality of experience. Not only is "that part of our duration very small of which we can truly call ourselves masters, or which we can spend wholly at our own choice,"[10] but once master of our moment in time we discover, as Johnson paraphrases Horace (*Satires*, I. I. lines 1–3), that "no man is pleased with his present state, which proves equally unsatisfactory... whether fallen upon by chance or chosen with deliberation."[11]

The intelligence and pressure under which these contradictory principles are brought together, distinguish Johnson from the positivistic and optimistic thrust of many other eighteenth-century critics and intellectuals, from John Dennis to Thomas and Joseph Warton.[12] Edward Young, for example, sees no impediments to the expression of natural genius, nor ever questions the supremacy of that faculty in his aesthetic, although he does articulate a rudimentary form of the anxiety of influence: "illustrious Examples *engross*, *prejudice*, and *intimidate*. They *engross* our attention, and so prevent a due inspection of ourselves; they *prejudice* our Judgment in favour of their abilities, and so lessen the sense of our own; and they *intimidate* us with the splendour of their Renown, and thus under Diffidence bury our strength."[13]

Johnson's sense of the circumstantial and compromised nature of intellectual life is central to his hermeneutics, the "disciplined understanding of understanding," as George Steiner calls it, and his thinking about memory.[14] Boswell does not really take up the critical value of this aspect of Johnson's self-reflexiveness in the closing pages of the *Life of Johnson*, where Johnson's intellectual and emotional division is recuperated into a view of heroic transcendence that reconciles and moralizes the contradictions of life. Johnson, however, is particularly interested in the present, and its temporal and narratological implications. In "Rambler" 41 he writes:

So few of the hours of life are filled up with objects adequate to the mind of man, and so frequently are we in want of present pleasure of employment, that we are forced to have recourse every moment to the past and future for supplemental satisfaction. (III, 221)

The present moment, however, is no simple or reified phenomenon, for it is usually experienced as *aporetic* – a positive, yet felt absence of anything solid or "present." In the same essay, he writes:

Almost all that we can be said to enjoy is past or future; the present is in perpetual motion; leaves us as soon as it arrives, ceases to be present before its presence is well perceived, and is only known to have existed by its effects which it leaves behind. (III, 223–24)

From this essay we learn, then, that, in terms of the structure of consciousness, both the past and the future are functions of the *absence* of the present moment, and become significant in this teleology by virtue of their differential relation to a reality and a meaning that seems always to be deferred.[15] This emptiness is both highly ethical, and instrumental, since it is the *locus* of memory, which is "the purveyor of reason" and "place[s] us in the class of moral agents" (III, 223). Within such a framework, as Richard Terdiman remarks, "memory is the modality of our relation to the past,"[16] but it is also the modality of our relation to the present. The present is the realm of human memory and of the historical, rather than of the divine and the transcendental (as Johnson notes when quoting Horace's 29th Ode of the Third Book), and his subsequent exploration of the issue identifies the present as *both* a function *and* an object of memory. In Johnson's hands this rhetorical conception of memory, I propose, mediates between origins and ends – that is, between memory-as-recollection and memory-as-repetition[17] – and, furthermore, it underwrites a specific narrative of temporality and history that characterizes much of his writing.

In developing these conceptions of memory and narrative, Johnson draws on a long European philosophical and scientific tradition.[18] For both Plato[19] and Aristotle,[20] memory is an engrammatological activity which envisages the aporia of memory as iconographic, and the human body as a place of mediation between the soul and the memory that inscribes itself on the soul.[21] While Augustine's *Confessions* sees memory as a cave with hidden and inexpressible recesses,[22] identified with God, it is also a forensic faculty that guarantees identity and continuity over time. Three different yet related kinds of memory operate in the *Confessions*: (1) rote memory, where we "memorize" something and have it by heart; (2) memory of experiences that have come to us through the senses which are consciously stored away and consciously recalled, used, and stored away again, with change necessarily occurring at each of these stages; and (3) a "principal memory" that neither partakes of the mechanics of rote memory, nor depends on external stimuli, but looks to an internal world, and shapes and creates truths according to a self already largely formed from memorial acts earlier in time and further back on a continuum.[23] As we shall see, all three levels of Augustinian memory find an echo in Locke, Johnson, and Hume.

Following the discussion of memory in *Confessions* Book 10, comes an important passage on narrative and time in Book 11. Memory here leads Augustine to the proposition that "it is abundantly clear that neither the future nor the past exist, and therefore it is not strictly correct to say that the three temporal times are past, present, and future. It might be more correct," he continues, "to say that there are three times, a present of things past, a present of things present, and a present of things future. Some such different times do exist in the mind, but nowhere else that I can see. The present time of things past is memory; the present time of things present is sight; the present time of things future is expectation."[24] Thus, as James Olney discusses, Augustine sees the power of memory as a story-telling faculty, and distinguishes human beings on this ground from other animals (a thought echoed by Johnson).[25] Memory thereby sustains a self-reflexive narrative linking the three temporal modes to each other, and makes a bridge between time and eternity, wherein the individual may discover God.[26]

Tracing the full Augustinian influence on concepts of memory in the eighteenth century would include Vico and Rousseau, whose mnemonics are no less complex and instrumental in their hermeneutics than is Johnson's. Yet their exclusive narrative concern with origins as a basis of historiography differentiates them from Johnson, whose thought is more orientated towards ends.[27] Locke, on the other hand, continues the Aristotelian and Augustinian sense of the discursiveness of memory. For him, memory is at once integral to perception, and basic to personal identity, and it is also aporetic in nature. As John Sutton has demonstrated, Locke's idea of memory in the *Essay Concerning Human Understanding* (1690) developed and broadened two distinct though related neurophilosophical arguments about the nature of memory (from Descartes through Kenelm Digby, Joseph Glanvill, Robert Hooke, and Henry More), one emphasizing distributive representation, the other local representation.[28] Yet, in the long chapter on personal identity added to the second edition of the *Essay* in 1694, memory comes to be the lynchpin of personal identity.[29]

For Locke, consciousness as it extends backwards in time is the sole criterion for sameness of personal identity. Personal identity thus depends not only on "that consciousness which is inseparable from thinking and, as it seems to me, essential to it," but also on memory (*Essay*, II.27.9). Locke first articulates his view of the sameness of personality over time in 1683,[30] and the first edition of the *Essay* sees memory more as a store house and repository (II.10.7). But animal spirits change over time, and his concepts of the soul and of memory-storage came under attack,[31] so in 1694 he sought identity by looking backwards and by appropriating one's past self and actions, adding the following disclaimer:

> But our *Ideas* being nothing, but actual Perceptions in the Mind, which cease to be any thing, when there is no perception of them, this *laying up* of our *Ideas* in the Repository of the Memory, signifies no more but this, that the Mind has a Power, in many cases, to revive Perceptions, which it has once had, with this additional Perception annexed to them, that it has had them before. And in this Sense it is, that our *Ideas* are said to be in our Memories, when indeed, they are actually no where, but only there is an ability in the Mind, when it will, to revive them again; and as it were paint them anew on itself.[32]

This is the cornerstone of Locke's idea of memory. Though essential to personal identity, memory is generated within a repetitive structure of mind (the mind has an *additional* perception that it has had these perceptions before), for which the mind writing on itself is a simile, and which means that such ideas are "actually no where." Locke thus articulates one of the fundamental ideas in the phenomenology of memory in Western thought by problematizing the relationship between aporia and representation in a form that many other writers (including Hume, Johnson, and Wordsworth) were to take up.

A threat to the Lockean self derives from the impossibility – on his model of implicit memory traces – of perfectly preserving motions and memories, which, in turn, threatens the notions of the substantial self and the insubstantial soul. These are issues that I take up in chapter 3 in conjunction with Hume's critique of miracles. At present, however, one might notice that Locke conceptualizes the problem in terms of an infinitely regressive and vulnerable childhood. A child who had lost her sight when very young, loses the idea of colors in time because her mind has been unable to repeat the sensations. This leads Locke to think of memories *as* children: "Thus," he writes, "the *Ideas*, as well as Children, of our Youth, often die before us: And our Minds represent to us those Tombs, to which we are approaching; where though the Brass and Marble remain, yet the Inscriptions are effaced by time, and the Imagery moulders away. The pictures drawn in our Minds, are laid in fading Colours; and if not sometimes refreshed, vanish and disappear" (*Essay*, 151–52).

Locke's metaphor suggests that, while the memories and ideas are in the mind, they are also one with the "Inscriptions," "Imagery," and "Colours." Remembrance, then, seems to mean becoming conscious of immanent ideas through inscription, when writing takes a particular repetitive form. Furthermore, the comparison of memories to children is especially poignant, for the implication is that to be without memory is to be like a child, because the effect of time on experience which makes for maturity, is also the process by which the individual is separated from her former childlike selves. Indeed, in the section on the association of ideas (II: 33), Locke returns to the notion of the child as an image for memory. This time, however, the child's death has a traumatic effect on the mother, whose repetitive mourning is now a *failure* of memory, and thus presents her as unable to separate the image of the child in her mind from the overwhelming image of death.[33] In this case true memory requires the intervention of time, for: "Till time has by disuse separated the sense of that Enjoyment and its loss from the *Idea* of the Child returning to her memory, all Representations, though never so reasonable, are in vain" (*Essay*, 398).[34]

Johnson was evidently impressed by Locke's imagery and narrative of memory because he appropriates it in the Preface to Shakespeare in developing his view of Shakespeare as a poet of nature. In the famous passage on dramatic illusion Johnson describes the imaginative, fictive experience of Shakespeare's drama in mnemonic terms, in which "we rather lament the possibility than suppose the presence of misery, as a mother weeps over her babe, when she remembers that death may take it from her."[35] That possibility becomes real and "natural" within the context of Shakespeare's drama by taking the form of a *recollection*. The mother, like a spectator or reader, is described as *remembering* her experience. One definition for "remember" in Johnson's *Dictionary* is "To recollect, to call to mind," illustrated by quoting Isaac Watts (who, in turn, paraphrases Locke's passage on memory quoted above): "We are said to remember anything, when the idea of it arises in the mind with a consciousness that we have had this idea before." This multiplicity of consciousness has something to do with a deepened and inflected consciousness in the Shakespearean spectator, in which an intuitive and immanent knowledge common to humankind (the knowledge of eventual death, for example, which, in Augustine's hermeneutics of memory, is the horizon of expectation) is experienced as a new and striking truth. Forgetfulness of our mortality is a common theme in Johnson's moral writing – "An even and unvaried tenour of life always hides from our apprehension the approach of its end"[36] – but some literature is marked by its capacity to penetrate the defenses of the mind that arise within the "even and unvaried tenour of life": "It was necessary to fix attention; and the mind can be captivated only by recollection or by curiosity; by reviving natural sentiments or impressing new appearances of things."[37] Recollection and curiosity seem here to be offered as alternatives, yet both clearly inhere in the same fictive Shakespearean experience, just as, as Olney discusses, the recollective narrative of Augustine's *Confessions* realizes itself in the course of time by bringing together memory and expectation.[38]

In Shakespeare's drama, memory is part of an experience that Johnson calls general nature, so there is no indication of the slippage surrounding the term. When memory itself is the object of consideration, as in "Rambler" 41, its phenomenology problematizes representation by pointing to its aporetic nature, as it does in Plato, Aristotle, Augustine, and Locke. Memory is a construction, insofar as we can read only those representations that consciousness has placed there, and which engrammatology permits one to construct each time, as if for the first time. Yet, memory is also conservation (retention), insofar as the icon is read with a view to a reality and a past that previously existed. Maurice Merleau-Ponty suggests that the problematic discrepancy between "the immanence and the transcendence of the past... can be reconciled only if we refrain from posing the problem in terms of representation."[39] In this vein, Johnson envisages the representativeness of memory as a form of difference, the contractual nature of which maintains his contact with Locke's political and his own legal thought. The "faculty of remembrance" now is placed in dialectical relation to the aporetic absence of the present moment, which is the object of memory. More, however, needs now to be said about Johnson's understanding of that presence.

The "present" under discussion here is for Johnson that which the mind almost never fully occupies; or, more accurately, it is the sign of a human situation in which present action is constantly elided by desire, restlessness, dissatisfaction, and imaginativeness, not to mention the formal limits of the human mind. The opening of "Rambler" 2 strikes a rueful note that is sounded in many of Johnson's other texts: "the mind of man is never satisfied with the objects immediately before it, but is always breaking away from the present moment, and losing itself in schemes of future felicity; and ... we forget the proper use of the time now in our power."[40] The present moment as perceived in "Rambler" 2, as it is at the opening of "Rambler" 5, is identified as a "point in time," the arrival of which comes without the desired satisfaction, therefore limiting the individual to a lesser, merely momentary temporal captivity. This lesser present is envisaged as a threat to virtue and reason, because it bears no conscious and remembered relation to past and future, and fails to engage the will. In such instances Johnson recommends that "the great task of him, who conducts his life by the precepts of religion, is to make the future predominate over the present."[41]

Claude Rawson observes that for both Johnson and Swift "restlessness was a radical perversity of the human mind,"[42] but "perversity" is not quite the right word for Johnson. Within the Renaissance Christian–humanist sceptical tradition, the disjunction of mind and world reflected in Johnson's thinking about time is felt rather as evidence of humankind's fallen state, and therefore also as a sign of its spiritual potential: "such is the inequality of our corporeal to our intellectual faculties, that we contrive in minutes what we execute in years."[43] Potentially tragic as such a formal disjunction might be, it is also incidental to hope ("the natural flights of the human mind are not from pleasure to pleasure, but from hope to hope"),[44] and thus fundamental to the psychological stimulus to action. This gap in human volition and contingency becomes a strategic and rhetorical dimension to Johnson's larger, more general "present" moment arising within his narrative of memory.

In "Rambler" 41, the double nature of the present – its absence and its power – is registered in two simultaneous stages of thought in a kind of double reading: the present leaves *as soon as it arrives*; the present is gone *before* it arrives. It is important to note that Johnson's syntax does not offer these observations as successive occurrences, but as one reality having two slightly different temporal relationships with experience. Paul de Man captures some sense of Johnson's perspective when he remarks that the "power of memory does not reside in its capacity to resurrect a situation or a feeling that actually existed, but it is a constitutive act of the mind bound to its own present and oriented toward the future of its own elaboration."[45] As Johnson understands it, the present is thus not an a priori or originary category, nor is Johnson necessarily interested in constructing an originary moment as a basis for meaning. Rather, the thrust of his argument is that the *presence* authorizing meaning is not simply mirrored in language, in the sense that it represents an already existing and fully accessible reality, but is itself a structure of thought and feeling brought into existence through language and writing. This presence, the historical product of memory, is, however, *still* a representation of a reality and of a truth, and bearing all the authority of Johnson's commitment to writing-the-truth that characterizes his works.

"Truth" has now been opened up, demonstrated as being hybrid and historically variable, subject to change and to various reinscriptions. It expresses Johnson's understanding of the limits of personal perspective in which "Life is not the object of science: we see a little, very little; and what is beyond we only can conjecture,"[46] as well as his conviction that language works as "the instrument of science."[47] While "science" (that is, "knowledge" or "any art or species of knowledge") exists within its various disciplinary structures, and has a historical and social life of its own, Johnson's handling of memory in "Rambler" 41 suggests that in some important sense "science" cannot come into being without language.

De Man's notion that in memory "the mind is bound to its own present" does not, however, quite reflect Johnson's thought, for at a crucial moment he invokes a transforming passage of Dryden's translation of Horace's 29th Ode of the Third Book by way of representing the present to which memory can provide access through its (re)constructive process:

Whatever we have once reposited, as Dryden expresses it, "in the sacred treasure of the past," is out of the reach of accident, or violence, nor can be lost either by our weakness, or another's malice:

> Non tamen irritum
> Quodcunque retro est efficiet, neque
> Diffinget, infectumque reddet,
> Quod fugiens semel hora vexit.
>
> Horace, ODES, III. 29.45–48.[48]

As part of this thought, Johnson gives an English version of Horace's lines, not from Philip Francis or James Elphinston, on whom he usually draws in the *Rambler* when quoting Horace in English, but from Dryden:

> Be fair or foul or rain or shine,
> The joys I have possess'd in spite of fate are mine.
> Not heav'n itself upon the past has pow'r,
> But what has been has been, and I have had my hour.[49]

Evidently, Johnson felt that Dryden's lines expressed his thought and feeling here most fully. The "secret happiness"[50] of this poem, and particularly of the lines quoted by Johnson, turn on the paradoxical denial of its explicit statements: an apparently passive and subservient relation to the past is transformed into a triumph over the acknowledged limiting facts of life and of the past. The past is irretrievably past ("what has been *has been*"), yet it is vitally present in the *way* Dryden seizes hold of his experience of difference in translating from one language and culture into another.[51] The historical distance between the past and present is accepted, and then effortlessly erased; and the sameness in difference, and the larger consciousness arising therefrom, are part of Johnson's perception of the present as this essay defines it.

The manner in which Dryden's passage and his whole translation are appropriated into Johnson's argument about memory, effectively narrates a transformation of *chronos* (the simple and inexorable successive moments of time) into *kairos* (time filled with significance derived from a conscious, structured relation to the end), which Frank Kermode has identified as the erotic consciousness of fiction. Plot works, according to Kermode, "to defeat the tendency of the interval between *tick* and *tock* to empty itself... the interval must be purged of simple chronicity, of the emptiness of... humanly uninteresting successiveness... [and] that which was conceived as simply successive becomes charged with past and future: what was *chronos* becomes *kairos*."[52] Stuart Sherman has pointed out that narratologists such as Kermode, E. P. Thompson, Benedict Anderson, Walter Benjamin, and Foucault have all seen the early modern period as one in which the messianic concept of time (*kairos*) actually gives way to a culture-wide acceptance of "homogenous empty time" (*chronos*),[53] a temporal concept much appreciated in the late-seventeenth and eighteenth centuries. This scenario certainly makes sense for Johnson, for his interest in *kairos* is not – nor ever could be – maintained without a corresponding concept and feel for simple chronicity, which forms the very site of his thinking about consciousness. Yet, Sherman's description of Johnson's construction of time as a "process whereby the imagination, operating upon time, discovers vacuity rather than fullness" (205) tells only half the story, for Johnson's writing generally finds fullness *in* vacuity when he remembers and narrates experience.

The collocation of eroticism (vis-à-vis Kermode's usage) and Johnson's appropriation of Dryden in "Rambler" 41 might surprise the reader, especially since highly elaborated symbolic structures (Dryden's baroque– "pindarique" form, Johnson's rhetorical prose) might be thought to move one *away* from the body, as verbal signs do.[54] Still, given the absence of presence (and the absence of body) in language, representation endeavors to make the body present and to create the felt illusion of body within language. It is the sense of the body's otherness – the paradigm, as a generation of feminist criticism has taught us, of gender and ideological differentiation – which informs the endeavor to bring it into language, so that it and its psychological and cultural significations can be endowed with meaning.[55] If desire is deliberately mapped against narrative temporality as narrative's way of postponing erotic denouement,[56] then Dryden's translation of Horace's 29th Ode of the Third Book collapses the attenuated temporal structure into a present moment of joy and energy, that seems to tap the creative possibilities of fortune.

These speculations about memory and the present all propose a specific, sophisticated kind of reading on Johnson's part – quite different from the common-sense, literal-mindedness that has often been taken as the hallmark of his perception – and Johnson himself names it: attentitiveness. Along with "nature" and "wit," "attention" is central to Johnson's critical project. However, because the term is usually subordinated to others, and since modern usage has hidden its connotations in Johnson's vocabulary, "attentitiveness" has largely escaped comment. "Idler" 74 argues that "[t]he true art of memory is the art of attention," and in terms that Wordsworth echoes in *Tintern Abbey*, "Idler" 44 proposes that memory is a "power to fill the attention, and suspend all perception of the course of time."57 The relevance of these forms of "attention" to time and memory is powerfully exemplified in Johnson's little epitaph for Hogarth.

TIME AND ATTENTION

As we know, after Hogarth's death (in 1764) his widow asked Garrick to write an epitaph for the painter's monument in St. Nicholas' Churchyard, Chiswick. Garrick sent three verses to Johnson for his comment, and Johnson sent Garrick his own version of the epitaph in a letter of 12 December 1771.58 The first verse of Johnson's epitaph is as follows:

> The Hand of Art here torpid lies
> That traced [wav'd] th' essential form of Grace,
> Here death has clos'd the curious eyes
> That saw the manners in the face.59

Some time later (we are not exactly sure when) Johnson recited his version of the epitaph to Mrs Thrale, and she recorded one verse in her journal for 28 May 1777.60

> The hand of him here torpid lies
> That drew th' essential Form of Grace;
> Here clos'd in Death th' attentive Eyes
> That saw the Manners in the Face.

The discrepancies between these two versions are unlikely to indicate Mrs Thrale's inaccuracy in recording Johnson. They seem rather to be due to Johnson's misremembering himself, or perhaps to a strategic recollection by Johnson to be explained in terms of the memory structuring the relation of the one text to the other.61 The later version substitutes "drew" for "traced" (or "wav'd") and "attentive" for "curious," with the consequence that the second version focuses more on an individual, while the first is more general, suggesting that Hogarth's activity touched the limits of art by responding to something larger than himself. "Drew" suggests personal volition, while "traced" captures the sense of following through a pattern in nature or the circumambient world. The later reading accords with Hogarth's own aesthetic, for it brings to mind the line of beauty which, as early as the 1740 self-portrait with Pug as well as in the *Analysis of Beauty* (1753), came for Hogarth to be symbolic of a method of drawing, a manner of seeing, as well as of suggesting the perpetual passing of time. "Curious," too, seems to be an apt word for Hogarth's art; it is more obviously active than "attentive" and, reinforced by Johnson's active syntax, appears to be responding to the energy of Hogarth's pictures.[62]

By contrast, the second version of Johnson's epigraph seems to have a greater intimacy: by making the third line passive, and eliminating the generalities of the second stanza, Hogarth seems to be brought closer to the reader. Hogarth was known to the Salusburys and the Thrales, perhaps better than he was to Johnson himself,[63] and in remembering Hogarth in Mrs Thrale's company Johnson may have been prompted to recollect him more as a man than as an artist. In the phrase "attentive eyes," "attentive" describes how the eyes perceive, as well as how they appear to others. Ronald Paulson describes Hogarth's self-portrait with Pug (1740), used as a frontispiece to the 1745 edition of his prints, as one in which the painter "has isolated himself from his attributes [as an artist], presenting himself as a lesser order of reality. The real man seems to be separated from the mask, the symbols, the aims, of the moralist-artist" (II, 4). This portrait, of course, presents Hogarth as the pugnacious and assertive entrepreneur he was, but there is also a tentativeness and an openness that is not there in other self-portraits (such as the "Head-and-shoulders with palette" of 1735–40), and we are met by eyes that are as attentive as they are curious.

Johnson's *Dictionary* defines "attentive" as "heedful, regardful, full of attention," and among his illustrative quotations are the two following from Hooker and Shakespeare: (1) "Being moved with these and the like your effectual discourses, whereunto we gave most *attentive* ear, till they entered even unto our souls;" and (2) "I'm never merry when I hear sweet musick / The reason is, your spirits are *attentive*." These contexts suggest that attentiveness is a rare quality of receptivity, capable of reaching the "soul" and the "spirits." In Hooker it is discourse that penetrates the mind through the attentive ear, in Shakespeare it is music.[64] This state of affairs is important because the felt immediacy of apprehension suggests a relationship of "word" to "thing" that counteracts the natural tendency of the human mind to be *dis*satisfied with "objects immediately before it."[65] It also draws to our attention the relationship between the two different historical moments in remembering Hogarth (1771 and 1777), and places them at a third remove from the life of Hogarth, which ended with his death in 1764. As David Venturo remarks, for Johnson "epitaph and elegy become a form of poetic biography, a means of telling compendiously the story of a dead man's life,"[66] and as such the temporal structure of Johnson's poem is similar to that of the biographies. The very repetitiveness of the two versions of Johnson's epitaphs therefore comprises a discursive, commemorative narrative, more critically inflected than the easy dichotomy attributed to Johnson's distinction between knowledge and opinion, and nature and custom by Kermode in his discussion of forms of attention.[67] Such repetitiveness is a manner of surveying Hogarth's completed life from the end, representing (as Hayden White remarks) "the aspects of time in which endings can be seen as linked to beginnings... link[ing] a terminus of a process with its origin in such a way as to endow whatever happened in between with a significance that can only be gained by 'retrospection.'"[68]

The narrative comprised by Johnson's recollection, and the very structure of temporality that he discovers in acts of memory such as the Hogarth epitaph and "Rambler" 41, impart a meaningful – though not logical or teleological – structure to an otherwise random or merely successive series of events. It also reenacts the movement from *chronos* to *kairos* which Kermode identifies as the erotic consciousness of fiction and that Ricoeur sees as the deep structure of temporality.[69] Recollection seems to bring Hogarth closer in the sense that it transforms the body as signified object into a fictively experienced reality, just as it does in Dryden's translation of Horace, woven by Johnson into the fabric of "Rambler" 41, where recollection takes the form of translation, and, I suggest, is consciously made by Johnson in his choice of Dryden's version as a *locus* of "remembrance" that places us in the "class of moral agents," and for the "memory" that "is the purveyor of reason" (III, 223). There are other significant moments in Johnson's criticism in which he brings together memory, reason, and the full experience of the present, as in his remarks on *Paradise Lost*, VIII, lines 66–197: "Raphael's reproof of Adams's curiosity after the planetary motions, with the answer returned by Adam, may be confidently opposed to any rule of life which any poet has delivered."[70]

While curiosity is essential to human knowledge for Johnson, a high *purpose* of intellectual endeavour is the quality of our daily experience. "The great praise of Socrates," Johnson notes, "is, that he drew the wits of Greece, by his instruction and example, from the vain pursuit of natural philosophy to moral inquiries, and turned their thoughts from the stars and tides, and matter and motion, upon the various modes of virtue, and relations of life."[71] Socrates' teaching (as mediated by Plato), like Montaigne's essays – where experience is invoked as a compensation for the limits of reason – securely locate themselves in experience. It is Milton's discovery of both morality *and joy* in the present moment (if not fallen experience) that increases the appeal of Raphael's passage for Johnson:

> Solicit not thy thoughts with matters hid,
> Leave them to God above...
> ...joy thou
> In what he gives to thee, this Paradise
> And thy fair Eve...
> (*Paradise Lost*, VIII, lines 67–68, 70–72)

At other moments in the "Life of Milton" Johnson uses the authority of Socrates on this issue of the present moment *against* Milton, indicating not only the complexity and circumstantiality of his account of Milton, but also the *instrumentality* of the present moment for Johnson. The style of writing within which the mind can happily exist within the constructed present is one that works deliberately with and within limits. Johnson's style often engenders the double consciousness of recollection – what Locke describes as the mind's power to "revive Perceptions, which it once had, with this additional Perception annexed to them, that it has had them before" – by working through difference, against and on the verge of endings, in both senses – death and the ends of activity:

In this work, when it shall be found that much is omitted, let it not be forgotten that much likewise is achieved.[72]

This secret horrour of the last is inseparable from a thinking being whose life is limited, and to whom death is dreadful. We always make a secret comparison between a part and the whole ... when we have done any thing for the last time, we involuntarily reflect that a part of the days allotted us is past, and that as more is past there is less remaining.[73]

The end of a particular life or particular undertaking can be a powerful image of human weakness for Johnson, but also a platform for re-energization.[74] The extent to which the reality of the *particular* pain penetrates his prose in the passage above, seems to correspond to a *general* energetic endorsement of life that emerges. While life is being lived, individual moments come and go, but when significant events provide occasions for retrospection and remembrance, those individual moments can be formed into a connected narrative, wherein they lose the inexorability and the logic of fate – or the tick, tick, tick structure of mere chronicity – and take on a timelessness that seems momentarily to release the participant from the anxieties of the immediate. Hence Johnson's recommendation to Boswell to keep a regular journal, for "it is by studying little things that we attain the great knowledge of having as little misery and as much happiness as possible."[75] While "Idler" 103 – the last in that series – strikes a rueful, even melancholy note, made poignant by Johnson's holding together so succinctly the particular moments of his life over the previous two years, with the inexorable movement of time which has now brought the series and, by extension, his life to an end, the quoted passage also has a certain lyrical strength, a satisfying absolution that belies the "secret horrour" of the last ending. Death certainly is a pervasive subject in Johnson's writing – every poet's death in the *Lives* finds a place in the narrative – but, as the last "Idler" suggests, Johnson has more than one attitude to death.

When encountering limits, the parallel structure of thought between Johnson's secular and his religious experience becomes clear. Just as the mind makes contact with a world "beyond" itself – or a past differentiated from the present – and constructs a present through memory, so Johnson's prayers and sermons work towards a dependence on God (as he defined prayer)[76] by playing off his past experiences against the uncertainties of Providence. The movement of thought in question is indicative of the structure of the prayers; for example:

Almighty God, who hast brought me to the beginning of another year, and by prolonging my life invitest to repentance, forgive me that I have misspent the time past, enable me from this instant to amend my life according to thy holy Word, grant me thy Holy Spirit that I may pass through things temporal as not finally to lose the things eternal. O God, hear my prayer for the sake of Jesus Christ.[77]

Past, present, future: passing through things temporal *so as*, through the intervention of the Holy Spirit, to achieve things eternal. The structure of memory is Augustinian. Such prayers represent one way Johnson has of living more in the present, of "redeeming the time," or so he hoped. The sermons on repentance follow the same pattern. The second sermon in the Yale edition, for example, whose theme (but not tone) resembles "Rambler" 110 on repentance, follows a central Anglican homiletic tradition, subscribed to by William Law and Jeremy Taylor, in emphasizing a change of life, that "reformation is the chief part of repentance," as part of a satisfactory repentance.[78] Johnson follows the homiletic tradition in associating repentance with the sacrament, by seeing the communion as the visible manifestation of an efficacious repentance: "But as this reformation is not to be accomplished by our own natural power, unassisted by God... we must implore a blessing by frequent prayer, and confirm our faith by the holy sacrament."[79] Jacques Le Goff points out that the typical Christian ritual of the communion in the Middle Ages lends itself to an eschatology of memory that *denies* temporal existence and history.[80] For Johnson, too, the sacrament of the communion is a dramatic representation of Christ's perpetual sacrifice for humankind, by which an ordering and a transforming principle was introduced into history, but for the purpose of redeeming the time past. Such temporal "redemption" is effected by people and takes place *in* history.

By participating in this sacramental drama, one is readmitted to the communion of the Church, from which sin severs people, and one becomes part of God's providential scheme.[81] In this advocacy, Johnson invokes the liturgical form of the 1662 Book of Common Prayer.[82] In the service of the communion in the Prayer Book the celebrant is asked to recall and examine his or her life, to confess his or her sins, to repent, to purpose amendment, and then to partake of the sacrament – "the Body of our Lord Jesus Christ" – symbolizing or dramatizing not a momentary but a *continual remembrance* of Christ's sacrifice, the manifestation of which is charity.[83] Both of Johnson's sermons about the communion (numbers 9 and 22 in the Yale edition) invoke a repetition, a recollection of an all-significant death: "Thus the sacrament is a kind of repetition of baptism, the means whereby we are readmitted into the communion of the church of Christ... which is therefore a renewal of our broken vows, a re-entrance into the society of the church, and the act, by which we are restored to the benefits of our Saviour's death" (*Sermon*, No. 9, 100).

The structure of many of Johnson's moral essays, sermons and prayers have in common this sacramental concern with the present moment as part of the mapping onto each other of the three temporal discourses of the past, the future, and the present (or the present of things past, the present of things present, and the present of things future), the coincidence of which characterizes Augustine's narrative temporality.[84] Moreover, the thematic organization and the rhetoric of Johnson's religious writing is that of the secular essays in that he describes the act of repentance and communion as a contractual one, and one of moving into the present moment: "We are in full possession of the present moment; let the present moment be improved."[85]

Though continuous with each other, Johnson's moral and religious thought are, at the same time, evidently not identical. Some scholars, like Philip Davis and Paul Alkon, see the relationship as being a rather close one, and argue that "[i]t is hardly possible to separate the religious and secular aspects of his advice on any part of the moral discipline of the mind without seriously distorting our vision of Johnson's achievement."[86] Others, like Michael Suarez and Blanford Parker, understand Johnson's humanist learning as relatively frivolous and profane in the light of what Parker describes as the "uncanny swerve towards the unreachable, divine object."[87] There is no entirely settling the question between such contending views. But, like Montaigne, Johnson's ethics is based on Christian worship and theology, though he distinguishes between absolute issues of religion and the relative matters of social and personal experience. The primacy of religious truth, more absolute and often discussed by Johnson as being *independent* of the mediating function of language and a historical framework, accounts for the difference in tone and rhetoric of the sermons and prayers, which do not have the anxious self-scrutiny of the *Rambler* essays. In response to Johnson's differentiation of religious from artistic thinking – "Of sentiments purely religious, it will be found that the most simple expression is the most sublime... The ideas of Christian Theology are too simple for eloquence, too sacred for fiction, and too majestic for ornament"[88] – Blanford Parker observes that "unlike in Herbert or Hopkins, there is nothing which connects creator to created in a seamless web of association."[89] So the motives to piety, rather than piety itself, are seen by Johnson as the appropriate subject for religious verse. Nonetheless, in the prayers and sermons Johnson relies on the liturgical form of the Prayer Book and the homiletic structures of the seventeenth-century Anglican clergymen as a means of facilitating religious discourse.[90] Because God is beyond nature, and because piety is beyond art, Johnson is convinced of the unlikelihood of *excellent* devotional poetry (though he was more accepting of the devotional poems of Watts than he was of those of Waller).[91] Psychologically one might see the complete repose-of-mind on God that is devotion, as fully *taking up* and *filling* his mind, in an experience of extraordinary attentiveness, necessarily and *willingly* leaving it without room to exercise its will and imagination.

At the same time, when Johnson shifts his attention from "the ideas of Christian Theology" to the conditions of life and the traces of human consciousness, he establishes an active and vital continuity between the memory and other forms of reasonable and imaginative activity. The transcendental power of Christian devotion which in the passage from the "Life of Waller" seems to suspend the memory and keep it *apart* from other aspects of the mind, does not mean that Johnson does not register religious experience in *other* forms. He certainly fully acknowledges the religious subject matter of *Paradise Lost*, and feels that *as* religious poetry it is far superior to and more acceptable than Cowley's *Davideis*. Allen Reddick has demonstrated that in the revised fourth edition of the *Dictionary* (1773) Johnson draws on *Paradise Lost* largely as a repository of religious sentiment of which he approves and which he uses polemically.[92] There are also many occasions – as in the treatment of the religious sensibility of Dryden, Watts, Addison, and Boerhaave, and the many conversations with Boswell – on which Johnson discusses social, moral, and personal aspects of religious behavior without any difficulty.

IRONY AND AT-ONE-MENT

To summarize Johnson's thought about memory is to recognize that it moves on two levels whose relatedness and separation are mediated by a humane irony. On one level he positively embraces human imperfection, taking personal responsibility for the inherent divisions in and the substance of his human nature – what theology calls "sin," in the sense meant by Karl Barth when he remarked that sin is the "specific gravity of human nature as such," and what most Johnson scholarship identifies as "guilt." But gravity is felt by Johnson as a writer, and not primarily as a theologian, and so Geoffrey Hill's description of what poetry can do is apt for Johnson: "it is at the heart of this 'heaviness' that poetry must do its atoning work, this heaviness which is simultaneously the 'density' of language and the 'specific gravity of human nature.'"[93] On this level – as I will discuss more fully in a later chapter on Johnson's legal thinking – human laws (limits, *nomos*) are challenged in order to affirm their humanizing necessity.

On another level, the personal bodily "presence" – or the fiction thereof – in Johnson's prose operates as a *freeing* device. The contact with the world of circumstantial evidence, has the effect of locating the mind and the body in some particular place, a here and now, while freeing the mind to be in the present.[94] This gives rise to a paradoxical presence of absoluteness-and-freedom, the authority of which is a kind of absolution. Yet this authority is *not* achieved *in spite of* the textuality and the rhetorical performativity of Johnson's prose, but within and through that very medium.

Geoffrey Hill considers that "the technical perfecting of a poem is an act of atonement, in the radical etymological sense – an act of at-one-ment, a setting at one, a bringing into concord, a reconciling, a uniting in harmony,"[95] yet Christopher Ricks' astute analysis of Hill is, as I have already tried to suggest, true of Johnson: "his art attains, among other things, an exact apprehension of what is for him unattainable," writing "not out of any perfected at-one-ment of atonement and at-one-ment, but out of the sense of honourably *not* being able to grasp such a perfect concord, such a true religious experience."[96] Johnson's "at-one-ment," unfulfilled as it might be, comes through the fictive and recreated presence of the body and the present in his prose, and through memory. In his moral essays, as well as the more explicitly religious writing, memory is a kind of repentance that "redeems the time," and in this sense he shares something essential with Eliot's *Four Quartets*.[97]

Johnson's openness to temporal and circumstantial change, and to human vulnerability, makes for a tragic awareness. The attrition of time on human effort registered in *The Vanity of Human Wishes* ("Time hovers o'er, impatient to destroy, / And shuts up all the Passages of Joy" [lines 259–60]), reveals, as many have discussed, a potentially tragic discrepancy between will and action. Action is a particularly human form of being[98] – "Rambler" 41 and Dryden's version of Horace's 29th Ode of the Third Book triumphantly declare that *neither* beast *nor* God, but only humankind can undo the past – yet the application of the will produces, in time, consequences different from intentions. The ends of action cannot be fully determined by the individual will, itself subject to nature and time. This tragic-oriented consciousness makes itself felt in the *Lives* in the implicit poetic failure of *every one* of the writers Johnson discusses, and this leads many to see "the pre-eminence of delusion and energetic self-destruction in human affairs" as "the great theme of the *Lives*."[99]

Yet, for all Johnson's melancholia in the works of the 1740s and 1750s, and various ironic attitudes in the *Lives*, this view does not quite describe either Johnson's tone or his intentions in the *Lives*. That tone is crucially modified by the rhetorical yet redemptive conception of memory elaborated above, which, I shall propose, informs a narrative structure full of grace. Given the hybridity of Johnson's writing, and though there may be no "at-one-ment" among the various discourses, grace reveals itself in the space where different temporal planes meet, and where the impermanent and imperfect details of a writer's life and writing confront the potentially permanent realm of experience represented by literature. Before turning to the structure of the *Lives*, however, I need to sketch in more fully Johnson's understanding of nature and the legal framework of his narrative within which those disparate realms are brought together in the *Lives*.

CHAPTER 2

Johnson and nature

> [L]iterary commentary may cross the line and become as demanding as literature: it is an unpredictable or unstable genre that cannot be subordinated, a priori, to its referential or commentating function.[1]

One of the arguments of this book is that memory is a structuring principle of the *Lives of the Poets*. Yet *how* it operates is problematic. Though distinctive in Johnson's œuvre, the *Lives* are continuous with his earlier critical practice and with other eighteenth-century texts, and any attempt to argue for a newly conceived structure in the later work needs to demonstrate the connections between Johnson's understanding of memory and his key critical terms – such as nature, wit, and attentiveness – and with his engagement with texts.

Many have written on the formal aesthetic traditions of the neoclassical concept of nature, and it is not my brief here to join that discussion. Although some of what follows addresses the critical and even theoretical sophistication of Johnson's reading, my concern is not to adduce a Johnsonian theory of criticism or of literature, or to classify Johnson within any of the historical or critical categories to which he might now conceivably belong. Just as memory is aporetic in Johnson's moral essays, operating as the framework within as well as the object of historical thinking, so, I would propose, the related term "nature" is a hybrid entity in Johnson's hands, porous and changing according to critical context and rhetorical intention. As a critical concept, nature in Johnson's writing is less positivistic, rational, and legalistic than the scholarship would have us believe, or that we automatically accept as obvious for Johnson. Like "memory" and the "present" that attends upon it, "nature" is textually mediated and created. Yet, like other key Johnsonian terms, rather than diminishing its importance, the textuality of "nature" makes it *more* significant, imbuing it with a power that is not merely relative, or devoid of truth-making properties.

By textuality I do not mean the infinite play of signs against each other that some of Derrida's work authorizes,[2] or the infinitely regressive acts of interpretation that Stanley Fish means by rhetoric.[3] These critical modalities see linguistic artifice as excluding so-called "essentials" such as truth. Johnson, however, develops rhetorical capacities worthy of a Cicero, and gives much weight to the historical and semantic properties of language, while maintaining a robust and intelligent belief in the existence of truth. The previous chapter argued that there is no mutual exclusion for Johnson between rhetoric and truth, for the rhetorical use of language is the medium within which truth is both found and made. Of particular interest, however, is how Johnson uses the *fictiveness and literariness* of textuality so as to build critical discriminations and experiential truths supporting judgments, and sustaining his distinctive authority. At the same time, it is of interest to examine how the textuality of nature sustains generality and operates as the counterpart to memory. How, in short, do memory and nature, in writing, operate as the two dialogically related sides of one mode of apprehending and inhabiting the present?

NATURE'S ARTIFICE

Whatever the classical and philosophical roots of the term itself,[4] Shakespeare's drama is the *locus classicus* of nature for Johnson as he uses the term in his literary criticism. Shakespeare was "above all writers, at least above all modern writers, the poet of nature." To base appreciation of Shakespeare on nature is to emphasize a certain kind of imaginative engagement with literature that privileges a certain moral–humanistic knowledge of life. Many, of course, have found "nature" to be a critically and historically limited paradigm for reading Shakespeare, leading, among other things, to a confusion of Johnson's feeling for nature with novelistic realism.[5]

In "Rambler" 4 (1750), written on the publication of *Tom Jones* (and not long after that of *Pamela* and *Joseph Andrews*), Johnson considers the moral power of what came to be known as realistic fiction. The ability of this fiction to imitate the details of common and domestic life with verisimilitude piques Johnson's appreciation of the persuasiveness of realism; its power, for example, to "take possession of the memory by a kind of violence, and produce effects almost without the intervention of the will." It also, however, awakens his concern for the moral impact of the form that was to become the English novel, for: "It is justly considered as the greatest excellency of art, to imitate nature; but it is necessary to distinguish those parts of nature, which are most proper for imitation: greater care is still required in representing life, which is so often discoloured by passion, or deformed by wickedness" (III, 22).

"Nature" in this essay is an evidently a smaller thing than it is in the context of Shakespeare and the *Lives*, where the emphasis is less on the anxious care in representing the details of life, and where the "instruction," "practical axioms," and "domestick wisdom" of which Johnson approves in Shakespeare's drama comes to the reader through "characters [that] are not modified by the customs of particular places, unpractised by the rest of the world."[6] Likewise, the nature of Shakespeare's drama differs from that in "Rambler" 4 by virtue of its generality – "the genuine progeny of common humanity" – and by the absence of a judgmental perspective in Johnson's appraisal of "the general passions and principles... by which all minds are agitated, and the whole system of life is continued in motion" (*Shakespeare* 1, 62). It has become axiomatic that Johnson's conception of literature is ethical, for "he that thinks reasonably must think morally" (1, 71), and even sympathetic critics find the moralism of the Preface to be problematic. But the imaginative engagement of Shakespeare's plays are to be found in the "progress of his fable, and the tenour of his dialogue," rather than in the "splendour of particular passages" or particular moral sentiments (1, 62). Johnson, thus, distinguishes between levels of thought in the Preface, making it clear that Shakespeare's attractions are not to be confused with the "system of civil and oeconomical prudence" which *may* (or may not) be collected from his works.

The drama of general nature, then, provides a different *kind* of knowledge and reading experience from that given by the realistic novel. Although Johnson greatly admired Richardson's novels, and distinguished his characters of nature from Fielding's characters of manners,[7] he usually differentiates the novel from drama as he does manners from nature, for it is the "just representations of general nature," as distinguished from "particular manners," that "can please many and please long" (*Shakespeare*, 1, 61, 62). Novelists are "engaged in portraits of which every one knows the original, and can detect any deviation from exactness of resemblance," so it is as "just copyers of human manners,"[8] providing minute knowledge of individuals and society (or the ideological *impression* of such knowledge[9]) that Johnson finds the peculiar power of the novelist. Johnson, however, emphasizes the transformational aspect of Shakespeare's drama that "approximates the remote and familiarizes the wonderful" (1, 65), that has the power to shape the mind, and to give readers or viewers a direct feeling for life that, paradoxically, goes beyond and deeper than the immediate, the empirical, or the realistic. This drama's generality has usually been conceived of as a kind of ideal order operating within the realm of the empirical,[10] with the implication that the general nature that Johnson found in Shakespeare is really a neoclassical paradigm deduced from – and more appropriate to – the poetic practices of Dryden, Pope, and Addison, and the empirical epistemologies of Bacon and Locke. But Johnson's admiration for Shakespeare actually emphasizes the felt life and materiality of writing that exhibits "the real state of sublunary nature" (*Shakespeare*, I, 66); all of the comparisons made in the Preface between Shakespeare and Restoration and eighteenth-century English and French writers are to Shakespeare's advantage. Part of the problem in grasping Johnson's use of the term "nature" in his criticism lies in the assumption that one's immediate experience – the "exploratory-creative use of words upon experience" that Leavis, Eliot, and the New Critics found to be an essential component of all great poetry – is always of *particulars*.[11] But the apparent contradiction between the general and the particular in Johnson's criticism diminishes when it is realized that "general nature" and "sublunary nature" are different ways of saying more or less the same thing.[12] For Johnson, it is an error to assume that our ordinary observation of the world is "immediate," or that the state of nature in which we live is a fully conscious part of our daily experience.

Quite the contrary. The "Rambler" essays testify to the near emptiness of human consciousness and to the discrepancy between the human will and action underlying Johnson's moral and critical thought: "The mind of man is never satisfied with the objects immediately before it";[13] "almost all that we can be said to enjoy is past or future; the present is in perpetual motion."[14] The vanity of human wishes and the gap between the hopes and the achievements of poets, are two versions of Johnson's skeptical belief that the human mind, human language, and the "things" of the world (to echo Locke's basic mental architecture) are not easily mapped onto each other. General nature is thus emphatically not part of empirical experience, but becomes accessible – both reflected and created – in writing. It is also not necessarily confined to specific genres, but is an experiential quality pertaining to literature.[15]

Knowledge and learning are obviously important for Johnson,[16] but the experience of general nature is distinguished in his writing by a particular kind of pleasure appropriate to literature. While ordinary empirical existence is marked by desire and restlessness – which has its own enjoyments – the "endless variety" of life in Shakespeare's drama gives Johnson not only the *sense* that we are contemplating "the real state of sublunary nature," but *also* a pleasure that make this text feel like a "*just* representation" (*Shakespeare*, 1, 66, 61). "Pleasure" is defined in Johnson's *Dictionary* as "in general... the consequent apprehension of a suitable object, suitably applied to a rightly disposed faculty," and (among other things) "just" (as a noun) is defined as "exact, proper, accurate." These two terms work together to imply a consonance between mind and its "objects," and mind and world, that are unusual in Johnson's writing.

This sense of the phenomenal, independent world coming through as *pleasure* in Shakespeare's writing is what is accessed in memory. As we have already seen, the experiential content of the dramatic illusion is described by Johnson in terms of remembrance: the reader or viewer feels towards the dramatic action just as the mother feels when she remembers that death may take her child from her (1, 78). The generality made available in the mother's feeling about the imagined, eventual death of her child takes the form of remembrance, and the general nature of the dramatic episode is both source and object of memory. It is remembrance that releases (in the "Life of Cowley" Johnson uses the word "relieves") and grounds the perceiving consciousness by enabling it to feel its experience as true of life, to have an independent, non-subjective quality, and to feel what it is like to be part of the species: "In the writings of other poets a character is too often an individual; in those of Shakespeare it is commonly a species" (1, 62).

When Johnson writes that the "reflection that strikes the heart" is like the sudden realization of the mother about to lose her child, he distinguishes the heart from the intellect or the mind, and chooses the word "reflect" to indicate the movement from manners to nature, and from empirical to general experience. Johnson's definitions of "reflection" (as well as of the cognate "reflect" and "reflex") suggest the mind observing itself, and *thereby* opening to feeling; for example, definition 4, "Thought thrown back upon the past, or the absent, on itself," illustrated by a quotation from Dryden: "This dreadful image so possess'd her mind, / She ceas'd all farther hope; and now began / To make *reflection* on the unhappy man;" and definition 5, "The action of the mind upon itself," illustrated by a quotation from Locke: "*Reflection* is the perception of the operations of our own minds within us, as it is employed about the ideas it has got." While most writers engage the reader's attention by "hyperbolical or aggravated characters, by fabulous and unexampled excellence or depravity" that "maze his imagination" (1, 64, 65), Shakespeare "finds the passes of the mind" and "awaken[s] those ideas that slumber in the heart,"[17] and this is an experience that brings with it a clarity and fittingness.

WIT

Fittingness brings me to wit. Johnson's formulation of general nature draws on Dryden's understanding of wit as "a propriety of thoughts and words; or, in other terms, thoughts and words elegantly adapted to the subject,"[18] and on Pope's lines in the *Essay on Criticism*:

> *True Wit is Nature* to Advantage drest,
> What oft was *Thought*, but ne'er so well *Exprest*,
> *Something*, whose Truth convinc'd at Sight we find,
> That gives us back the Image of our Mind.
>
> (lines 297–300)

Johnson's criticism effectively assimilates, moralizes, and broadens Dryden's and Pope's conception of wit in the lives of those poets and as one of his general criteria in the *Lives*. Johnson's manner of evoking a sense of general nature in the Preface is like Pope's in writing true wit in the *Essay* – the recognition that the only way of talking about true wit is to manifest the quality.[19] Pope's wit depends upon the transforming yet transparent function of poetic language to awaken an immanent knowledge in such a way that the mind becomes cognizant of it as if were a phenomenal object, a *thing*, outside yet inside the mind. This linguistic engagement is a means of knowing the self and the self's relation to the world more fully than would otherwise occur. Pope's poetry, that is, becomes a mirror in which the individual mind can know itself, and know its experience to be true.

In formulating his lines on wit, Pope was assimilating an impressive body of thought about poetry and wit from Aristotle, Horace, and Longinus to Boileau, Dryden, and Walsh,[20] and they sound very Johnsonian. Johnson, who thought the *Essay on Criticism* "one of [Pope's] greatest ... works,"[21] is sometimes taken as simply replicating his terms. His poetic horizons are sometimes thought of as being shaped by the couplet art of Dryden and Pope, and his conception of wit is seen as necessarily limited to theirs.[22] But Johnson thought that "Pope's account of wit is undoubtedly erroneous; he depresses it below its natural dignity, and reduces it from strength of thought to happiness of language."[23] Johnson's distinction between "language" and "thought" here, stands in the Renaissance tradition of the relation of *res* to *verba*, but also inflects that tradition by grafting on to it the thought of the French classical writers Bouhours and Boileau,[24] and especially appropriating Montaigne's notion – in writing of the "nervous and solid eloquence" of Virgil and Lucretius: "When I see these brave methods of Expression, so lively, so profound, I do not say that 'tis well said, but well thought."[25]

Pope's lines seem unable to effect such a transition between language and thought. Even though nature for Pope (and for Johnson) is "At once the *Source*, and *End*, and *Test* of *Art*" (*Essay on Criticism*, line 73), there is a sense in Pope's lines that the relationship between nature-as-fact and nature-as-value is too narrow, suggesting embellishment ("well *Exprest*"), rather than the Montaignian (and the Johnsonian) ravishment, and something less than engagement between the words and the substance for which they aim (that which "oft was *Thought*").

The "Life of Pope" is sensitive to the social nuances of Pope's poetry, yet the lines on wit seem to leave Johnson with a sense of individual consciousness – commensurate with "man in his particular manners" rather than in his "general nature." The passage's refinement and linguistic balance has the effect of dissolving the "things" of the world ("*Something*" whose truth convinces us) into the image of the mind, suggesting Pope's closeness to Marvell's "Mind, that Ocean where each kind / Does streight its own resemblance find" ("The Garden," lines 43–44). Beguiling as this effect is, it is not the substantiality, variety, and comprehensiveness that Johnson discovers in Shakespeare's "mingled drama," in which, "at the same time," many different events are depicted as happening, and "many mischiefs and many benefits are done and hindered *without design*."[26]

The *Dictionary* defines "comprehensive" as "having the power to comprehend or understand many things at once," and quotes as illustration Dryden's description of the "most wonderful comprehensive nature" of Chaucer's *Canterbury Tales*.[27] Part of the pleasure of such a literary effect lies in the sense of the independence of the world of things and emotion from any single principle, as well as in the resistance of the mind to the different realities depicted by, say, Shakespeare's or Chaucer's texts. Hawkins and Hazlitt might both be responding to a similar profoundly comprehensive grasp when detecting a problem in the parallel structure of Johnson's prose: "in all Johnson's disquisitions, whether argumentative or critical, there is a certain even-handed justice that leaves the mind in a strange perplexity."[28] Yet this "resistant" aspect of Johnson's thought is a form of recognition that no complex truth can be rendered in any definite or single proposition, and that truth is more likely to be grasped by the creative use and rendition of one's intellectual boundaries and preconceptions.

More, however, needs to be said about Johnson's understanding of wit and how it functions in his critical reading, and this necessitates a consideration of its place in Johnson's engagement with the metaphysical poets in the "Life of Cowley."

The "Life of Cowley," was the first of the *Lives* to be written (1777), and it stood first in the *Prefaces, Biographical and Critical, to the Works of the English Poets* when the first four volumes were published in 1779.[29] According to Boswell, Johnson considered it to be the best of the *Lives* "on account of the dissertation which it contains on the *Metaphysical Poets*" (*Life*, IV, 38) and, according to Hawkins, because of its "investigation and discrimination of the characteristics of wit" (537). The critical nature and contextual function of the section on the metaphysical poets is complex. It consists of just fourteen paragraphs (numbers 49–63 in G. B. Hill's edition) in a text that totals two hundred; it is preceded by a chronological biographical sketch of Cowley's life, and followed by two sections of detailed commentary and quotation, the first offering specific examples from Donne and Cowley to exemplify Johnson's general criticisms (paras. 64–101), the second concentrating on Cowley's main poems, from the *Miscellanies* to the *Davideis* (paras. 102–202). The section on the metaphysical poets represents Johnson's statement about the poet's intellectual and poetic character, and as with many other lives, this central section of "Cowley" addresses issues of significant critical and historical implication.

In the case of Cowley, Johnson was moved to cast his critical net relatively wide, to offer not only a recontextualization and revaluation of the works of Cowley (after almost a century of critical neglect), but also self-consciously to formulate a mini critical tradition (Aristotle to Johnson), to imply a mini literary history (Jacobean Age to the Georgian), all in the process of defining a specific poetic style. Since Cowley's life had been more fully treated (by Sprat, for example) than his poetry, Johnson subordinates biographical questions to poetic ones.[30] While never offering the section on the metaphysical poets as a manifesto ("To circumscribe poetry by a definition will only shew the narrowness of the definer"),[31] it does make a powerful statement of principles.

Eliot famously thought that "a thought to Donne was an experience; it modified his sensibility," and his interest was to trace the poetic process, the "mechanism of sensibility which could devour any kind of experience."[32] But Christopher Ricks points out that "'The task of criticism' was, for Johnson, to 'establish principles,' and he everywhere made clear that his refusal to elaborate and concatenate the needed concepts beyond a certain point... was not a refusal to think, but a decision to think thereafter about the application of the principles."[33] The application of principles in Johnson's criticism is usually registered in terms of effect rather than interpretation. While there are occasions on which a moral*izing* judgment on Cowley as on Shakespeare outweighs the registering of what we would call a literary effect, Johnson does not privilege *purely* literary effects, but is rather concerned with the "effect upon the mind"[34] – experience that supports "representations of general nature." It is such experiential criteria, *brought to bear* on the particular stylistic qualities of the metaphysical poets, that lead Johnson to formulate his thought about wit:

If by a more noble and more adequate conception that be considered as Wit which is at once natural and new, that which though not obvious is, upon its first production, acknowledged to be just; if it be that, which he that never found it, wonders how he missed; to wit of this kind the metaphysical poets have seldom risen. (para. 55)

While this is a general statement, it is not offered as a universal one, for this line of thought begins with a *historical* observation as part of a *historical* exercise: "Wit, like all other things subject by their nature to the choice of man, has its changes and fashions, and at different times takes different forms" (para. 50). Wit, thus, is registered as relative, how different historical periods tell different jokes and also produce and enjoy different types of literature. It is precisely because of the social and linguistic changes over time that Cowley in the 1770s needs to be rehabilitated: during the seventeenth century he had been admired and revered as a poet – Milton, for example, ranked Cowley with Spenser and Shakespeare, Dryden thought him "elevated... copious, and full of spirit," and Pope commended the "language of his heart"[35] – but by the 1770s his poetry had become decanonized (para. 49). Johnson links this revolution in reputation to Cowley's "narrow views" and "temporary prejudices" (para. 49), yet also attempts to create a context in which Cowley can be more "adequately" estimated. What is said of Cowley in this section of the text is implied of Donne, since both poets share some stylistic and intellectual characteristics, and since Johnson is also aware of challenging the prevailing opinion of Donne in the context of his reputation in the eighteenth century.

While it is true that Johnson's conception of literature is representational, one should notice that he invokes Aristotle not as an original, theoretical standard against which all other subsequent positions should be measured, but as one of *several* ways of defining poetry ("*If* the father of criticism has rightly denominated poetry... an imitative art," then the following propositions hold). By the time we arrive at the statement about wit being at once natural and new, Johnson's version of "true wit" is offered not as a subset of "wit" (as opposed to poetry), but as another way of understanding poetry, a "more noble and adequate conception." The judgments that then follow from that conception of wit exemplify *several* ways in which Johnson applies a set of his critical principles, and reveals different ways in which the metaphysicals are felt not to fulfill the criteria of nature. In terms of critical response, this judgment means that the metaphysicals are unable, for Johnson, to evoke deep human feeling (para. 57) or to fill and expand the mind (para. 58).

Donne's love poetry is, of course, dialectical, subtle, argumentative, erudite, and fantastic; it is also vividly realistic in its depiction of passion, which is not the ideal Petrarchanism of the sonnets of Spenser, Sidney, and Drayton, but love as an actual experience in all its various moods (anger, scorn, repulsion, rapture, joy, tenderness, and sorrow). All of these qualities contribute to Donne's wit. Carew had praised "the awe of thy imperious wit" which

> Our stubborne language bends, made only fit
> With her tough-thick-rib'd hoopes to gird about
> Thy Giant phansie[36]

– and it is that wit, in its relation to language and experience, that is the hinge of Johnson's account of Donne. When Johnson remarks that in Donne's poetry "the most heterogeneous ideas are yoked by violence together; nature and art are ransacked for illustrations, comparisons and allusions" (para. 56), he is, presumably, thinking of the idiom of such quintessential poems as "The Extasie," "Twicknam Garden," "Valediction: Forbidding Mourning," "The Good Morrow," "The Canonization" – poems which, to quote Frank Kermode, are "full of *mind*."[37] Johnson, of course, *admired* many of Donne's intellectual qualities – his learning and subtlety ("their learning instructs, and their subtlety surprises," para. 56), his great labor and abilities (para. 60), his capacity to stimulate the reader to "recollection or inquiry" (para. 61), and his originality – for "to write on their plan it was at least necessary to read and think. No man could be born a metaphysical poet, nor assume the dignity of a writer by descriptions copied from descriptions" (para. 60). Indeed, Donne is felt as having *risen above* the mediocre and merely traditional qualities of Elizabethan poetry. These general qualities of his poetry immediately associate him with writers Johnson more explicitly admires – Milton, Dryden, Pope, Cowley, and perhaps Thomson and Akenside – placing him far above the other poets featured in the *Lives of the Poets*.

But at one with these qualities of Donne is the conceited inflection of his wit. This wit underlies the violent yoking together of heterogeneous ideas (para. 56), it "broke every image into fragments" (para. 58) and tended towards hyperbole (para. 59), leading Johnson to exclude it from his notion of wit as being at once natural and new: "Their thoughts are often new, but seldom natural; they are not obvious, but neither are they just; and the reader, far from wondering that he missed them, wonders more frequently by what perverseness of industry they were ever found" (para. 55).

> On a round ball
> A workman, that hath copies by, can lay
> An Europe, Afric, and an Asia,
> And quickly make that, which was nothing, all,
> So doth each tear,
> Which thee doth wear,
> A globe, yea world, by that impression grow,
> Till thy tears mixt with mine do overflow
> This world, by waters sent from thee my heaven dissolved so.

Johnson quotes this stanza (para. 77) from "A Valediction: Of Weeping" as an example of the far-fetched (and "perverse") nature of the heterogeneous "ideas" of the metaphysicals (see para. 71). Eliot thought that this stanza exemplified "a development by rapid association of thought which requires considerable agility on the part of the reader,"[38] but his observation only registers the metaphoric movement of the lines, a facet Johnson notices too: "The tears of lovers are always of great poetical account, but Donne has extended them into worlds" (para. 77). But Johnson *also* registers the effect and the implications of the lines: "Their attempts were always analytick: they broke every image into fragments" (para. 58). This is one reason why Donne "was not successful in representing or moving the affections" (para. 57). "A Valediction: Of Weeping" certainly moves with a quickness and ingenuity from one image to another, touching lightly and with a hint of humor on different emotions, thoughts, and observations. While the poem addresses a moment of parting between two lovers that occasions their weeping, the moment is obviously not meant to be taken with complete seriousness (though also not with complete levity); the movement from vulnerability and emotional honesty ("Let me pour forth / My tears before thy face") to final resolution ("Since thou and I sigh one another's breath, / Whoe'er sighs most, is cruellest, and hastes the other's death"), is a triumph of language in which, typically, the lovers' tears are all and nothing. While manifesting the power of Donne's language, the poem declines the opportunity to explore either what it feels like for one to weep for the parting of one's lover, or what it might mean.

This is probably why Johnson remarks that "as they were *wholly* employed on something unexpected and surprising they had no regard to that uniformity of sentiment, which enables us to conceive and to excite the pains and the pleasure of other minds" (para. 57 – my emphasis). The experience of weeping is energetically kept at bay by the act of looking at the tears, and then working with the *word* and with the *idea* "tears."[39] The Johnsonian reader, therefore, is kept on the outside of the poem, admiring its dexterity and its language but unable to feel the connection with the actual drama of the senses and of the soul. Hence, "their learning instructs, and their subtlety surprises; but the reader commonly thinks his improvement dearly bought, and, though he sometimes admires, is seldom pleased" (para. 56).

For Eliot, and many twentieth-century readers, this analytic bent of mind marked "a direct sensuous apprehension of thought, or a recreation of thought into feeling";[40] yet it is precisely the relation between thought and feeling in Donne's poetry that is problematic for Johnson. His distinction between admiration and pleasure, when applied, for example, to "A Nocturnall upon S. Lucies day," registers the difference between the breathtakingness of the metaphorical concentration with which the poet renders his deprivation and alienation –

> Were I a man, that I were one,
> I needs must know; I should preferre,
>   If I were any beast,
> Some ends, some means; Yea plants, yea stones detest
> And love; All, all some properties invest;
> If I an ordinary nothing were,
> As shadow, a light, and body must be here.
> But I am none.

– and the feeling of participating in the grief that a person feels at the loss (or death) of a loved one. This poem has been highly regarded for its impassioned exploration of a state of loss, penetrating into the realms of nature, science, medicine, alchemy, and astrology, and thereby highlighting the interpenetration of the soul and the body, and the mind and the senses that so captured the Renaissance imagination. Yet it is, as Helen Gardner has observed, "essentially a style in which individuality is expressed."[41]

Johnson's response to the poem draws attention to the constrictions of individuality. The self-absorption of the passion ("Study me then . . . But I am by her death . . . But I am none"), together with the eclipse of grief by that passion, leads Johnson to argue that "they were not successful in representing or moving the affections." Precisely because the poem represents the individual consciousness, the reader has some difficulty in entering the poem, adopting its priorities, and feeling like a species ("In the writings of other poets a character is too often an individual; in those of Shakespeare it is commonly a species").[42] If, as Johnson says of Cowley's *Davideis*, "we find wit and learning unprofitably squandered. Attention has no relief; the affections are never moved" (para. 170), it is because of the poem's inability to form a larger, freeing, pleasurable experience for the reader.

Thus far, Johnson's thought suggests that Donne was unable to move the deep affections of the reader because he was unable to represent them. That is, the observation on the moral and experiential paucity of the poems is of an artistic failure, and in this Johnson echoes his observation on "Lycidas" that: "In this poem there is no nature, for there is no truth; there is no art, for there is nothing new."[43] But Johnson also comments on an experiential problem he sees in the metaphysicals, who "wrote rather as beholders than partakers of human nature; as beings looking upon good and evil, impassive and at leisure; as Epicurean deities making remarks on the actions of men and the vicissitudes of life, without interest and without emotion. Their courtship was void of fondness and their lamentation of sorrow" (para. 57).

The force of this criticism clearly has much to do with the metaphysicals being like "Epicurean deities." Johnson's *Dictionary* definitions of epicureanism stress luxuriousness, sensual enjoyment, and "gross pleasure," thereby identifying the hedonistic and un-Christian strand of the Epicurean philosophy that saw the gods as living in remote contentment from the world and indifferent to its suffering. However, Walter Charleton's *Epicurus' Morals* (1656) and Thomas Stanley's *History of Philosophy* (1660) had introduced a different Epicurus into English thought: they distinguished the freedom from anxiety, simple happiness, and lasting pleasure that characterized the Epicurean doctrine (as mediated by the French philosopher Pierre Gassendi), from the Cyrenaic propagation of corporeal pleasure, indulgence, and the immediate present as the ultimate end of Epicurus' teaching. Several passages in Cowley's *Essays in Verse and Prose* show him as attracted to Epicurus' ideals of retirement, abstemiousness, and spiritual tranquility, and to be interested in a philosophy that "rationally guides" one's pleasures.[44]

While one might observe that Johnson's Review of *A Free Inquiry* (1757) identifies Jenyns with the remoteness of Epicureanism, he distinguishes between Jenyns' position and the sensibility he found in Cowley's *Anacreontiques*, songs he notes, "dedicated to festivity and gaiety, in which even the morality is voluptuous, and which teach nothing but the enjoyment of the present day" ("Life of Cowley," para. 115). There is nothing problematic for Johnson in the pleasure of these little poems, to which he gives full utterance. They are like Shakespeare's comedy (*Shakespeare*, 1, 70) in that their "familiarity of language" and "dialogue of comedy ... [are] transcribed from popular manners and real life" (para. 117), and are felt by Johnson to take pleasure in the ebb and flow of ordinary feelings, without any temptation to be pseudo-heroic or indecent. The *Anacreontiques* are distinguished by their human sentiment and their continuing freshness – they "give now [1777] all the pleasure which they ever gave" [para. 118]).[45] However, the Epicurean distance of metaphysical wit leads Johnson to formulate the following notion:

But Wit, abstracted from its effects upon the hearer, may be more rigorously and philosophically considered as a kind of *discordia concors*; a combination of dissimilar images, or discovery of occult resemblances in things apparently unlike. (para. 56)

This is not a definition of all wit, but particularly of that pertaining to Donne, a manner whose appreciation requires an inner abstraction in the reader. In order to know this kind of wit, the reader has to separate himself from the experience of the poetry – "Wit, abstracted from its effects upon the reader" – which, by implication, are themselves problematic, disjunct, "harsh." Although Johnson is able to *imagine* a poem "abstracted from its effects upon the hearer," and to formulate that unrelatedness, he clearly does not like being made to *feel* that way.[46]

Valuation partly entails making an implicit comparison between Donne's wit and the writing of others, as Johnson does when he formulates the *absence* of a particular kind of sublime experience in Donne and the metaphysicals:

> Nor was the sublime more within their reach than the pathetick; for they never attempted that comprehension and expanse of thought which at once fills the whole mind, and of which the first is sudden astonishment, and the second rational admiration. (para. 58)

Hagstrum – setting the tone for half a century of Johnson criticism – finds Johnson's criticism to be governed by three critical discourses – the beautiful, the pathetic, the sublime – and for each of these qualities to be exemplified by a different writer (Pope is beautiful, Shakespeare is pathetic, Milton is sublime).[47] But the force of Johnson's observation on the sublime and the pathetic lies in the discovery of interpenetrating qualities and discourses that are commonly thought of as being mutually exclusive: sudden astonishment along with rational admiration.[48] A poem like "A Nocturnal upon S. Lucies day" is, for Johnson, neither sublime nor pathetic, because, unlike (for example) Ben Jonson's "On my first Sonne," it is unable to move the affections of the reader, *or* to fill the reader's mind with a sublime experience – that is, one that almost (but not quite) leaves the reader breathless, and then finally focuses his astonishment in a rational experience of one's connections to (rather than separation from) life.[49] Pathos and sublimity are thus not characteristics of different poems, but different ways in which the same poem might be a "just representation of general nature." In Jonson's "On my first Sonne," the struggle between faith and reason is inseparable from the speaker's personal loss. Even though the poet knows that death is natural and even to be envied, he cannot *not* feel deep personal loss – "O, could I loose all father, now." But to lose his humanity now, easeful as it might be, would be to betray his love for the dead son, so the pain is transformed in a monumental effort into a commemoration of the child and of the father's powerlessness – "Rest in soft peace, and ask'd, say here doth lye / Ben. Jonson his best piece of poetrie" – in a poem that measures with unusual clarity the irrevocable distance between father and poet, child and poem.

The event of Jonson's little poem is no less serious than that of Donne's, yet it achieves its effects with a fulness that belies its engagement with life. For Donne, the loss seems to be so strangely, so frantically felt that it becomes a kind of bravura that astonishes the reader but does not ground him: "As they were wholly employed on something unexpected and surprising they had no regard to that uniformity of sentiment, which enables us to conceive and to excite the pains and the pleasure of other minds" (paras. 57). The reader witnesses the dramatization of "Donne's" grief, but Jonson's poem not only moves the affections, it does so by filling and expanding the mind. (Jonson's "manner," we are told, "resembled that of Donne more in the ruggedness of his lines than in the cast of his sentiments" [para. 62].) It enables, I suspect, even the childless and the female reader to feel what it is to be a father, and in so doing it rises to the grandeur of generality. This perhaps is an example of what Johnson understood by true wit being at once natural and new.

Donne and Cowley, on the other hand, "in forming descriptions... looked out not for images, but for conceits" (para. 98); "their attempts were always analytick: they broke every image into fragments" (para. 58). Some have assumed that Johnson lacks the requisite sensibility and critical vocabulary to appreciate Donne's intellectual agility. Donald Greene, for example, states that "there can be no question" that "image" for Johnson "meant little more than 'a mental picture.'"[50] But when placed in the broader context of Johnson's usage, his understanding of the term is obviously quite subtle, as his discussion of famous night pieces suggests.[51] Comparing Dryden's description of night (in *The Indian Emperor*, III. ii) with Macbeth's meditation before the murder of Duncan –

> All things are hush'd as Nature's self lay dead;
> The mountains seem to nod their drowsy head;
> The little birds, in dreams, their songs repeat,
> And sleeping flow'rs beneath the night-dew sweat.
> Even lust and envy sleep; yet love denies
> Rest to my soul, and slumber to my eyes.
> (*Indian Emperor*)[52]

> Now o'er one half the world
> Nature seems dead, and wicked dreams abuse
> The curtain'd sleep; now witchcraft celebrates
> Pale Hecate's offerings   (*Macbeth*, II.i. 49–52)

– Johnson notes that "*this image*... is perhaps the most striking that poetry can produce," and then elaborates: "Night is described by two great poets, but one describes a night of quiet, the other of perturbation. In the night of Dryden, all the disturbers of the world are laid asleep; in that of Shakespeare, nothing but sorcery, lust, and murder, is awake. He that reads Dryden, finds himself lull'd with serenity, and disposed to solitude and contemplation. He that peruses Shakespeare, looks around alarmed, and starts to find himself alone" (*Shakespeare*, II, 769–70). Whether or not one agrees with this judgment, it is clear that Johnson's use of the term "image" refers to the *whole* of the imaginative effect, generated by these dramatic moments, in which the mind either finds itself at home in nature, or is forced to inhabit the dark space between the heart and civilized norms.

There is no reason to assume that Johnson uses the term any differently in the "Life of Cowley." Donne is a poet whose originality and powerful hold on the language ("our stubborn language bends") *challenges* Johnson to formulate a decisive statement, the emotional force of which *counters* (rather than coincides with) Donne's genius. When Johnson asks the reader to compare Donne's description of night (quoted by him, para. 98) with the passage of Dryden's quoted above, he hardly has to make his judgment explicit, since "in forming descriptions [Donne] looked out not for images, but for conceits" (para. 98).

METAPHOR

The function of "image" in Johnson's critical thought is an aspect of his metaphoric grasp of the critical enterprise itself. To say as much is to question the established body of criticism on Johnson's reading of literature, which, in the words of René Wellek, tends to believe in "Johnson's incomprehension of the centrally metaphorical character of poetry."[53] Both Wellek and Allen Tate[54] identify metaphoric limitation in Johnson's supposed desire to have both tenor and vehicle derive from the same, preferably abstract realm. The test passage chosen by Wellek and Tate are the famous lines from Denham's *Cooper's Hill* and Johnson's comments on the passage:

> O could I flow like thee, and make thy stream
> My great example, as it is my theme!
> Though deep, yet clear, though gentle, yet not dull,
> Strong without rage, without ore-flowing full.
> (lines 189–93)[55]

Johnson's comment on the passage is as follows:

The lines are in themselves not perfect, for most of the words thus artfully opposed are to be understood simply on one side of the comparison, and metaphorically on the other; and if there be any language which does not express intellectual operations by material images, into that language they cannot be translated. (*Lives*, I, 78)

Both Wellek (98) and Tate (493) believe that Johnson betrays a rationalistic literal-mindedness, and that his real objection to Denham's lines is that they cannot be translated into "abstract language." It is difficult to see how such a view can be derived from Johnson's words, especially if his comment is taken in context, and not judged in terms of a post-Romantic theory of metaphor. That context consists partly of other comments on the passage in the "Life of Denham," other contingent remarks on poetry, and the history of the reception of Denham's famous quatrain.

In understanding Johnson's remarks on Denham's lines *as metaphor* one needs to recognize that, since Dryden's time, the passage had been discussed by critics almost solely in terms of prosody. In the Preface to his translation of Virgil's *Pastorals* (1697), Dryden had set his contemporaries a task: quoting lines 191–92 of Denham's poem he remarked that "there are few who make verses, have observed the sweetness of these two lines... And there are yet fewer who can find the reason of that sweetness."[56] The list of critics who tried to answer that question included John Hughes, John Mason, James Burnet, and Samuel Say.[57] Johnson, too, could be answering Dryden's question, not by confining himself to the passage's versification (essential as that is to its "sweetness"), but by noticing its metaphoric effect. Far from wanting his metaphors to derive both tenor and vehicle from the same, "abstract" realm, Johnson's usual understanding of metaphor stresses the *difference* of those prosodic elements. For example, in discussing the simile of the angel in Addison's *The Campaign*, Johnson remarks that: "A poetical simile is the discovery of likeness between two actions, in their general nature dissimilar, or of causes terminating by *different operations* in some resemblance of effect" [my emphases].[58] The simile is more excellent as the lines of comparison "approach from greater distance." Why? Because "the mind is impressed with the resemblance of things generally unlike, as unlike as intellect and body" (II, 130). Heterogeneous ideas are yoked together, but not by violence, and not according to "occult resemblances in things apparently unlike."[59]

Tate thinks that Johnson means: "it is the fault of the passage that the intellectual qualities which Denham desires cannot be 'translated' into nonmaterial images," and that this means that for the tenor of the figure to be convincing it "ought to have translatability into a high degree of abstraction; it ought to be detachable from the literal image of the flowing river" (493). But what Johnson says, first, is that *if* there is a "language which does not express intellectual operations by material images," then "into that language they [the lines] cannot be translated."

This is precisely true – but it is a situation which does not arise in English: Denham's lines are manifestly able to translate intellectual operations and material images.

Johnson's second point is that the particular strength of Denham's lines have to do with their not *actually* translating intellectual operations and material images: this, after all, is a *metaphor* not translation or lexicographical definition. Translation is for Johnson (and Dryden and Pope), a *kind* of metaphor, and subject to similar lexical and cultural barriers and limitations as all writing. In lexicography, Johnson ran into the problem of defining simple words – "the idea signified by them has not more than one appellation... names, therefore, have often many ideas, but few ideas have many names" – and this, in turn, suggested to him the inescapably diachronic, and metaphoric, nature of language: "It was therefore necessary to use the proximate word... [but] the sense may easily be collected entire from the examples."[60] Contrary to Locke's findings, names and ideas for Johnson are not synchronized, not even simple ones, a relationship that becomes still more disjunct once things (or "material images," to use Johnson's words in the "Life of Denham") are introduced into the equation. The "examples" in the *Dictionary*, however, permit an *approximation*, and taken thus Denham's passage is an *almost* "perfect" example of such an approximation.

Its action as metaphor derives from its *seeming* – but only seeming – to translate one realm into another, and not actually doing that. Donald Davidson's contentious understanding of metaphor is, in some ways, parallel to Johnson's here: "metaphors mean what the words, in their most literal interpretation, mean, and nothing more... Metaphor makes us see one thing as another by making some literal statement that inspires or prompts the insight."[61] Hence the fine distinctions in Johnson's praise of the lines:

so much meaning is comprised in so few words; the particulars of resemblance are so perspicaciously collected, and every mode of excellence separated from its adjacent fault by so nice a line of limitation; the different parts of the sentence are so accurately adjusted; and the flow of the last couplet is so smooth and sweet – that the passage however celebrated has not been praised above its merit. It has beauty peculiar to itself. (I, 79)

"[T]he mind is impressed with the resemblance of things generally unlike, as unlike as intellect and body." Approximating intellect and body would seem to be the central business of metaphor for Johnson, just as, of semantics, it is approximating sign and signified. For Johnson, the power of resemblance (Davidson's "seeing one thing as another") is inseparable from the poet's knowing the difference between intellectual operations and material images, between intellect and body (Davidson's "literal statement"). In fact, Johnson's terminology indicates how *much* mind and world have become mirrors for each other in Denham's lines, anticipating Empson's notion of "sympathetic magic" – called out by the fact that "some of the adjectives apply more directly to the river, some to the poem, and... your attention is kept moving from one to the other."[62] This conviction is confirmed by Johnson's sense of Denham's fine discriminations ("the particulars of resemblance are so perspicaciously collected... the different parts of the sentence are so accurately adjusted"), and his sense that the poetic effect is something that could not be willed and cannot be accounted for by the sum of its parts: "It has beauty peculiar to itself, and must be numbered among those felicities which cannot be produced at will by wit and labour, but must arise unexpectedly in some hour propitious to poetry" (I, 79).

What we effectively have in Johnson's remark on Denham is a reflection on the nature of language as such. The point about the translatability or non-translatability of Denham's lines, of course, is that they draw attention to their metaphoric nature and of language itself. For Johnson knows that there is *no* such language as he hypothesizes! It is in the nature of language to be separated from the "objects" it signifies, whether material or immaterial. Contrary to Hagstrum's view that Johnson wants metaphor to derive both its vehicle and its tenor from the "real" world, and Abrams' that Johnson is unable to respond to a metaphor whose "foundation... [is] difficult to discover,"[63] Johnson's criticism of the metaphysicals failure at metaphor is that it is the excessive, even exclusive *concern* of Donne and Cowley with the so-called real world which is the problem: "all the power of description is destroyed by a scrupulous enumeration; and the force of metaphors is lost, when the mind by the mention of particulars is turned more upon the original than the secondary sense, more upon that from which the illustration is drawn than that to which it is applied" (I, 45). Denham's lines, presumably, are *almost* perfect because the original and the secondary senses are *almost* equally balanced, whereas the habit of Cowley and Donne "is that of pursuing [their] thoughts to their last ramifications, by which [they lose] the grandeur of generality" (para. 133). The grandeur of generality is what comes from employing the "force of metaphors."

JOHNSON'S POWER OF PERFORMANCE

Johnson's account of the metaphysicals is perhaps *more* sympathetic and *more* critical of Donne's poetry than I have suggested. As part of the "Life of Cowley," the section on the metaphysical poets is designed to identify Cowley's general style, but then Johnson finds Cowley to be the best of the metaphysicals because he has "as much sentiment and more musick" as his predecessors (para. 63). Cowley is the best of the metaphysicals for Johnson because he has less "metaphysicalness" – or conceitedness – and more nature than Donne and Cleveland. This finding is sustained by the unusual praise Johnson gives to Cowley's *Miscellanies, Anacreontiques, Essays in Verse and Prose,* and some of the *Pindaric Odes,* as well as by what he says of Cowley's innovativeness ("he was the first who imparted to English numbers the enthusiasm of the greater ode, and the gaiety of the less"), his poetic variety ("he was equally qualified for spritely sallies and for lofty flights"), and his contribution towards developing poetic translation ("he was among those who freed translation from servility, and, instead of following his author at a distance, walked by his side") (I, 64).

At the same time, this text gives Donne serious consideration. In 1690 Francis Atterbury had used his edition of Waller's poems[64] to define Waller's achievement in polished and civilized versification *against* Donne's "barbarity." "If any man doubts of this [Waller's great achievement]," Atterbury suggests, "let him read ten lines in *Donne,* and he'll be quickly convinc'd."[65] Aside from the occasional and routine praise of the satires, Atterbury's view of Donne prevailed throughout the eighteenth century. Johnson, however, was not so easily convinced: while Dryden was complimenting the Earl of Dorset by elevating him *above* Donne ("You equal Donne in the variety, multiplicity, and choice of thoughts; you excel him in the manner and the words"),[66] Johnson knew that Dorset's poems were nothing more than "the effusions of a man of wit, gay, vigorous, and airy."[67] Although Johnson acknowledges Waller as having "added something to our elegance of diction, and something to our propriety of thought,"[68] he also sees him as a poet not "much elevated by nature, nor amplified by learning" (I, 294), and in a lesser category from that of Donne.

Donne engaged Johnson in deeper and more stimulating ways than either Waller or Dorset, and most other poets he encountered. Not only does Donne's poetry have qualities that Johnson genuinely admires – learning, logic, argumentativeness, subtlety, genius – but he also becomes sufficiently inward with Donne's imaginative world to formulate an imaginative critical statement that participates in the very qualities it criticizes. Paradoxically, though Cowley is more congenial to Johnson's sensibility than Donne, Cowley without Donne would probably not have stimulated Johnson to write the dissertation on the metaphysical poets. What Johnson says of Dryden's prose is true of his own remarks on the metaphysicals, that it is "the criticism of a poet; not a dull collection of theorems, nor a rude detection of faults, which perhaps the censor was not able to have committed; but a gay and vigorous dissertation, where delight is mingled with instruction, and where the author proves his right of judgement by his power of performance."[69] In this Johnson answers Geoffrey Hartman's epitaphic proposition with which I began this chapter, that "literary commentary may cross the line and become as demanding as literature," a proposition which, one might add, fueled much of the best (and much of the worst) theoretical criticism in the wake of Derrida.

So, when Johnson writes of the metaphysicals, "[t]heir attempts were always analytick: they broke every image into fragments, and could no more represent by their slender conceits and laboured particularities the prospects of nature or the scenes of life, than he who dissects a sun-beam with a prism can exhibit the wide effulgence of a summer noon" (par. 58), the metaphoric form of the statement is both a joke at Donne's expense, as well as a sensitive echo of the *kind* of wit Johnson found in Donne:

> And as no chemic yet the elixir got,
>   But glorifies his pregnant pot,
>   If by the way to him befall
> Some odoriferous thing, or medicinal,
> So, lovers dream a rich and long delight,
> But get a winter-seeming summer's night.
>   ("Love's Alchemy," lines 7–12)

Splitting a sunbeam with a prism in order to demonstrate the beauty of a summer's day, and then making *that* a metaphor for "the scenes of life," is exactly the kind of thing Donne does!

Furthermore, when Johnson writes that Donne and Cowley "were wholly employed on something unexpected and surprising [and] had no regard to that uniformity of sentiment, which enables us to conceive and to excite the pains and the pleasure of other minds" (para. 57), the measured deliberateness and the eloquence of the sentence swell and open the mind, suggesting something of an *equivalence* to the experience

Johnson does *not* find in the poetry itself. The parallel clauses, the internal rhymes, and the rhythm ("enables us to conceive and to excite the pains and the pleasure") open the mind, and suggest some experience beneath the level of conscious thought (awakening those ideas that slumber in the heart) which Johnson generally does not find in the metaphysicals.

Yet, his particular project needs what he *does* find in Donne, and in a typical yet surprising gesture of reciprocity Johnson actively appropriates, even translates, the antithetical wit of Donne, his language, in order to create his own memorable critical formulation. His remarks stress the absence of a certain feeling in the poetry: but this is no mere censure, for his prose at the same time manifests its own sadness. This is a sadness *of* the poetry, that which the poetry of Donne and Cowley lacks ("Their courtship was void of fondness and their lamentation of sorrow," para. 57), but it is also Johnson's sadness *toward* the human attitude implied by the poetry. Christopher Ricks has observed, in writing of the endings of Donne's poems, that "Donne at times wrote more deeply than he meant, or than he could bear, and what we then engage with is ... imaginings which – beyond the poet's final digressive powers – the poem is forced to spit out and spit upon."[70] The reciprocity of Johnson's critical style and procedure in this life – marking it as a cutting edge and sign of intelligence in his criticism – is a kind of response to the painful tension remarked by Ricks: "in the mass of materials, which ingenious absurdity has thrown together, genuine wit and useful knowledge may be sometimes found, buried perhaps in grossness of expression, but useful to those who know their value" (para. 61).

The general nature by which metaphysical poetry is implicitly tested, and found "inadequate" (to adapt Johnson's own term), is, then, something towards which Johnson has to work; it is neither entirely part of his given experience, nor entirely outside and beyond it. It is, in short, the product of his imaginative engagement with literature, and a version of Wordsworth's creating the taste by which he is judged. The only wonder is that commentators have found this rhetorical authority to be somehow odd and illicit. That authority, as I have now argued, rests partly on the qualities of nature that Johnson himself articulates in the Preface to Shakespeare and the "Life of Cowley," and nature, in its turn, is a manifestation of a form of memory. But Johnson's authority – his preference, for example, for poetry of nature over other kinds of poetry, and his willingness to put himself behind such preference – also entails an attitude towards authorship, that is, literary character, which, in the *Lives of the Poets*, comes to be an expression of and a vehicle for different kinds of memory. Cowley's familiarity as a poet, Milton's sublimity, Dryden's ease and energy, Pope's heroic aspiration, Addison's politeness, Watts' devoutness, Parnell's simplicity – all these are ways of describing poetic character in Johnson's terminology, each of which bears its own distinctive relation to memory. But before I move into a discussion of the ways in which Johnson uses poetic character to establish the parameters and the horizon of memory in the *Lives*, I need to address Johnson's association of legal narrative with critical judgment and historical experience.

CHAPTER 3

Law, narrative, and memory

On the morning of Tuesday 17 June 1783, Johnson (in his 73rd year) awoke to discover that he had suffered a stroke and had been deprived of the power of speech. He wrote the following note to his neighbour, Edmund Allen:

Dear Sir,
It hath pleased Almighty God this morning to deprive me of the powers of speech; and as I do not know but that it might be his further good pleasure to deprive me soon of my senses, I request you will, on receipt of this note, come to me, and act for me, as the exigencies of my case might require. I am sincerely your's,
Sam Johnson[1]

There is something iconic about this moment in Johnson's life: it tells of a long series of afflictions, both mental and physical; it tells of his courage in facing a death that always troubled him; and it tells of his wry humour – for a few days later (19 June 1783) he described the stroke to Hester Thrale by writing: "I was alarmed, and prayed God, that however he might afflict my body he would spare my understanding. This prayer, that I might try the integrity of my faculties I made in Latin verse. The lines were not good, but I knew them not to be very good, I made them easily, and concluded myself to be unimpaired in my faculties" (*Letters*, IV, 151). Above all, however, the moment in which Johnson's voice is silenced, as he imagines it, by a more powerful voice than his own, and he records God's writing – as manifested in the physiological life of his own body – in the simple and restrained eloquence of his letter, this moment dramatizes the inextricable relationship between identity, speech, and writing in Johnson's works, as it does the residual, almost instinctively textual manner in which he deals with the limits of the reality revealed to him by this occurrence. This powerful moment in Johnson's life is also, I would like to suggest, an example of *legal* thinking, in its broadest liberal terms, in that in the eighteenth century law helped to produce the personal identity of the civic, reasonable, and juridical individual.[2]

I have already begun to suggest how Johnson's authority as a writer is textually and historically inscribed within mnemonic terms. I now wish to broaden the consideration of Johnson's textual authority by establishing a connection between memory and law in Johnson's thought. My general proposition is that law, and various forms of legal understanding, underlie most of Johnson's thinking, including his thinking about language and memory. This chapter focuses particularly on ways in which Johnson's legal rhetoric and legal knowledge contribute textually towards a construction of personal identity, which, in turn, underwrites Johnson's general understanding of the function of human limits in relation to human experience.

JOHNSON'S LEGAL UNDERSTANDING

Johnson had a formidable autodidactic legal knowledge which informed the intellectual and moral fabric of his thinking. Hawkins, Boswell, Burke and many other contemporaries recognized his great competence in legal matters, which had formed early, under the tutelage of Gilbert Walmsley, continuing throughout his life, and which Johnson attempted, unsuccessfully, to turn into a professional direction in 1745.[3] Johnson took many opportunities to advise friends like William Hamilton, Robert Chambers, and Boswell on legal, constitutional and historical matters.[4] His collaboration with Robert Chambers between October 1766 and spring 1769, in writing the lectures on the English law (given 1767–1773) as part of the Vinerian professorship at Oxford, is only the most significant example of his extraordinary learning in this field.[5]

While it is unlikely that Johnson was entirely responsible for any single lecture given by Chambers,[6] the consensus is that he was actively involved in their composition, especially in the first twenty lectures of the course. These lectures comprised the general Introduction, providing a consideration of the metaphysical and practical foundations of all law as well as the Saxon and Norman roots of the English common law; and it included Part I of the course, a history of the public law tracing the ancient and modern structures of British government. The Vinerian lectures echo views, and exhibit some of the stylistic and rhetorical organization of Johnson's canonical works. A partial list of topics covered suggests the broad range of topics addressed in the lectures: natural law, feudal government and law, public law (including the law, history, and constitution of the monarchy, the royal family and the aristocracy, parliament, the Privy Council, the judiciary, civil, canon, and maritime courts, diplomacy, the colonies, and corporations), criminal law, and private law. While Johnson's personal supervision clearly benefited Chambers in this significant undertaking in the history of the English law, the collaboration also, by all accounts, had an impact on Johnson's thinking. The legal and jurisprudential knowledge he had acquired while working on the Harleian Library (1743) and then on the *Dictionary* (1745–55) was supplemented and increased by his secretarial work for William Hamilton[7] and collaboration with Chambers. Some scholars emphasize the generality of Johnson's interest in this field – "the social, moral and historical aspects of law"[8] – and Curley remarks that Johnson's "collaboration with Chambers seems to have augmented his already profound knowledge of government and to have facilitated that peculiar density of philosophical disquisition found in his travel book and pamphlets of the 1770s" (*Lectures*, I, 69).

Johnson's engagement with legal issues and with what jurisprudential theorists have identified as the narrativity of law, began as early as his work at the *Gentleman's Magazine* (1739) and the Parliamentary Debates (1741). It touched many of the aspects of social life discussed in the *Rambler* and of the history of language in the *Dictionary*; in various ways it was central to the *Journal of a Tour to the Hebrides* (1775) and the *Lives of the Poets* (1779–81). Johnson's considerable knowledge of constitutional law has been appropriated by literary historians who identify Johnson as a Jacobite,[9] and, whatever one's estimation of Johnson's attitude towards Jacobitism, it is clear that the law was never for him a marginal or optional undertaking: he considered a knowledge of the law as necessary to the fulfillment of one's civic duty as an Englishman. Johnson's remark to the young Boswell – "I know not how you will make a better choice than by studying the civil Law as your father advises"[10] – is taken up in his Preface to Dodsley's *The Preceptor* (1748):

This Knowledge by peculiar Necessity constitutes a Party of the Education of an *Englishman*, who professes to obey his Prince according to the Law, and who is himself a secondary Legislator, as he gives his Consent by his Representative, to all the Laws by which he is bound, and has a Right to petition the great Council of the Nation, whenever he thinks they are deliberating upon an Act detrimental to the Interest of the Community. This is therefore a Subject to which the Thoughts of a young Man ought to be directed. (*P & D*, 187–88)

Not only the thoughts of a young man, however, for as Johnson himself grew older he came increasingly to believe, in the words of one of the Vinerian lectures, that "the end of law is to promote the happiness of the world, partly by obviating the corruptions of human nature, and partly by supplying its defects."[11] Like Locke and Hume,[12] the *Lectures* see law as positively conducive to the development of civic and political, though not necessarily to personal, freedom. Law, for both Chambers and Johnson, necessitates the assimilation of personal freedom to social and political order. The "unwritten law of social nature . . . the great and pregnant principle of political necessity" for Johnson, is that "government is necessary to man, and where obedience is not compelled, there is no government. If the subject refuses to obey, it is the duty of authority to use compulsion. Society cannot subsist but by the power, first of making laws, and then of enforcing them."[13]

This emphasis on the enforceability of law should not necessarily be thought of as a sign of Johnson's heavy-handedness or illiberal disposition, for Grotius, Pufendorf and other eminent jurists all saw the effectiveness of law as implying enforceability. Derrida, too, notes that "the word 'enforceability' reminds us that there is no such thing as law (*droit*) that doesn't imply *in itself, a priori, in the analytic structure of its concept*, the possibility of being 'enforced,' applied by force. There are, to be sure, laws that are not enforced, but there is no law without enforceability, and no applicability or enforceability of the law without force."[14] It is in response to the corruptions, the weaknesses and the sheer inventiveness of human nature that the political, social, and civil institutions of the country have evolved and from which they derive their historical and their continuing meaning: "In sovereignty there are no gradations. There may be limited royalty, there may be limited consulship; but there can be no limited government."[15]

The basis of law for eighteenth-century jurists is the English common law. As Johnson points out under the definition for "common law" in the *Dictionary*, many things that begin as common law become statute law, and many parliamentary statutes reverse the trend and become common law.[16] In seventeenth- and eighteenth-century England the common law constituted a powerful popular and cultural memory, consisting, as Chambers writes, "of customs derived from immemorial tradition, and of maxims established by immemorial practice."[17] As Sir Matthew Hale discussed, the English common law embodied "values shared by people who identify with each other across the barriers of individuality and class, values learned by imitation, confirmed by habit, transmitted through national history."[18] The common law, resting on natural or divine law and the human reason that Hale, Locke, and Chambers saw as constituting the foundation and integrity of law itself, was thus identified as universal in character.

However, the common law's immutability did not disable it from adapting to changing circumstances without forgoing its ability to foster national identity. In some ways this body of law operated as Benedict Anderson describes print-culture as doing in enabling people to imagine and forge the nation in the eighteenth century.[19] The civil and political institutions of England evolved, and took their meaning and their strength partly from their capacity to adapt to changing historical circumstances. Neither Johnson nor Chambers subscribed to a rationalistic or historically fixed concept of the common law as articulated, for example, by Sir William Blackstone's *Commentaries on the Laws of England* (1765–1769) and Sir Edward Coke's *Reports* (1600–1615) and *Institutes of the Laws of England* (4 Parts; 1628–1644), notwithstanding the use of Blackstone and Coke as sources for the lectures.[20] More in the vein of Locke and Hale, the Vinerian lectures emphasized the evolving and flexible nature of English law over time: "We now live at a time when by diffusion of civility and circulation of intelligence the manners of the whole nation are uniform, when by determinations of acknowledged authority, the limits of all jurisdictions are fixed, when a long course of records and precedents has furnished models for almost every civil transaction, and experience has supplied what reason wanted in the art of government."[21] And because experience recognises "reason" as significantly limited when it comes to cultural and even constitutional history, the nature of such institutions as the House of Commons cannot be determined by a priori categories or a hegemonic notion of origins: "young enquirers into the origin of our government" are cautioned "against too great confidence in systematical writers or modern historians," who "deceive themselves and their readers when they attempt to explain by reason that which happened by chance, when they search for profound policy and subtle refinement in temporary expedients [and] capricious propositions."[22]

This sceptical, genealogical attitude toward governmental institutions implicitly recognizes, I would propose, the invented nature of the "origin" and the commonly metaleptic structure of the reasoning that seeks to anchor the authority of present institutions in a clearly perceived and stable past.[23] Johnson demonstrates this kind of sophistication in dealing with the function of legal language and structures. I have already suggested how adeptly he handles legal advocacy and judgment in discussing the ethics of legal rhetoric with Boswell. In response to Boswell's concern that lawyers argue unjust cases, as I remarked, Johnson's analysis emphasized the contingent nature of the truth produced in a juridical venue, and the highly rhetorical nature of the advocate's argument. Both of these issues are taken up by Johnson in other, more complex instances of legal advice he offered Boswell, two of which I wish to discuss here, the first dealing with property law and inheritance, the other with slavery. These are issues that might be said to go to the heart of eighteenth-century self-conception and authority, and reveal a residual political and legal engagement in Johnson's thought.

In late 1775 the longstanding dispute between Boswell and his father about the Auchinleck estate came to a head. Lord Auchinleck planned to entail the estate in ways that he believed would maintain its integrity and profitability, and protect it from Boswell's waywardness, so he proposed to include within such an entail all of his natural heirs, including women. To entail inherited lands, Lord Auchinleck needed Boswell's consent. Although an entail might actually exclude Boswell from inheritance, he nonetheless supported the idea, but believed that his father should emulate the practice of David Boswell (the fifth Laird and Lord Auchinleck's great-granduncle) who had bypassed his four daughters in order to settle the estate on his nephew, Lord Auchinleck's grandfather. Boswell, for his part, wanted to include his son, Alexander (born in October 1775), but to bypass his two daughters (a third was born in 1780), and to reach back to entail the estate on the male heirs of Thomas Boswell, the founder of the estate (1504).[24] During the disagreement, Boswell wrote to Johnson (2 January 1776) seeking his "friendly opinion and advice" on the case, and Johnson replied to Boswell in six letters in 1776, that of 15 January, 3 February, 9 February, 15 February, 24 February, and 5 March.[25]

Johnson's attitude towards property was not uncomplicated. As a man of his time he saw property, as Roy Porter puts it, as the "soul of eighteenth-century society,"[26] and would not have disagreed with Locke's proposition that "the great and *chief end*... of Mens uniting into Commonwealths, and putting themselves under Government, *is the Preservation of their Property.*"[27] Johnson attached great cultural importance to safeguarding the inheritance of landed estates and when staying with Lord Errol at Slains Castle on his Scottish journey he "spoke well in favour of entails, to preserve lines of men whom mankind are accustomed to reverence."[28] At the same time, Johnson brought to bear on specific questions of property an independent legal understanding that often cut against his more conventional assumptions. Though asserting, in the matter of entailing Auchinleck, a need for "more knowledge of local law, and more acquaintance with the general rules of inheritance, than I can claim" (*Life*, II, 416), Johnson's letters to Boswell actually exemplify precise knowledge of the matters at hand, and also engage in a complex rhetoric for the attainment of certain ends.

One of Johnson's purposes is to alleviate Boswell's melancholic fixation on the necessity of a *specific* course of action. Boswell "apprehended that we were under an implied obligation, in honour and good faith, to transmit the estate by the same tenure which we held it, which was as heirs male, excluding nearer females" (*Life*, II, 415). But Johnson's discussion repeatedly questions the logic of this assumption, pointing out that "[p]rovidence is not counteracted by any means which Providence puts into our power," and marshalling various kinds of evidence to free Boswell from "the supposed necessity of a rigorous entail" (II, 421). Johnson seems to see Boswell's *psychological* difficulty – a zealous, over-*rational* attempt to replicate the past – as misunderstanding the *legal* issues involved. Just as Boswell cannot "hope wholly to reason away [his] troubles" (II, 423), so he cannot expect to fully know the motives and intentions of the ancestor whose action he wishes to imitate:

Intentions must be gathered from acts. When he left the estate to his nephew, by excluding his daughters, was it, or was it not, in his power to have perpetuated the succession to the males? If he could have done it, he seems to have shewn, by omitting it, that he did not desire it to be done; and, upon your own principles, you will not easily prove your right to destroy that capacity of succession which your ancestors have left. (II, 417)

Origins are obscure, perhaps irretrievable, and original intentions are known only by historical effect. Since we cannot know that David Boswell intended to exclude females from inheritance in perpetuity, Boswell is under no moral obligation to institute such a measure. Nor is he legally bound to do so, for "the rules of succession are, in a great part, purely legal, [and] no man can be supposed to bequeath any thing, but upon legal terms." There is no clear legal ground for "limit[ing] that succession which descended to you unlimited" (II, 418, 417).

Johnson's legal arguments, however, are informed by a broader historical understanding of Boswell's proposed entail that implies Johnson's sense of temporality and cultural memory: "As times and opinions are always changing, I know not whether it be not usurpation to prescribe rules to posterity, by presuming to judge of what we cannot know" (*Life*,

II, 417). "Usurpation" is "forcible, unjust, illegal seizure or possession," and, as Johnson's *Dictionary* illustrations indicate, it implies a long history of English (and Scottish) constitutional law. Particularly interesting, however, is Johnson's manner of placing the legal question within the context of time and the limits of human knowledge and institutions. The structure of thought here is analogous to the narrative of temporality and memory in "Rambler" 41, discussed in chapter 1, for the nature of the mind and human experience within temporal change seems to distance and problematize both past and future, both of which become functions – and creations – of present choice. Thus, Johnson agrees with Lord Hailes's suggestion that "entails are encroachments on the dominion of Providence," but, surprisingly, he pushes Hailes's thought further in observing that his principle "may be extended to *all* hereditary privileges and *all* permanent institutions" (my emphases): "I do not see why it may not be extended to any provision but for the present hour, since all care about futurity proceeds upon a supposition, that we know at least in some degree what will be future. Of the future we certainly know nothing" (II, 420).

Johnson's argument is offered as the effect of probable reasoning upon the facts themselves, yet it is carefully crafted to achieve uncommon ends, such as the vindication of the rights of woman. Not that the legal rights of women in the eighteenth century were not as Johnson advocates, for he is clear that "women have natural and equitable claims as well as men, and these claims are not to be capriciously or lightly superseded or infringed" (*Life*, II, 419); but his legal and historical focus has the effect of bringing to the fore those "equitable claims" which Boswell wishes to suppress.[29] What authorizes Johnson's interpretation of the law is his sense of memory, that "as manners make laws, manners likewise repeal them" (II, 419). Manners change not only in time but also according to circumstances. This may be why Johnson allows himself to laugh at the female beneficiaries of Bennet Langton's will, when, in a famous episode (10 May 1773) in Boswell's *Life of Johnson*, he calls them the "three dowdies" and asserts that "an ancient estate should always go to males" (*Life*, II, 261).

It is not clear, however, how much of Johnson's "bold feudal spirit" on this occasion is due to his beliefs or to Boswell's manner of presenting the event, since Boswell is evidently puzzled by the nature of Johnson's subsequent laughter at Langton's will-making: "He now laughed immoderately, without any reason that we could perceive, at our friend's making his will; called him the *testator*, and added, 'I dare say, he thinks he has done a mighty thing'" (*Life*, II, 261). True, Johnson's laughter, as

Fussell suggests, is probably directed at Langton's self-importance, and at the discrepancy between human mortality and the attempt at keeping that reality at bay through fictive constructions. Hence the careful, comic use of the technical term "testator" for one who makes a will.[30] But the laughter is perhaps also about the law's rhetorical power, the *necessary* and freeing fictive structure of the English legal system within which individuals are made into the "internally coherent and self-regulating subject" mentioned by John Zomchick.[31] Hence the irony of a legal will, which is willed into existence by the testator even as he is made into a "testator" by the legal discourse itself: "He believes he has made this will; but he did not make it: you, Chambers, made it for him" (*Life*, II, 262). Johnson had already explained to Boswell that the legal system works by creating its own truths: "Sir, you do not know it [a cause] to be good or bad till the Judge determines it" (II, 47).

However ambiguous Johnson's attitudes sometimes are towards women's legal rights, the consensus now seems to be that his understanding of women's experience in society was genuine and far-reaching.[32] Johnson uses similar arguments against slavery – towards which he was always implacably opposed – as he does against Boswell's plan to entail his estate by excluding women. In the case of the Caribbean slave Joseph Knight, who sued John Wedderburn for his freedom under Scottish law (1777–78),[33] Johnson expresses a general moral disapprobation of slavery, but, importantly, supports that position with specific historical and legal arguments. While his moral argument is based on natural right and natural justice – "men in their original state were equal . . . no man is by nature the property of another" (*Life*, III, 202, 203) – his legal perspective is historical and, as before, linked to a sense of temporality: "An individual may, indeed, forfeit his liberty by a crime; but he cannot by that crime forfeit the liberty of his children. What is true of a criminal seems true likewise of a captive. A man may accept life from a conquering enemy on condition of perpetual servitude; but it is very doubtful whether he can entail that servitude on his descendants" (III, 202). Just as entailing property presumes a control of the future, and is thus a fundamental form of inauthenticity and hubris, so is the enslavement of people.

Self-evidently rational and ethical as Johnson's antipathy to slavery might be, it was not so to Boswell, whose metaleptic rationalization of slavery saw it as "a *status*, which in all ages God has sanctioned, and man has continued," and who thus saw Johnson's position as "prejudice" and as undermining the commercial well-being of the country (*Life*, III, 204). Johnson "lamented that moral right should ever give way to political convenience" in the matter of commercial gain. Boswell's point of view, however, highlights the extent to which Johnson's position here, and on the question of entail, are produced through an active interpretation of law, emphasizing a temporal and historical framework which stresses one's precarious hold on the realities of the present moment. English (and Scottish) law for Johnson was evidently an important form of cultural memory, contributing to the sense of national identity of both countries. Yet the culturally embodied form of the law clearly speaks to its historical changeability, and contributes to its flexibility and its enduring strength. Like Hans-Georg Gadamer, Johnson seemed to understand the intimate intrinsic relationship between rule-governance and concrete–contextual interpretation. On these grounds there is considerable intellectual continuity between Johnson and recent thinkers. Of the original connection between philological, theological, and legal hermeneutics, Gadamer wrote:

In both legal and theological hermeneutics there is the essential tension between the text set down – of the law or of the proclamation – on the one hand and, on the other, the sense arrived at by its application in the particular moment of interpretation, either in judgment or in preaching.[34]

According to Gadamer, the nexus of text and exegesis operates in different ways in philological, theological, and legal contexts, but the common ingredient is that textual meaning only discloses itself in concretely engaged interpretation which, in turn, remains embedded in a social fabric of understanding.[35]

Johnson's moral and legal thought is most authoritative when focused in such specific social, ethical, and linguistic contexts. It is from within such contexts that he develops a historical narrative, which remains sensitive to the randomness and variousness of life identified with Shakespeare's nature, which inscribes its own legality and legitimacy. To the "intimate relationship that ... exists between law, historicality, and narrativity," Hayden White sees a link with "narrativity, whether of the fictional or the factual sort, [which] presupposes the existence of a legal system."[36] Legal theorists have increasingly seen a link between narrative development and law, or in Richard Weisberg's words, "the rise of formal nation-states that must narratively control their histories in order to impose legal order on their peoples ... [T]he desire to narrate is the desire to represent authority, whose legitimacy depends on establishing certain grounding facts."[37] Such "facts" have become the subject of discussion among modern cultural theorists like Homi Bhabha in defining the colonial consciousness and the cultural difference that comes with postcoloniality,[38] as indeed they are for Johnson in his anthropological depictions of Scottish history and culture in *A Journey to the Western islands of Scotland*.

My concern at present is not with the construction and critique of nationhood in Johnson's thought (to which I turn briefly in the final chapter), but with his practical and imaginative deployment of legal theory to inform his sense of temporality and historicality. For the nexus between his legal thought and the social and experiential truths he sees the English legal system as existing to support, partakes of the differential materiality that characterizes his grasp of language and of time. In bringing together rhetoric and truth ambiguously yet so convincingly, his legal opinions demonstrate the dialogical interdependence of "words" and "things" of which he wrote in the Preface to the *Dictionary*. "Language is only the instrument of science, and words are but the signs of ideas," yet, as Johnson demonstrates, "things" are inaccessible to meaning without words, and "science," though representative of an independent body of knowledge, cannot come into being without "language" – indeed, science is ultimately constructed *in* language.[39] If law, then, as Locke argues, exists to facilitate human happiness, Johnson understands the necessity of taking the notion of "happiness" with a sceptical lightness of touch, not expecting the term in itself to yield anything very substantial, but to seek its personal meaning at the points where expectation and desire encounter the limits of experience.

THE DISCURSIVENESS OF LIMITS

When Imlac tries to explain grief to Nekayah (lamenting the loss of Pekuah), his mythical story of the "fabulous inhabitants of the new created earth," who might have "put out their eyes when it was dark,"[40] raises the importance of perspective and narrativity in the tale, and centers in questions both of law and evidence. Putting out our eyes when it is dark is to act according to a totalizing narrative, in the belief of the indivisibility of the world and self. If such literalism is the state of mind of the "fabulous inhabitants," it also characterizes the inhabitants of the Happy Valley, who operate with the "enlightened" empirical view of a necessary relationship of cause to effect – between discrete events, between ideas and reality, and between words and things. Although "every desire was immediately granted" (3) in the Happy Valley, Rasselas is distressed when his appetites are not satisfied as automatically as the animals' are (5–6), and surprised when his fantasies come to nothing (10).

The disappointment arising from frustrated desires, however, is fundamental to two of the text's main insights. When Rasselas laments that "I can discover within me no power of perception which is not glutted with its proper pleasure, yet I do not feel myself delighted" (6), he posits a certain governing relationship between mind and body (and between material sense and spiritual substance), that echoes Locke's thought on memory. In a characteristic complication of Locke, Johnson also suggests that "proper pleasure" lies in the *nexus* of the various human faculties of the experiencing individual, rather than in their individual existence. *Difference*, therefore, becomes important in the narrative's meaning, because every effort to escape their private world and command a more effective mode of action seems to lead the characters to forgetfulness – yet every forgetfulness seems to re-energize their attempts at grasping something real within or just beyond the rim of their lives. While it is desire for the otherness of the world that stimulates the escape from the Happy Valley, once outside the characters reverse their energies and become bent on a rational pursuit of right action – making a priori "enlightened" assumptions about a rational and ethical life ("Surely all these evils may be avoided by . . . deliberation"; 70) – which turns out to be an unconscious effort at recapitulating their original conditions. In depicting the resulting disappointment[41] Johnson appropriates a Lockean epistemological schema about how the world is configured in terms of three related but not co-incident dimensions – language, mind, and world.

The light tone and narrative movement circumscribe and place the consciousness and verbalizations of the characters. They suggest an appreciation of the material awkwardness of language as a record of momentary experiences – not to mention absolute or trans-historical truths – as the characters appropriate things of the world ostensibly in order to choose a happy way of living, but really to maintain an atemporal dream. Both Johnson and Locke are commonly understood as holding a theory of language privileging meaning over discourse. A theory of language cannot easily be deduced from a rhetorical style,[42] yet Locke's rhetoric paradoxically underwrites a view of meaning that identifies "*figurative speeches* and allusions" as obstructive in speaking of "things as they are."[43] As earlier discussed, Johnson's appropriation of Locke in the Preface to the *Dictionary* lends itself to two general extrapolations about language and meaning: (1) signs and signifiers are relative and mutable; and (2) in its fictive and tropological forms, writing gives access to experience that is real, true, and general.[44] Johnson's characters, however, resist such ideas and use language to compel order from their world, identifying Rasselas as a Quixotic figure who (according to Foucault) is intended by Cervantes to symbolize "the rupture of a world based on analogy and thrust into differentiation."[45] Don Quixote was a suggestive, archetypal figure for Johnson, who enabled readers to reflect on their own natural follies: "very few readers, amidst their mirth or pity, can deny that they have admitted visions of the same kind; though they have not, perhaps, expected events equally strange, or by means equally inadequate. When we pity him, we reflect on our own disappointment."[46]

Rasselas is an enlightenment Quixote, trying to hold together the world of things and words, while the text in which he finds himself continually prizes them apart. It does so partly by *enacting* rather than merely documenting a differential procedure that questions the rational, even "Johnsonian" ideologies of its characters. The differential structure of the narrative thus produces a general knowledge from the relation of particular experiences of disappointment: "Thus it happens when wrong opinions are entertained, that they mutually destroy each other, and leave the mind open to truth" (68) – a psychological opening up much like Peter Brooks's notion that the "the frame of the framed tale comes to represent Freud's 'real life,' that outer margin that makes the life within narratable, figure it as the 'artificial illness' treated for what it has to say about the story written by unconscious desire."[47]

While such "framing" escapes the binary structures identified with enlightenment,[48] narrative "framing" does *not* simply amount to "no clear choice ... [or] an endless, directionless oscillation between opposites."[49] Johnson's narrative, rather, enacts a series of confrontations (between characters, character and event, mind and world, words and things) by which meaning is both undercut *and* generated. In much the way "Rambler" 41 constructs memory out of emptiness, the *more* fragmented the experience of the *characters* becomes, the more substantial and engaged the *narrative itself* seems to be.[50]

Failure, therefore, becomes a technology to reflect on the emptiness of language, and the culturally relative and constructed nature of the social institutions within which the characters operate. But we should be clear about the import of this idea: it is not that the text's narrative movement says that *life* is empty, or that truths do not exist; it rather suggests that, even though the technologies available are not entirely adequate to desire and hope, we have no other, metaphysically sanctioned, unmediated means of knowing the world and the self.

This is why Johnson frequently focuses on the *specific* contact of mind with world, of nominal self with other, and the "framed" resistance between the two, as we see in Nekayah's observation, when considering the necessity of choice, to "Flatter not yourself with contrarieties of pleasure. Of the blessings set before you make your choice, and be content. No man can taste the fruits of autumn while he is delighting his scent with the flowers of the spring: no man can, at the same time, fill his cup from the source and from the mouth of the Nile" (72). Noticeable in this observation on the limits of the will, is the tropological and metaphorical form of the observation, suggesting that, notwithstanding the *talk* about limits (and even their syntactical inculcation), the emotional logic of the paragraph does otherwise. Its emotional trajectory moves in the opposite direction to its overt statement. There is a sense of expansiveness and freedom in this passage which, strangely, is inseparable from its sobering message. The definite lift given by the metaphor to the implied temporal narrative (you cannot be in two places at once) has the effect of countering the explicit argument, so that the *experience* of human limitation is, curiously, a freeing one and a bit like drinking from the source and the mouth of the Nile at once. It is not that the eloquence of the prose here *merely* gainsays the explicit statements, making it magically possible to transcend material conditions by invoking an aesthetic power. Johnson has a far greater respect for the real and the material to argue thus. Rather, the metaphoric shape of the thought breaks down the dichotomy of "mouth" and "source," subverts the dualistic habit of mind that sees and constructs the world in that way. Charles Hinnant suggests that Johnson's metaphor "only partly resolves the dilemma, since it implies that the issue is finally undecidable"; but then, problematically, he maintains, it asserts "that we must make a choice, even though we lack the wisdom of deciding which of the two alternatives should be given priority over the others."[51] But this formulation retains the dichotomy between source and mouth (while gesturing towards its "undecidability"), and so does not register that the narrative works within the text's dualistic structure to free the mind from its constraints *even while* observing the laws of nature. For it is precisely because *some* choice is made – with all the implied recognition of reasonable boundaries of law and self – that our ignorance as to priorities becomes irrelevant, and "undecidability" becomes moot.

The characteristic Johnsonian narrative effect is that reality is felt to be reconfigured, permitting the self to expand in a quasi-sublime movement that is *not* like the fearful and repressive power of the oriental sublime and oriental despotism,[52] but more akin to Johnson's idea of a "natural" sublime: "that comprehension and expanse of thought which at once fills the whole mind, and of which the first effect is sudden astonishment, and the second rational admiration."[53] The self implied here is not Cartesian, but a continuous consciousness which Johnson found in Locke's discussion of memory, and which he developed into his own nuanced form of historical and social being, not unlike that identified by Hayden White as the *locus* of the specific knowledge of historicality: "history has always been less an object of study, something to be explained, than a mode of being-in-the-world that both makes possible understanding and invokes it as a condition of its own deconcealment."[54]

Though very brief, the episode in the catacombs (ch. 48), in which the characters visit mummified bodies, is crucial in the structural development of the narrative: it mediates between the episodes featuring the mad astronomer (chs. 40–44, 46–47) and the paradoxically conclusive inconclusiveness of the final chapter. Furthermore, in its concentration upon finitude, endings, and death, the episode stands in dialectical relation to both the Happy Valley (human life under the gaze of the eternal and the undifferentiated) and the Egyptian Pyramids symbolizing for the characters the inaccessible otherness of pre-history, as well as (for Imlac) "that hunger of imagination that preys incessantly upon life" (78).

Chapter 48 pushes the limits of language and reason to the heart of eighteenth-century evidentiary experience by questioning the existence and the nature of the soul. Locke's notion of the soul and of personal identity (in Bk. II: 27 of the *Essay*) is historically significant because it contravened the substantialist understanding of the individual which had characterized seventeenth-century orthodox thought.[55] When Locke argued that "consciousness always accompanies thinking, and 'tis that, that makes every one to be, what he calls *self*; and thereby distinguishes himself from all other thinking things, in this alone consists *personal Identity*,"[56] he dislodges the notion of the soul as immaterial, abiding substance as the basis of personal identity, and disrupts notions of moral accountability and providential omnipotence implied by spiritual continuity.[57] Locke believed that personal consciousness was probably annexed to one indivisible and *im*material substance, but his empiricism recognized the limits to knowing the indivisibility or the continuity of that substance. So he developed a notion of consciousness that incorporated a tripartite conception of personal identity – the (spiritual) substance, the man, and the person – each term of which had its own mode of existence. These terms are all held together, within the context of temporal and personal change, by memory: "as far as this consciousness can be extended backwards to any past Action or Thought, so far reaches the Identity of that *Person*; it is the same *self* now it was then; and 'tis by the same *self* with this present one that now reflects on it, that the Action was done" (*Essay*, II, 27, 9).

Unlike Descartes and Cudworth on the question of identity, Locke's argument, as Charles Taylor asserts, does not assume that consciousness could be clearly distinguished from its embodiment,[58] but rather develops a self that incorporates instability and materiality within the temporal sphere.[59] It is this historical aspect of Locke's thought, I believe, rather than some strictly theological or philosophical tenet, to which Johnson might have been responding in the catacombs episode of *Rasselas*. There the characters go underground and contemplate the mummified bodies. Unlike the pyramids episode (chs. 30–32), where all are stimulated to sweeping cultural and psychological speculations and judgments, the pure *materiality* of the dead bodies in chapter 48 raises questions that see beyond formal philosophy. The attempts to define the issues quickly run into obstacles as the characters realize that their language, like Locke's, cannot adequately account for their *sense* that they have souls, and their *belief* that the soul continues to exist after death.

Johnson knew that "belief" in this context was highly problematic, for, more sceptical than Locke, Hume had argued in "Of Miracles" that "if the spirit of religion join itself to the love of wonder, there is an end to common sense; and human testimony, in these circumstances, loses all pretensions to authority."[60] In Hume's terms, no conviction, however strong, amounts to a reasonable proof of the existence of anything solid, let alone an idea as vague and as ideologically fraught as the soul, for: "We have no perfect idea of any thing but of a perception. A substance is entirely different from a perception. We have, therefore, no idea of a substance."[61] Hume's urbanity clearly invites the agreement of the reasonable person, so it is important that Johnson's response to questions raised by his characters is not to argue a contrary case from Hume through logic or assertion, but rather to draw on a very different praxis of personal experience, memory, and language to make his point.

In Johnson's text questions about God and the soul are raised by the complete *absence* of life in the dead bodies. Illogically, yet convincingly, something in the futile attempt at finding verbal equivalents for the human response to these momentous questions seems to convince the characters of the reality of the soul they cannot define. Johnson's extensive treatment of the concept of "soul" in the *Dictionary* suggests how ready he was to enter a philosophical discussion on this subject,[62] but his purpose in *Rasselas* was to further a different kind of liminal knowledge, more represented by silence and infinite repetitiveness: "The whole company stood awhile silent and collected. 'Let us return, said Rasselas, from this scene of mortality... Those that lie here stretched before us... were, perhaps, snatched away while they were busy, like us, in the choice of life'" (121–22).

Rather than opting for a denouement of Christian resignation and teleology, such as Boswell and many recent critics see as common to the tale,[63] Johnson maintains the fictional framework of the narrative in order to open up a spiritual dimension *within* the temporal and the material.[64] If there is any irony here it concerns the extraordinary ease with which this deeply religious man blended discussion of the soul with a completely material world and historical experience, without feeling any necessity for resolving inner contradictions. This is a crucial, yet typical space in Johnson's narrative, developing out of a retrospective and repetitive movement that responds to the human finitude displayed in the catacombs. Standing in relation to all the earlier moments of disappointment, this episode links the soul – that presence whose effect is felt only in its absence – with the historicality and the temporality of the foregoing narrative, and inflects Imlac's earlier truisms about history and the pyramids: "To know any thing... we must know its effects; to see men we must see their works... The truth is, that no mind is much employed upon the present" (73).

Whereas the pyramids gave rise to a typically sententious Johnsonian proclamation – "I consider this mighty structure as a monument of the insufficiency of human enjoyments" (78) – the catacombs, held dialectically *in relation to* the pyramids, establishes a limit, a horizon to thought that generates a more differentiated, more modest and yet more real, and even legal knowledge that problematizes rather than settles the nature of human experience. As the concluding narrative doubles back on itself, returning the characters to Abyssinia (though not necessarily to the Happy Valley), there is the suggestion that, if the soul exists, it does so not as a logically deduced entity or, *pace* Hume, as a "perfect idea," but as an *absence* arising at the *intersection* of the past and the future, and of mind and body, and within the present on which "no mind is much employed."

Curiously, it is in the *in*adequacy of particular choices to the present moment that the soul is recognized as being both (as Johnson notes in the *Dictionary*) "the immaterial and immortal spirit of man," and (as Locke argues in the *Essay*) the personal identity of some person. Like "happiness," however, "soul" is a sign that stands for no single reality, yet both signs have exercised an extraordinary power over the civilized Western mind.

But neither term, nor any of the normative laws of time and history arising from the tale's deep repetitiveness, are reified by Johnson. The nexus of mind and world in *Rasselas* produces a soul that is independent of specific religious dogma and philosophical terminological determinants, for its medium is narrative, and its ontological status that of human law and history. There are no eternal laws here, except, perhaps, that none are to be expected, and life is neither just nor logical nor divinely organized. Still, the narrative imparts a sense of coherence to events that might otherwise seem meaningless or merely indeterminate, and they thus enact an essential "legal" function of civil discourse: in the words of James Boyd White, "creating a rhetorical community over time."[65]

THE RHETORIC OF EVIDENCE

The continuity of radically different states of mind is based in Johnson's sense of the circumscribed nature of the reason, the energy of imagination, and the constantly changing nature of experience. Somewhat like Hume, Johnson is very reasonable about the near impossibility of reason. Hume observes, "Nothing in this world is perpetual; every thing, however, seemingly firm, is in continual flux and change." For Johnson, "Definition is, indeed, not the province of man; every thing is set above or below our faculties."[66] In mathematical problems everyone agrees because we perceive "the whole at once"; but we differ from ourselves as we differ from others, "when we see only part of the question as in the multifarious relations of politicks and morality."[67] Disagreement, according to Johnson, arises not because we are irrational, but "because we are finite beings,"[68] and all non-mathematical knowledge is relative, comparative, and historical. Contrary to other eighteenth-century critics on Shakespeare, Johnson opens the Preface by suggesting a comparison with Homer, the greatest poet of nature that he knows.[69] In *Rasselas* he uses the pyramids and the catacombs dialogically as cultural phenomena between which historical understanding is produced.[70] "Where reason is wanting," as Montaigne says, in determining truth, "we therein employ Experience," and although experience is itself flawed and multifarious, "*Truth* is so great a thing, that we ought not to distain any Mediation that will guide us to it."[71] For Johnson, too, experience is an essential component of reason and supports the moral capacities of human beings, because memory both reflects and shapes experience, and because it is "the purveyor of reason." It is the "faculty of remembrance, which may be said to place us in the class of moral agents."[72]

Yet experience is heuristic for Johnson, never self-evident or even empirical, in the sense of being clearly accessible to the senses or understanding, and it functions within a complex system of legal protocols contributing to cultural and personal identity. *Rasselas* and the *Rambler* essays all raise questions about the *evidence* for experience, recognizing various ways in which circumstances, history and genre all contribute towards making experience known and usable. Alexander Welsh discusses the growing distrust of personal testimony in eighteenth-century legal practice in favor of circumstantial evidence as a means of deducing facts.[73] The increasing trustworthiness of circumstance as a sign of truth was linked to the narrative form circumstances were commonly given in legal testimony, thereby drawing a direct relation between legal evidentiary narrative, novelistic realism, and rhetorical purpose.[74] In no field of inquiry was the use of circumstantial probability more marked than in natural religion, since Christianity valued its scriptures and the testimony of its saints so highly and placed great stake in the reality of things unseen. Joseph Butler's *The Analogy of Religion* (1736) framed one of the earliest uses of the phrase "circumstantial evidence" in discussing belief and natural religion:

No one who is serious can possibly think these things to be nothing, if he considers the Importance of collateral things, and even of lesser Circumstances, in the Evidence of Probability, as distinguished, in Nature, from the Evidence of Demonstration. In many Cases indeed it seems to require the truest Judgment, to determine with Exactness the Weight of circumstantial Evidence: but it is very often altogether as convincing, as That, which is the most express and direct.[75]

No deist, Johnson nonetheless appreciated the qualified reasonableness of Butler's discussion of the Christian evidences, yet his own use of circumstantial evidence as mediate to truth has its intellectual origins in his resistance to Hume's philosophical scepticism. While there is very little overt engagement with Hume in Johnson's published writings, it is arguable that Boswell detected something essential about Johnson's moral thought when, on one level, he structured the *Life of Johnson* as an implicit opposition between Johnson and Hume, the great English man and the great Scottish man of letters of the century, exemplars of Christian humanist and humanist enlightenment cultures. Boswell shrewdly understood that much of Johnson's thought constituted an implicit response to Hume's sceptical critique of the Christian evidences, the authority of Christian morality, as well as the nature of human experience. It might also be argued that Boswell's dramatic portrait of Johnson's character recognized that an unconscious part of Johnson's response to Hume was an attempt to handle the Humean side of himself.[76] Johnson's declaration that "Every thing that Hume has advanced against Christianity had passed through my mind long before he wrote" (*Life*, 1, 444), reveals a degree of bravura on Johnson's part, but also points to a serious dialogue between the two in Johnson's mind.

Eighteenth-century Anglican apologetics traditionally appealed to argument and revelation in support of religious belief. Revelation was not primarily individual perception of the deity ("enthusiasm"), but the testimony of the New Testament, which, it was held, guaranteed the authenticity of revelation. New Testament revelation fulfilled Old Testament prophecy and was attended by "miracles" (e.g., crucifixion, resurrection, redemption, the real presence) that could only have been effected by God, and these events were taken to be rational grounds for accepting Christian revelation as true.

In "Of Miracles," chapter 10 of the *Essay Concerning Human Understanding* (1748), Hume interrogates the Christian evidences in two ways.[77] He argues a priori that a rational person proportions his belief to the evidence: a certainty always overbalances a probability: "A miracle is a violation of the laws of nature; and as a firm and unalterable experience has established these laws, the proof against a miracle, from the very nature of the fact, is as entire as any argument from experience can possibly be imagined."[78] Furthermore, Hume argues a posteriori that there is insufficient evidence to substantiate belief in miracles, and, consequently, "that a miracle can never be proved, so as to be the foundation of a system of religion" (88). Consequently, since the resurrection cannot be proved as fact, it cannot become a rational basis for Christian revelation. While Hume's argument never openly attacks the foundations of Christianity, his rhetoric clearly works towards that end: "When, therefore, these two kinds of experience [proof of miracles and proof of the laws of nature] are contrary, we have nothing to do but subtract the one from the other, and embrace an opinion, either on one side or the other, with that assurance which arises from the remainder" (87–88). Yet, the "remainder" is immaterial, and the "assurance" of the position is evidently the "entire annihilation" that is the fate of "all popular religions." (88).

Hume's arguments are based on the logically simple yet rhetorically complex principle that: "It is experience only, which gives authority to human testimony; and it is the same experience, which assures us of the laws of nature" (87). Accordingly, Hume reasons from causes to effects, but finds no justification at all for reversing the procedure and deducing a cause *from* an effect: "When we infer any particular cause from an effect, we must proportion the one to the other, and can never be allowed to ascribe to the cause any qualities, but what are exactly sufficient to produce the effect" (93). Because we can know nothing certain beyond our own momentary experience, there is no rational basis for metaphysical or foundational truths, nor, indeed (as he argues in the *Treatise of Human Nature*) for our moment-to-moment connection with the world, or even for the contiguous experiences that comprise our sense of self. What gives coherence and meaning to our disparate experiences is the force of habit, a mnemonic and imaginative fiction which discloses occurrences in the mind, and not necessarily in the world itself, or in our actual connection to that world.

Boswell was both troubled and impressed by Hume's philosophical acumen, especially by his ability to entertain the notion of a decentred self[79] and his arguments against the fear of death. Boswell reports three occasions on which Johnson responds to Hume's arguments on the Christian miracles and on death (21 July 1763; 26 October 1769; 16 September 1777).[80] Each of these occasions are, of course, reported conversations, representing *ad hominem* responses on Johnson's part to questions raised by Boswell (and others), and not formal, philosophical texts. On each occasion Johnson responds to Hume's ideas (as presented in conversation by Boswell) with a variety of arguments. Notably, Johnson makes no attempt at a systematic or logical *answer* to Hume, but offers rather a series of qualifying statements that have the effect of opening up a substantially different notion of experience located within a framework of circumstantial evidence.

On 21 July 1763, Boswell mentions Hume's idea (in "Of Miracles") that it was more likely that witnesses to "miracles" were mistaken, or had lied, than that they had accurately reported what had happened. Johnson, in response, acknowledges the need for caution – "the great difficulty of proving miracles should make us very cautious in believing them"(*Life*, I, 444) – and unlike Hume, who proceeds confidently from a strict concept of nature, Johnson is more cautious, suggesting that "although God has made Nature to operate by certain fixed laws, yet it is not unreasonable to think that he may suspend those laws" (I, 444). He thus seems to be arguing from effects to causes, rather than from known causes to effects. Evidently the "light and certainty" of Christianity – the effects – authorize him metaleptically to argue the reasonableness of the suspension of the laws of nature "in order to establish a system highly advantageous to mankind" (I, 444). However, in a qualifying step he invokes history and human testimony by noting that miracles were "attested to by men who had no interest in deceiving us; but who, on the contrary, were told that they should suffer persecution, and actually lay down their lives in confirmation of the truth of the facts which they attested"(I, 445). This historical testimony branches out to enlist Old Testament prophecy, as does Gibbon, when, in arguing the views of non-believers, his criticism of miracles tacitly acknowledges their existence.

On another occasion (22 September 1777), Johnson acknowledged to Boswell that "Hume, taking the proposition [against the probability of miracles] simply, is right," but qualified this by invoking Christian teleology: "revelation is not proved by the miracles alone, but as connected with prophecies, and with the doctrine in confirmation of which the miracles were wrought" (*Life*, III, 188). James Force argues that the traditional eighteenth-century connection of the miracles with prophecies did not escape Hume's argument in "Of Miracles," which links prophecy with "miracles" as "events" that violate the course of nature, and are therefore useless as evidence.[81] Johnson, however, does not cite prophecy as self-sufficient evidence for miracles, but offers the *complementariness* of prophecy and miracles as representing a composite knowledge within the realms of language and history which (Johnson implies) strengthens them as evidence.

In the conversation on 21 July 1763, Johnson concludes with a statement that does two things at once: it asserts his own personal belief in the existence of miracles (including his belief in their spiritual efficacy); and it registers the grounds on which doubt might be entertained: "Supposing a miracle possible, as to which, in my opinion, there can be no doubt, we have as strong evidence for the miracles in support of Christianity, as the nature of the thing admits" (*Life*, I, 445). In other words, miracles are *not* phenomena about which a reasonable person can be certain, certainty not being in the "nature of the thing." This concession fundamentally divides Johnson from Hume, for notwithstanding *some* truth to Hume's argument, it is his argumentative insistence on *certainty* that weakens his case for Johnson. Furthermore, it seems that Hume-the-sceptic is less willing to trust himself to history than is Johnson-the-believer.

Johnson occasionally emphasizes the historical basis of revealed religion,[82] yet the epistemologically uncertain status of miracles – in conjunction with the observation that "the human mind is so limited, that it cannot take in all the parts of a subject" – prompts him to produce *several* forms of evidence for miracles (personal testimony, historical documentation, Old Testament evidence), rather than one philosophical argument. Johnson's argument actually echoes aspects of Hume's own views on evidence, whose criticism of Macpherson's *Ossian* employs standards of "scientific" history: since Macpherson gives no provenance and presents the Ossianic texts as translations of extant poems, Hume urges Blair to acquire evidence that the poems existed even five years earlier, if he wants to enforce their credit.[83] Johnson's criticism of Macpherson also focuses, among other things, on the question of evidence: if Macpherson claims an antiquarian and traditional textual basis for the Ossianic poems he should be able to provide manuscripts.[84]

Johnson's acceptance of the uncertain status of miracles paradoxically strengthens rather than weakens his case against Hume. It corresponds to the contingency of knowledge which Hume himself invokes as a reason for philosophical humility ("In vain would our limited understanding break through those boundaries, which are too narrow for our fond imagination").[85] But Johnson is not convinced by Hume's declared modesty: "Hume, and other sceptical innovators, are vain men, and will gratify themselves at any expence" (*Life*, I, 444). He sees a rich store of meaning in the term "vanity," and in the *Dictionary* defines it as follows: (1) Emptiness, uncertainty, inanity; (2) fruitless desire, fruitless endeavour; (3) trifling labour; (4) [*sic*] falshood, untruth; (5) empty pleasure, vain pursuit, idle shew, unsubstantial enjoyment, petty object of pride; (6) ostentation, arrogance; and (7) petty pride, pride exerted upon slight grounds, pride operating on small occasions. Several of these meanings seem to be pressed into service against Hume: vanity is the complete fruitlessness of human endeavour when measured against the *actual* natural order ("There are objections against a *plenum*, and objections against a *vacuum*; yet one of them must be true" [*Life*, I, 444]); but in Hume it is perhaps more the vaingloriousness of the efforts to overthrow a system that had been found by generations to be sufficient to their spiritual needs ("after a system is well settled upon positive evidence, a few partial objections ought not to shake it" [*Life*, I, 444]).

Vanity of character implies not only heroic self-sufficiency – about which Johnson himself knew something – but also an absurd willfulness ("Truth, Sir, is a cow which will yield such people no more milk, and so they have gone to milk the bull" [*Life*, I, 444]). Johnson's argument links the limits of human reason with existential vulnerability and spiritual need in a thought whose emotional power is a product of its surprising counter-intuitiveness: "The human mind is so limited, that it cannot take in all the parts of a subject... the Christian religion is a most beneficial system, as it gives us light and certainty where we were before in darkness and doubt." This is to make human *need* for support and grace an integral evidentiary aspect of the reasonableness of revelation. Johnson, a man with powerful, self-centred emotions, acknowledges his spiritual vulnerability; Hume, a brilliant, vain man, imagines himself in need of nothing. In short, the understated quality of Johnson's response to what he sees as the vanity of Hume's position follows the advice of one of the quotations, from Raleigh's *History of the World*, he chooses to illustrate "vanity" as "trifling labour": "To use long discourse against those things which are both against scripture and reason, might rightly be judged a vanity in the answerer, not much inferior to that of the inventor."

The relation of vanity to human need also suggests why Johnson doubts the sincerity of Hume's indifference towards death. Hume had argued in print against the immortality of the soul,[86] but, for Johnson, writing and living are different realities, and "it is not difficult to conceive ... that for many reasons a man writes much better than he lives."[87] Boswell twice brings up Hume's attitude to death, the first (26 October 1769) before his "death-bed" interview with Hume; the second (16 September 1777) after the interview.[88] On both occasions in the *Life* Boswell draws attention to Hume's relaxed attitude at the approach of death and his Lucretian contention that death is nothing but annihilation. In the interview itself Boswell is "shocked" that Hume is "placid and even chearful" (*Extremes*, 11), as he responds to Boswell's "curiosity to be satisfied if he persisted in disbelieving a future state even when he had death before his eyes," by applying his published skeptical principles to that question, and by engaging Boswell in banter (*Extremes*, 11–13).[89]

Boswell is shocked by the possibility that Hume might be *right* in his belief that death is mere annihilation, but he is also, typically, made anxious by the possibility that Hume is *wrong*, that one will eventually have to face a judgment consequent to one's actions. Of the interview with Hume, Boswell writes that "I maintained my faith. I told him that I believed the Christian religion as I believed history." But to Hume's, "You do not believe it as you believe the Revolution?," Boswell responds with, "Yes ... but the difference is that I am not so much interested in the truth of the Revolution; otherwise I should have anxious doubts concerning it" (*Extremes*, 13). In other words, Boswell does *not* believe in revelation in the way he believes in history, that is, as fact, but he can find no means of formulating the difference other than by using his anxiety as a yardstick.

Anxiety about death is real but also instrumental for Johnson. As before, however, he does not attempt to refute Hume philosophically, but resorts to a number of different circumstantial scenarios to illuminate the matter under consideration: Hume is either mad or untruthful; he has a vanity in being thought easy before death; death is an unknown state in which anything might await one – who is to know?[90] But Johnson's own fears of death and his long experience cannot permit him an easy refutation. Instead, he incorporates his understanding of human needs – phenomena, significantly, taken by Hume as evidence of the *invalidity* of testimony (people testify to miracles because they are lacking in "experience") – into an image of human beings as naturally located in history and in the material and moral circumstances of life. This enables him to reflect that, "[w]hen he [Hume] dies, he at least gives up all he has" (*Life*, II, 106), and that "[i]t is more probable that he should assume an appearance of ease, than that so very improbable a thing should be, as a man not afraid of going (as, in spite of his delusive theory, he cannot be sure but he may go,) into an unknown state, and not being uneasy at leaving all he knew" (III, 153).

This is, once again, to direct Humean principles with a vengeance against Hume himself. For Johnson, to "leave all one knows," one's manifold connections to the particularities of life, is highly poignant and looms large in his own biography.[91] Death is one of Milton's Adam's few fears. Johnson notes that "Milton has judiciously represented the father of mankind [*Paradise Lost*, XI, 461–65], as seized with horror and astonishment at the sight of death, exhibited to him on the mount of vision. For surely, nothing can so much disturb the passions, or perplex the intellects of man, as the disruption of his union with visible nature."[92] Johnson and Milton both evoke a vision of nature (reminiscent of Augustine and Pascal) as fallen and imperfect, but susceptible of both secular and religious redemption, in time and in the hereafter. Hume's apparent refusal to value his connections to life, echoed in his extraordinary autobiography – in which he writes about his own life and death with remarkable dispassionateness – is the outcome, for Johnson, of a philosophical logic lacking in humanity.[93] Boswell's shock at Hume on his deathbed points to a similar inadequacy in Hume. Because, it might be argued, Hume's insouciance provides no moral support in the face of the individual's helplessness at moments of finality, for Boswell it is almost as troublesome as the fear of endings and likely judgment that it is designed to obviate. Ernest Mossner sees Johnson's response to Hume's indifference towards death as "illogical,"[94] but its illogicality is precisely the instrument of Johnson's critique. It acknowledges the uncertainty when belief and reason are brought into conflict with each other: "we have as strong evidence . . . as the nature of the thing admits."

At the same time, Johnson's rhetorical handling of circumstantial evidence suggests that the discrepancy between evidence and the "truth" of miracles lies in a fictive dimension of discourse that accommodates hope or belief to the "nature of the thing" itself.

Johnson's rhetorical use of circumstantial evidence in countering Hume, and especially his willingness to entertain the fictionality of the structures of Christian belief, suggest not only his legalistic turn of mind, but also that eighteenth-century thought saw circumstantial evidence as a *more persuasive* element than personal testimony. While Johnson was a believing and even devout Anglican, his account of the Christian evidences is what Alexander Welsh calls a "strong representation," by which he means "those of the later eighteenth and nineteenth centuries that openly distrust direct testimony, [and] insist on submitting witnesses to the test of corroborating circumstances, and claim to know many things without anyone's having seen them at all."[95] In these instances of quasi-theological controversy, as in more purely legal and historical matters already touched on, Johnson understands that the "facts" of evidence remain ineffective and *un*circumstantial without the rhetorical shaping necessary to create the narrative that will convince the listener of their truth.

Importantly, however, Johnson's performativity does not undercut or diminish his conviction of the truth of the Christian evidences and of historically accumulated experience. Though Johnson adheres to Saint Paul's tenet that faith is "the evidence of things not seen,"[96] he is aware that experience in itself is less persuasive, indeed, in some way less "factual" than the representations that make it signify. In short, he knows that representations are *made* and not found, and, like recent legal theorists, knows that "truth is not the property of an event; rather, it is a property of an account of an event."[97] His instinctive thrust against Hume therefore employs this rhetorical knowledge to support it.

The crucial relation between representation and truth in this aspect of Johnson's thought bears repetition. For Johnson, the realms of history and revelation are separate, and revelation – Christ's advent in human history – is a "matter of fact."[98] For Hume, by contrast, there seems to be no difference between history and revelation, because all revelation is history by another name. If Hume attributed belief in "miracles" to a lack of experience, Johnson attributes *his* lack of belief to the same cause. What we have here are two different concepts of experience. Johnson's is clearly inflected by the *inscribed* quality of thought, testifying to the discursive and impure nature of evidence, yet, paradoxically, to the way in which such phenomena sustain the truths of Christian doctrine through history.[99] Hume's style, on the other hand, cultivates and tolerates uncertainty, yet, as Jerome Christensen remarks, his is a "literary practice aimed at attaining a reputation exempt from contingency."[100] In Hume's philosophy the application of a rigorous empirical principle has the effect of emptying the notion of experience as a lived phenomenon: in the *Treatise*, not only can reason not penetrate beyond one's rigorously delimited experience, but neither can it provide any knowledge of the self! In terms of personal identity (and, by extension, historical and cultural continuity) Hume's argument leaves the individual precariously balanced "betwixt a false reason and none at all" (*Treatise*, I, vii, 268). Maintaining that the knowledge of things "in themselves," and of the relation between causes and effects, amounts to nothing but knowledge of our own mind, "cuts off all hope" by reducing the self to a series of contiguous impressions: "For my part, when I enter most intimately into what I call *myself*, I always stumble on some particular perception or other, of heat or cold, light or shade, love or hatred, pain or pleasure. I never can catch *myself* at any time without a perception, and never can observe any thing but the perception" (*Treatise*, I, iv, 252).

Self-reflexively Hume thus moves back on his own skeptical thinking, anticipating Adam Smith's arguments about the instrumentality of spectatorship in the creation of the ethical self.[101] In Hume's writing, however, the metaphor of the self watching itself as a spectator watches an actor on a stage leads to rational detachment – supposedly the grounds for moral judgment – but it also has the effect of removing external and moral sanctions for action and identity:[102] "The mind is a kind of theatre, where several perceptions successively make their appearance; pass, re-pass, glide away, and mingle in an infinite variety of postures and situations" (*Treatise*, I, vi, 253). With powerful results: "The *intense* view of these manifold contradictions and imperfections in human reason has so wrought upon me, and heated my brain, that I am ready to reject all belief and reasoning, and can look upon no opinion even as more probable or likely than another" (I, iv, 268–269).

Like Johnson's astronomer in *Rasselas*, whose over-conscientious application to experience of the principles of cause-and-effect leads him to conclude that he can control the weather, and so seals himself into a private world of loneliness and doubt, Hume's narrator finds himself in an alien world through the systematic application of a reasonable, "experiential" skepticism. Johnson's deluded astronomer may indeed have been modelled on these passages in the *Treatise*, for, as Mark

Temmer remarks, the "Astronomer's delusion... relates unquestionably to the history of causality in Western civilization... Hume's contention is precisely what Johnson's story shows, [in that]... logic is incapable of creating a foundation for causal connection based on reason."[103] But Johnson's story shows *more* than Hume contends, by drawing out the human predicament raised by his skepticism.

The alien world of Hume's passage is that of his own self. In a Montaigne-like gesture, where reason fails for Hume to heal the breach that reason causes, nature steps in (*Treatise*, I, iv, 269), but the movement towards nature represents a rhetorical means of undercutting his own skeptical principles, problematizing the demands of thinking and living. However, the questioning of identity ("Where am I, or what?") leads not to a qualification and adaptation of ideas, but to a formal, half-ironic gesture of regression: "I may, nay I must yield to the current of nature, in submitting to my senses and understanding; and in this blind submission I shew most perfectly my sceptical disposition and principles" (I, iv, 269).

"Nature," however, turns out to be nothing more (nor less) than public opinion, and leads Hume's protagonist to resolve "to live, and talk, and act like other people in the common affairs of life" (I, iv, 269). The disengaged insouciance with which these various entities are held together suggests a perpetually possible state of dissolution.[104] My point, however, is not to dispute the sophistication of the rhetoric but to draw attention to its *effect*, and consequently to its value within the social and philosophical contexts implied by the rhetoric itself. The structure of assumptions, to recall Fish, within which Hume's philosophy finds itself, is that within which the rhetoric is made to *mean*, but also within which it is to be judged.[105] Hume's rhetorical performance, thus, implies a position that cannot believe in a whole, integrated self, *nor* in a decentred, disintegrated self; his urbane, civilized poise is a way of being between these states, inhabiting neither.[106]

Johnson's astronomer also finds himself having to resort to nature in order to restore his mental health and perspective (*Rasselas*, ch. 46). Imlac's advice is not to "stand to parley, but [to] fly to business or to Pekuah" (*Rasselas*, 115), and the narrative subsequently draws the astronomer into relationship with others, and with a more circumstantial set of expectations which confirm Imlac's observation that: "you are only one atom of the mass of humanity, and have neither such virtue nor vice, as that you should be singled out for supernatural favours or afflictions" (*Rasselas*, 114). This principle takes the plenitude and the evolving universalism of nature seriously. Rhetorically accomplished as Hume is, Johnson sees him as a writer who considers himself above others, resistant to the idea that he might be "only one atom of the mass of humanity." This is actually how Hume sees or pretends to see himself: when registering the *effect* of his skepticism upon his feelings, he is "affrighted and confounded with that forlorn solitude, in which I am plac'd in my philosophy, and fancy myself some strange uncouth monster, who not being able to mingle and unite in society, has been expell'd all human commerce, and left utterly abandon'd and disconsolate" (*Treatise*, 1, vii, 264).

Finally, for Johnson, no single author could (or should) have the power to disrupt a whole system of thought and practice, built up by the incremental experience of generations over time: "Always remember this, that after a system is well settled upon positive evidence, a few partial objections ought not to shake it. The human mind is so limited, that it cannot take in all the parts of a subject, so there may be objections against any thing" (*Life*, 1, 444). Johnson found Hume a dangerous thinker. His endorsement of James Beattie's *Essay on Truth* (1770) and William Adams's *Essay on Mr. Hume's Essay on Miracles* (1751) as successful challenges to Hume suggests that he was willing to use whatever means were at his disposal to attack Hume's thought.[107] However, Johnson's response to Hume is no mere argument for victory, as Donald Siebert would have it.[108] Like his relation to Swift, the tension in Johnson's critique of Hume indicates a degree of self-criticism, rooted in a strong feeling that he shared some of the philosopher's attitudes and ideas:[109] "Every thing which Hume has advanced against Christianity has passed through my mind long before he wrote" (*Life*, 1, 444).

Crucially, however, Johnson chose to maintain the difference. An abiding sense of human imperfection and human needs, of the limits of the mind and powerful bodily inclinations, are written into what experience *was* for Johnson. Its efficacy within discourse depends upon its relation to the law of limits, and so to Johnson's legal grasp – as I have defined it in this chapter – of language and memory. Notwithstanding the mediated and rhetorical nature of religious and secular truths – implying the narratological and circumstantial nature of evidence – "truth" for Johnson is not merely equivalent to language. But neither is it equivalent to empirical fact. Rather, it is known in experience through the *encounter with* and realization of the attendant circumstantiality of fact, which is what mediates and relates the mind to history and the world of the present.

CHAPTER 4

Narrative, history, and memory in the Lives of the Poets

The notion that people more often need to be reminded than informed is central to Johnson's thinking about human experience.[1] Anticipating the basic recollective structure of psychoanalysis, in which the past through "repetition" seeks re-emplotment in a newly imagined narrative,[2] Johnson's idea speaks to the relationships among memory, knowledge, writing, and character which inform the structure and experiential content of the *Lives of the Poets*. These are relationships which make for the constitutive and "redemptive" functions of biographical memory. Such theoretical terms have long been used to describe Boswell's biographical writing, and, while the fictive nature of biographical writing – most obviously, the use of tropes and figurative language in recording a life – has been widely accepted in other areas of literary studies,[3] we have insisted on seeing Johnson as wedded to a theory of positivistic verisimilitude. Oddly, we have not registered Johnson's insistence on the imaginativeness of life writing. In "Rambler" 60 he notes that, like high forms of literature, biography succeeds in proportion to its capacity to draw on and appeal to common human experiences, for "[a]ll joy or sorrow for the happiness or calamities of others is produced by an act of imagination, that realises the event however fictitious, or approximates it however remote... Our passions are therefore more strongly moved, in proportion as we can more readily adopt the pains and the pleasures proposed to our minds" (III, 318–19).

The sympathetic experience described here is no different in kind from that of poetry or fiction. Evidently, all good writing for Johnson appeals to human passions, and "Rambler" 60 assumes that a biographer fulfills his purpose in proportion to the creativity of the writing. He may be able to conceive the pains and the pleasures of other minds, but must also *excite* them – "uniformity of sentiment...enables us to conceive and to excite the pains and the pleasure of other minds" (*Lives*, I, 20). In doing so we are able to distinguish a mere "chronological series of actions and preferments," depicting only the "most prominent and observable particularities, and the grosser features of his mind," from a "living acquaintance."[4]

For Johnson this portrayal implies a moral purpose, which, in "Idler" 84, he identifies under the rubric of "prudence," designating "not how any man became great, but how he was made happy." Good life-writing is prudential in both subject and manner, and considers how experience manifests itself in action in a person's life. Johnson defines "prudence" as "wisdom applied to practice," and illustrates it by quoting Peacham: "Under prudence is comprehended, that discrete, apt, suiting, and disposing as well of actions as words, in their due place, time and manner"; and Hale: "Prudence is principally in reference to actions to be done, and due means, order, season, and method of doing or not doing." Commensurate with this notion of "prudence" as pertaining to the rightness of words and actions Johnson's life-writing establishes relations between particular conduct and temporality, and the ends of action. "Ends" here are multiple, comprehending the idea of consequences, aims or ideals; and achievement. "Ends" in Johnson's life-writing also, of course, signify the structural importance of death in each of the *Lives of the Poets*,[5] for their subjects are writers who have employed their energies in representing *some* truth of their lives, whatever that might be, and Johnsonian life-writing represents (among other things) whatever truth a writer has realized in the ends of his activity – that is, in writing – and also at the end of his life.

This link between writing, action, and ends constitutes one of the ways Johnson's life-writing participates in a broadening of historiographical discourse in the eighteenth century, bringing a bourgeois sentiment to bear on classical ideals of the *vita activa* underlying the neoclassical conception of history.[6] It is a link implying a multidimensional structure for the *Lives*. As we know, the individual lives all generally follow a similar pattern: a biographical and chronological sketch of the writer's life and writings is followed by a critical dissertation on the works, except that the larger lives – of Cowley, Milton, Dryden, Pope, Addison, and Gray – complicate the structural relationship between the biographical and critical sections by introducing a mediating character sketch, a discourse on the writer's poetic identity that addresses his intellectual behaviour, and considers ways in which (if at all) the particular writer's efforts have become authoritative, that is, taken on the identity of an author. Many of the middle-size lives, such as those of Waller, Butler, Rochester, Otway, Congreve, Thomson, Shenstone, and Gay, also have the tripartite structure (biography, character, criticism), but on a reduced scale. But the question of the function of the narrative structure in the *Lives*, especially the encoded relations between the writer's life and work, are central to Johnson's understanding of temporality and memory.

Years before Boswell's *Life of Johnson*, now routinely identified as the first modern, self-reflexive biography, Johnson understood that biographical truths are specific and relative, and are most effectively deployed within the biographer's narrative. Richard Holmes' remark that "the inventive, shaping instinct of the storyteller [namely, the biographer] struggles with the ideal of a permanent, historical, and objective document,"[7] would seem also to describe Johnson's theoretical project as a biographer. Certainly, Johnson knows that biography cannot *reproduce* a life that has been lived and is over; rather than verisimilitude, his biographies confer a fictional presence on the fragments and traces of a writer's life and works.

BIOGRAPHY'S FICTIVE ENTERPRISE

The notion of "fictional presence" raises the complex issue of the relations among biography, history, and the novel in the eighteenth century, and especially the attitudes towards referentiality. A substantial scholarship has already described the shifting boundaries and relations between the novel and history in the eighteenth century,[8] but significant similarities between the forms of referentiality of the novel and history, and Johnson's biographical practice remain to be explored. All three modes as they evolve during the eighteenth century ask the reader to consider the realities to which historical or factual writing refer, and what the proper function of language is in recording and constituting specifically historical realities. The verifiably referential had become the norm in determining the truth in history writing by the early eighteenth century, yet the rigorous application of that standard had revealed gaps in historical knowledge that fiction writing aimed to fill. Both forms of writing, of course, retained a private perspective from their common roots in biography, autobiography, memoir, and familiar letter,[9] but the empirical claims of history implied an epistemology of the particular and of the factual that undercut its larger narrative and interpretive claims. The Renaissance conflict between antiquarian and humanist historiography (still implicit in Gibbon's practice[10]) was partly mediated by the novel's dual commitment to observation of the particular and the quotidian, and to an elaboration of meta-narratives of personal, social, and cultural life. In doing so, novelists such as Defoe, Richardson, and Fielding employed different forms of probabilistic fiction, combining accumulated experience, traditional historical knowledge and anecdote, and invented "historical" scenarios to circumvent the confines of empirical verifiability, and to construct their sense of the fullness and reality of the social world.[11] Eighteenth-century fiction thus opportunistically filled the gaps created by historical method in its emphasis on immediate documentary evidence, and in the process turned attention to the authority of the narrator, the coherence of the "historical" narrative, and the very evidentiary foundation of the view of the historical world offered.

The narrative authority of both Defoe and Richardson is maintained through a series of narratological maneuvers – employing the persona of an editor and the structure of journals and letters – to ensure the historical authenticity of their texts and the stable foundations of the historical world presented. However, the realism of *Crusoe*, *Pamela*, or *Clarissa* was, in Jules Law's words, a "highly rhetorical cultural enterprise, concerned with persuasion as much as demonstration, with social vision as much as scientific inquiry, and with 'coherence' as much as 'correspondence.'"[12] But it was not the rhetoric of fiction per se that separated novels from history, for all the evidence points to the truth-value of *both* discourses, rather than the different *ways* of collecting and verifying evidence of the historicality of the world.

When Johnson animadverts on the exemplary force of the new fiction in "Rambler" 4, and raises concerns about its moral effect – leading many to think him obtuse about fiction – he is not objecting to the rhetoric of Richardson's or Fielding's writing or to the fact that their novels simulate a historical narrative. Johnson clearly finds these features to *enhance* the efficacy of the realism which, when well done, is so powerful "as to take possession of the memory by a kind of violence, and produces effects almost without the intervention of the will" (*Rambler*, III, 22). In comparison to Addison (e.g., "Spectator" 411), whose aesthetic finds only urbane entertainment in fiction, Johnson finds the realistic novel, or "familiar histories," to be "of *greater use* than the solemnities of professed morality, and [to be able to] convey the knowledge of vice and virtue with *more* efficacy than axioms and definitions" (my emphasis – *Rambler*, III, 21–22). But this ideological power makes novels dangerous. Here Johnson considers the moral purpose of the novelist in relation to his putative audience – "the young, the ignorant, and the idle" (III, 21) – and proposes the possibility of shaping fiction so as to blunt the harmful impact of the real (when it is harmful), while still offering equally powerful but educative examples of characters and events.[13] This may not be a modern attitude to public expression, yet it is not a "subordination of fiction to truth," for Johnson is entirely aware that the novel's power is predicated on its ability to deliver truth – or what *resembles* truth. The real issue for Johnson is the *kind* of fictional representation offered, and whether it is *read* with appropriate critical awareness:[14] "What I cannot for a moment believe, I cannot for a moment behold with interest or anxiety."[15]

The relation between belief and imitation is more complex than this assertion might suggest, as the example of Charlotte Lennox's *The Female Quixote* indicates. Whether or not Johnson ghost-wrote Book IX, chapter 11 of *The Female Quixote*,[16] the purpose of the Doctor at the end of that novel is not to humiliate or discredit Arabella, but to enable her to appreciate the fictional rather than the literal truth of the old romances on which she is fixated. This does not invalidate romances as legitimate reading – as we know, Johnson himself greatly enjoyed such reading[17] – because awareness of their fictiveness makes possible a more critical and sophisticated reading and pleasure.

The Doctor – whether Johnson or not – holds romance to have a *lesser* impact on the mind than realism, yet Arabella's yearning for significance forces a literal construction from a genre that declares its own fictitiousness, forcing the Doctor, in turn, to depict the deleterious moral effect of romance *when taken* literally, and *as the basis for action*. Arabella's assertion about authorial intention – "he that writes without Intention to be credited, must write to little Purpose"(*Female Quixote*, 376) – elicits the Doctor's proposition about the relation between fiction and truth: "Truth is not always injured by Fiction. An admirable Writer of our own Time [i.e. Richardson], has found the Way to convey the most solid Instructions, the noblest Sentiments, and the most exalted Piety, in the pleasing Dress of a Novel." Arabella's response to this idea not only reveals a critical awareness, but echoes one of the main operational principles of early realistic novels: the Fables of Aesop, she says, "are among those of which the Absurdity discovers itself, and the Truth is comprised in the Application; but what can be said of those Tales which are told with the solemn Air of historical Truth, and if false convey no Instruction?" (IX. xi, 377). Arabella eventually recognizes that the truth-effect of the fiction is *enhanced* by its declared artifice, when artifice operates within a narrative context in which "absurdities" are read ("applied") against other events as well as against a normative sense of life in order to arrive at a trustworthy "instruction."[18]

In differentiating between romance and realistic fiction – taking realism as the basis for serious historical representation, against the fantasy (albeit entertaining) of the old romances – Johnson's views about historical narrative are (surprisingly) consonant with those of Bolingbroke and Godwin. All three were sceptical of what passed for history. Bolingbroke believed in the power of history to teach by example but emphasized the fabulous nature of most history writing: "The very best is nothing better than a probable tale, artfully contrived, and plausibly told, wherein truth and falsehood are indistinguishably blended together."[19] For Godwin, likewise, "all history bears too near a resemblance to fable" and "the reader will be miserably deluded if, while he reads history, he suffers himself to imagine that he is reading facts."[20] But he maintains a respect for history and argues that realistic fiction (what he calls romance) when "strictly considered, may be pronounced to be one of the species of history," because the "romance" writer is free to choose his materials from a greater range of sources, while the historian is confined to "individual incident and individual man"(370). In short, both Bolingbroke and Godwin see the exemplariness of history as a function of its narrative and its ability to connect individuals and society together into a coherent scheme.

Politically, Johnson stands at a distance from Bolingbroke[21] and Godwin, but he shares their grasp of the ideological effect in so-called factual works. History and life-writing are near relatives not only in seventeenth- and early eighteenth-century historiography but in Johnson's own writing, and both modes share narratological and epistemological characteristics with realistic fiction.[22] Although there is little systematic analysis of history-writing in Johnson's work, a considerable body of thought on various aspects of the emerging discipline can be compiled from his writings.[23] For the most part, when Johnson uses the term "history" or "historical narrative" he understands a "scientific," factual text that descends from seventeenth-century antiquarianism, and that will eventually become the heir of the post-Romantic positivist disciplines of Macaulay, Carlyle, Burkhardt, and F. H. Bradley.[24] As early as 1751, however, Johnson's usage suggests an inclination towards a humanist historiography, a modernity exemplified by Machiavelli, Bacon, and Clarendon, and that eventually comes to fruition in the histories of Hume and Gibbon.[25] Humanist historiography argued the central shaping importance of people in civil and political affairs, and Johnson's discourses increasingly reflect that view, also echoing Bacon's belief that historical discourse was not only a way of knowing but a way of acting in the world.[26] "'Books,' says Bacon, 'cannot teach the use of books.' The student must learn by commerce with mankind to reduce his speculations to practice, and accommodate his knowledge to the purposes of life."[27] Johnson's view in "Rambler" 122, however, seems to eschew the interpretation of established facts and the elicitation of underlying general human principles, implied by humanist historiography. He seems willing to confine history to an uninflected, factual, and authoritative account of past events, to that strand of history-writing that came to be known as scientific.

The stylistic and philosophical qualities enumerated by Johnson in "Rambler" 122 all seem to pertain to relatively simple forms of historiography (he himself calls it a "simple narration"): chronicle, and political and national history. Of course, Raleigh's *History of the World*, Clarendon's *History of the Rebellion*, and Knolles' *History of the Turks* – the illustrative texts on which he draws – all more or less fall into these categories, though with some important qualifications.[28] Such history, as Johnson describes it, would nonetheless seem to rise no higher than the documentary, to appeal to relatively simple rules of verifiability, and to imply a clearly accessible past, for the historian "has only the actions and designs of men like himself to conceive and to relate; he is not to form, but to copy characters." His style, accordingly, need not rise to the highest levels of invention: "The difficulty of making variety consistent, or uniting probability with surprize, needs not to disturb him; the manners and actions of his personages are already fixed; his materials are provided and put into his hands, and he is at leisure to employ all his powers in arranging and displaying them" (IV, 288).

Significantly, this essay was written (18 May 1751) before the publication of any of the more fully developed humanist histories of Robertson, Gibbon, Hume, and Ramsay, and before the full development of Johnson's historical thought.[29] It is also typical of Johnson, however, that his thinking about history is not always limited to formal, generic parameters. Indeed, Johnson's own historiographical practice – to be found usually in texts that are not formal histories – *exceeds* his theory, such as it is, and the apparent ambiguities of his thinking about history reflect the flexibility and the generic porousness that characterized the various historical discourses of the time.[30] It is in a liminal area between formal genres and in Johnson's reflexive skeptical mode – especially in his writing about time and memory – that we look for a more sophisticated modern historiographical understanding. Thus, even "Rambler" 122 gives the impression that the correspondence between historical narrative and past events is not nearly so straightforward and "scientific" as Johnson declares. His praise of Knolles' narrative[31] suggests that history is not as transparent as the rhetoric implies: "A wonderful multiplicity of events is so artfully arranged, and so distinctly explained, that each facilitates the knowledge of the next" (IV, 290).

The subtext here is that Knolles' historical coherence results from his having artfully orchestrated complex and multifarious materials. In 1779, in the "Life of Milton," Johnson sees history as supplying "the writer with the rudiments of narration" which he then " must improve and exalt by a nobler art, must animate by dramatick energy, and diversify by retrospection and anticipation" – that "nobler art" including historical narration.[32] However, when the past and those who dwelt within it are no longer accessible to personal memory or empirical observation, the historian's art ceases to be one that merely records, and necessarily becomes one that also invents, but invents truthfully. Here Johnson's thinking about history joins his thinking about life-writing. Aware of the historiographical priorities of such writers as Bacon, Clarendon, Hutchinson, and Baxter, which accept life-writing as an important historical form,[33] Johnson develops narratological principles for biography that begin to resemble those of eighteenth-century history- and novel-writing.

One of the compelling features of biography for Johnson is that, like the realistic novel, it addresses "those parallel circumstances, and kindred images, to which we readily conform our minds," and which can be found in "narratives of the lives of particular persons" (*Rambler*, 60, III, 319). In terms of the emotive appeal and moral effect, scientific history stands in relation to biography as romance stands to the novel: "Histories of the downfal of kingdoms, and the revolutions of empires, are read with great tranquillity," as opposed to "a judicious and faithful narrative" of an ordinary life that "lead the thoughts into domestick privacies" (*Rambler*, III, 319, 320, 321). Yet history and biography share an epistemological and an evidentiary problem in the form of the ever-receding and contestable past. If Johnson believed that "the incidents which give excellence to biography are of a volatile and evanescent kind, such as soon escape the memory, and are rarely transmitted by tradition" (III, 323), we also know how little of this kind of information he had (or sought) in composing the *Lives of the Poets* and his earlier biographies. The *Life of Savage* is exceptional in being based on much personal experience, and one might argue that in comparison to the later lives *Savage* is consequently less finished. The "Life of Addison" records an epistemological problem that is paradigmatic of all the *Lives*, when Johnson notes that "History may be formed from permanent monuments and records; but Lives can only be written from personal knowledge, which is growing every day less, and in a short time is lost for ever ... The delicate features of the mind, the nice discriminations of character, and the minute peculiarities of conduct, are soon obliterated" (*Lives*, II, 116).

Even formal history (like Clarendon's) incorporates the depiction of personal and public lives (equally susceptible to time), and on such occasions the historian has to resort to the biographer's methods, and both deal with matters of evidence, coherence, and truth by mimicking techniques of the realistic novel. Johnson counters the absence of personal testimony and the gradual loss of personal memory by using various forms of circumstantial evidence, including anecdotal information from contemporaries and other forms of historical documentation, but most notably by resorting to the individual's own writings. This is one of the ways in which he is able to register a fictional approximation and hence a *continuity* of life and work in the *Lives* that anticipates a modern focus on the transformative power of life-writing, "that meeting point between mind and work," as Frederick Karl notes, where "[b]iography [becomes] . . . the reconstruction of a human model who seems suitable for the work created."[34]

Drawing upon the literary output is Johnson's primary way of making such a "reconstruction." Because "there is always a silent reference of human works to human abilities" (*Shakespeare*, I, 81), Johnson's biographical method moves (like his legal thinking) from effects to causes, from the work to the mind that created it, rather than by constructing an interpretation of a writer's work based on his biography.[35] Writing of biography, Fish argues that all literary interpretation is necessarily inseparable from the act of assigning intention,[36] yet Johnson's methodology emphasizes the increasing inaccessibility of historical fact, and hence of the origins and intentions of a text. If the gap between the present and the past points to the limits of human reason, and to a tragic view of life, the ubiquitous presence of failure and death, and the individual's inadequacy to his own aspirations and to the events of his time, are *also* instrumental in Johnson's process of imagining characters for his poets.[37] From the biographical point of view, all of the *Lives* take as their subject a mortal life that has passed and is over; correspondingly, the larger biographical narrative of the *Lives* takes a retrospective mode, frequently highlighting the irony in the discrepancy between intentions and achievements and between the personal consciousness of the character and a larger narratological perspective.

However, for all the irony of Johnson's moral consideration of human mortality (as witness the careers of Wolsey and Swedish Charles in the *Vanity*), of which his occasionally rueful treatment of literary and political failure is part, my proposition is that Johnson's proto-tragic view is transformed in the narrative structure of the *Lives* which operates with secular, commemorative redemptiveness.[38] There are many examples of local, distributive memory in the *Lives*, in which the commemorative voice of the biographer recollects some personal event, as Johnson does when he recalls his father, "an old bookseller,"[39] or when he remembers Gilbert Walmsley at the end of the "Life of Edmund Smith": "Of Gilbert Walmsley, thus presented to my mind, let me indulge myself in the remembrance. I knew him very early; he was one of the first friends that literature procured me."[40] Memory also frequently takes the form of anecdote, as when Johnson makes a telling symbolic use of the story of Dryden's social habits at Will's Coffee House,[41] or the story of Pope's rejection by his one-time friend and putative lover Martha Blount.[42] These forms of memory further the plot and the historical density of the *Lives*, and also provide some important insight into the character of the poet under consideration. Both forms of memory have the effect of placing individual moments of experience or particular events in the context of a longer historical perspective, but they also confer a reality on them by virtue of having *been* remembered and because they are given a significant place in a chronologically ordered sequence comprising Johnson's larger narrative.[43] These memories – and others like them – all exercise a certain redemptive function, where "redemption" is understood as a spiritually oriented form of secular philosophical thinking which draws attention to the nature of temporality by opening up a powerful present moment.[44]

However, in terms of the structural memory of single lives, as well as the overarching narrative of all fifty-two *Lives* as a single work, the deficiencies of historical evidence are acknowledged and compensated for by Johnson's manner of bringing together the individual's life and writing within a larger temporal and experiential continuum. In Lawrence Lipking's words, Johnson discovers how poetry "can constitute the experience of a life," and how a great poet "makes his own destiny; makes it, precisely, with poems."[45] The distinctive combinations of criticism and biography of the *Lives* discover not only some of the lost delicacies of mind and discriminations of character in the *works* of the writers dealt with, but they also mitigate the vanity of human wishes. Johnson thereby imparts to the structures of the *Lives* a value and a function not present in any one part of a life by itself. He discovers in human limitations and the historical realm a dignity and grace which moves his writing from proto-tragedy, emphasizing the helplessness of the individual in the face of the universal laws of life, into a "mingled," "natural" mode, reminiscent of Shakespeare's dramas (*Shakespeare*, I, 66).

There is obviously no literal correspondence between living and writing for Johnson: it is not in the nature of language to provide such correspondence; and, moreover, "it may be shewn much easier to design than to perform... It is the condition of our present state to see more than we can attain."[46] Yet he creates a continuous though differential structure out of the biographical and critical elements in the *Lives*, and this artifice is a function of the recollective and repetitive narrative action, in which the linear and successive particular moments of time (chronos) become filled with a supra-personal temporal significance (kairos). This transformation in the temporal dimension of experience is articulated in the *Lives* most clearly by Johnson's creation of the literary character, a principle of coherence that makes his narrative into a genuine cognitive instrument in the spirit of Louis Mink's idea that "the cognitive function of narrative form... is not just to relate a succession of events but to body forth an ensemble of interrelationships of many different kinds as a single whole."[47] Johnson's literary characters, in the context of "an ensemble of interrelationships," address the question of how a writer makes something of himself, and how he makes (or, crucially, does *not* make) a memory of and for himself.

The *Lives* seriously commemorate all of their subjects, but there is more than one way in which memory functions in the *Lives*. Those lives with a clearly developed character sketch mediating between biography and criticism (of Cowley, Milton, Dryden, Pope, Addison, Gray) record how poets "realize" their character (or their "genius," as Johnson calls it) in and through writing, and then how literary genius transforms the temporal into the timeless. Central to each of these lives is Johnson's interest in the circumstances under which the writer transforms his personality into an author, and how he thereby contributes towards the formation of a national English literature.[48] This discourse of canonization is linked by Johnson to a certain kind of generality and memorability and it distinguishes his position from the prevailing mid eighteenth-century concepts of the canon as developed by Joseph and Thomas Warton, Richard Hurd, and John Upton.[49] The death of the author seen by Foucault as incidental to the rise of a historical or archaeological discursiveness in the late-eighteenth century is, in Johnson's *Lives*, undone by a biographical criticism as sophisticated as any that Foucault imagined.

For Johnson, making a character is tantamount to remembering or making an authorial self out of personal experience, the historical and cultural past, and fragments of contemporary life. Poets who achieve this level of articulation do so in their own distinctive ways. Johnson's narrative typically records and constitutes that event, in a manner similar to the novelist's and historian's; but his characters are not of the "realistic" kind found in either Richardson's or Fielding's novels. His biographical method does, however, make similar distinctions about character he employed when discussing *their* characters. Johnson's two singular critical comments on Richardson and Fielding can with some latitude be applied to his own characters in the *Lives*. He employs a common metaphor distinguishing between characters of nature and characters of manners when comparing Richardson with Fielding: "Characters of manners are very entertaining; but they are to be understood, by a more superficial observer, than characters of nature, where a man must dive into the recesses of the heart." Employing another metaphor with a long life in the eighteenth century, Johnson told Boswell "that there was as great a difference between [Richardson and Fielding] as between a man who knew how a watch was made, and a man who could tell the hour by looking on the dial-plate" (*Life*, II, 48–49).

Exactly how the metaphor of the clock is to be applied to the relative qualities of the novelists in question is not at issue at moment;[50] what is, is that Johnson's own biographical characters can be described in these terms. For some characters, like Milton, require of Johnson that he dive into the recesses of the heart in order to conceptualize and to describe them, while Butler, Halifax, and others – entertaining and instructive as they may be – leave the biographer's invention and critical judgment relatively unengaged. Likewise there are some characters, like Dryden and Pope, who exemplify the dynamic of the clock metaphor, but, as with Fielding and Richardson,[51] it is no simple matter to decide exactly *how* the metaphor applies to the poets in question. Even in the case of characters of manners, however, Johnson's biographical method is memorable – that is, it creates a memory for the poet. But *how* characters are known in Johnson's narrative, and *what* is known about them, evidently differs from the novelistic style that characterizes Boswell's *Life of Johnson* or the realism of Richardson.[52]

Ralph Rader describes the Richardsonian novel as "involving a focally autonomous illusion of a world like all of our life worlds, but informed by a subsidiary registration of the fact that the substance of the apparently autonomous fictional world is everywhere instinct with the author's intention to give it affective meaning and point."[53] To some degree the worlds of Johnson's biographies partake of a similar illusory autonomy, but, except for the occasional perception into human motive and feeling, Johnson's method involves no sustained psychological exploration of character; there is very little "focal illusion of characters acting autonomously as if in the world of real experience" ("The Emergence of the Novel," 72). Although Johnson's methods reveal and produce several *different* kinds of character in the *Lives*, his narrative voice stands outside rather than inside the human psyche of his characters, as it does in *Rasselas*, developing a historical–biographical narrative rather than a psychological–novelistic one.

Notwithstanding this uniformity, individual *Lives* differ from each other in important ways. Just as Shakespeare's dramas are not uniformly natural, so not all of the writers in the *Lives* are poets of nature. Donne is metaphysical, Milton is sublime, and Pope is idealist; only Dryden and, to lesser degrees, Cowley and Parnell are felt to be poets of nature, although the term is also used with various degrees of critical urgency and pressure to describe a wide range of commonplace literary effects across the whole spectrum of the *Lives*, from the observation that Pomfret's *Choice* "exhibits a system of life adapted to common notions and equal to common expectations" to the conviction that the famous scene in Congreve's *Mourning Bride* lets us "enjoy ... for the moment the powers of a poet."[54] My proposition, then, is that Johnson's power of performance, and his critical engagement in the lives and works of these writers, is such that each of the *Lives* manifests a distinctive style and intellectual engagement as a result of Johnson's response to the writer with whom he is dealing. Thus, the "Life of Milton" is monolithic and intellectual, the "Life of Pope" subtle and minutely discriminatory, and the "Life of Dryden" easy and capacious, as if – notwithstanding the severe criticism of the debilitated aspects of Dryden – Johnson were in the company of a kindred spirit. There is a remarkable resistance among professional critics to this notion of the serendipitous performativity of Johnson's writing, yet this is to say no more (but no less) than that Johnson is, as he says of Dryden, "another and the same,"[55] and capable of writing imaginatively and sensitively in response to the characteristics and otherness of the writer under consideration – even while maintaining his *own* stylistic character. "Literary commentary," Geoffrey Hartman observes, "may cross the line and become as demanding as literature: it ... cannot be subordinated, a priori, to its referential or commenting function,"[56] and the *Lives* demonstrate as much.

However, Milton's sublimity, Pope's idealizing artifice, and Dryden's numinous energy (to mention only three of the larger lives) all testify, as

Johnson says in the "Life of Gay," to the "*mens divinior*," the "divine soul" of the poet.[57] Yet Johnson does not reify reason, invention, good sense, judgment, or any other intellectual, stylistic, or psychological characteristic. Just as Shakespeare is used as a standard of nature in the *Lives*, whose drama is implicitly recollected in various critical judgments as a means of distinguishing different qualities of writing, so other poets with the "*mens divinior*" operate as touchstones or embodiments of memory in the *Lives*. The "Life of Milton" in particular depicts the production of memory more symbolically than any of the other lives, and Milton marks an important horizon and standard in the *Lives of the Poets*.

REMEMBERING MILTON

Read with awareness of Johnson's interest in the relations between memory and character, it becomes clear how highly Johnson thought of Milton. The hostility towards Milton implied by Johnson's association with William Lauder's forged *Essay on Milton's Use and Imitation of the Moderns* (1749),[58] the sharp-edged tone of the "Life of Milton," and the negative contemporary reviews of this life,[59] have all weighed heavily in the critical estimation of Johnson's Milton. We have been quicker to register his grudging, even misconceived evaluation of Milton's life and writing, than we have been to remark his extraordinary praise of Milton's mind, his estimation that *Paradise Lost* rivals Homer's epics, and that the poem is used in the *Rambler* and the *Lives* as the embodiment of some of the very finest poetry. The undervaluation of this life has perhaps been cemented by the Whig literary history inherited from the likes of Macaulay,[60] compounded by the association of Milton with romanticism and the opposition seen between romanticism and neoclassicism[61] – and by critics like Eliot and Leavis,[62] whose notion that Milton was primarily responsible for the "dissociation of sensibility" in the seventeenth century effected twentieth-century appreciation, at least until Christopher Ricks' *Milton's Grand Style* (1962) and Christopher Hill's *Milton and the English Revolution* (1977).

For Johnson, however, Milton was extraordinary and exemplary in more ways than one. Unlike any of the other poets in the *Lives*, Milton undertook a monumental body of work, *and* he completely realized his poetic aims, for "to display the motives and actions of beings thus superior [as those featured in *Paradise Lost*]... is the task this mighty poet has undertaken *and performed*" (para. 213 – my emphasis).[63] Johnson takes as truth Milton's declaration while on the Grand Tour that he would "perhaps leave something so written to after-times, as they should not willingly let it die" (para. 25).[64] Furthermore, there is no hint, at least as far as *Paradise Lost* is concerned, of the inevitable discrepancy that exists in all of the other lives between intellectual effort and actual production.

As remarkable, given Johnson's skepticism of grand pronouncements, is his willingness to accept Milton's life – at least, his character – as commensurate with his writing, noting that "Milton... *with great reason* congratulates himself upon the consciousness of being found equal to his own character, and having preserved in a private and familiar interview that reputation which his works had procured him (my emphasis)."[65] In Johnson's critical lexicon these are signs of Milton's having obtained an extraordinary level of articulation that intrigued him, even though the "Life" registers other issues to which he is less attracted. In short, Milton was one of the very few English writers with a European reputation, a man who, like Johnson himself, from humble beginnings rose to make a national and historic contribution in literature. Even though Milton's life had been written many times,[66] and his writing had by the 1770s already been absorbed and appropriated into the English poetic imagination,[67] Johnson took the opportunity of providing a "new narrative," ostensibly to meet the requirements of "the uniformity of this edition,"[68] but really to engage Milton.

It is now recognized that the organization of the life entails "continuities" generated not so much in the literary character (paras. 157–75), but in the critical section (paras. 176–277) – especially in the passages devoted to *Paradise Lost* (paras. 207–64) – where Johnson detects qualities common to Milton's life and poetry.[69] Notwithstanding his disapproval of Milton's egotism, aloofness, and republicanism, he also recognizes the same qualities as nurturing and expressing a mind peculiarly apt for writing *Paradise Lost*. Milton's poetic "character" in this life is not a given – as it is in the early lives of Milton – but it is created by the confluence of the personal, the political, and the poetic as co-ordinated in Johnson's text. Thus, the biographical part of the life reflects in detail Johnson's hostility to Milton's politics, but it also registers bafflement at the way a transcendent imagination enslaves itself to a political program whose fancied good entails the destruction of all that's worthy in civilization. The force of Johnson's critique of Milton's politics is partly determined by the historical facts and the hagiographic attitude of Milton's early biographers. When Milton's politics is seen as a manifestation of his imaginative powers, Johnson's treatment becomes more inclusive, and speaks to Milton's "character" and not merely to his opinions.

However, Milton's politics are obviously very challenging for Johnson: deeply rooted in principle, they spoke to a completely contrary tradition to that to which Johnson adhered, and, contrary to his treatment of the similar politics of Admiral Blake and Francis Cheynel, Johnson identifies Milton's as capricious and perverse. Still, there is a significant historical and symbolic difference between Milton's views and those of Blake and Cheynel – or Edmund Waller. In comparison to Milton's formidable justification of the revolution and regicide, Waller's support of Cromwell is merely the weakness of an ordinary man, bending in the winds of political change.[70] But for one who so dislikes Milton's politics, Johnson certainly quotes him frequently. In citing the *Reason of Church Government*, the *Doctrine and Discipline of Divorce, Of Education*, the *Judgment of Martin Bucer, Tetrachordon, Areopagitica, The Tenure of Kings and Magistrates*, "Remarks on Articles of Peace between Ormond and the Irish Rebels," *Eikonoclastes, The 2nd Defence of the People*, and *Smectymnius*, he draws on Milton's politics more extensively than he does on other bodies of writing.

Not only does Johnson refer to Milton's political texts, he probes their reasonableness, in the process employing a narratology which *both* appropriates *and* critiques Milton's own language and polemical methods. Eighteenth-century attitudes to Milton's prose were generally divided between those who, like Addison and Warburton, denounced their "abominable" virulence and "unnatural" forced grandeur[71], and those, like Edward Phillips, Toland, and Macaulay, who saw in Milton's prose "the full power of the English language."[72] Both sides, however, present Milton as a figure divided between the material, polemical demands of politics and ecclesiastical policies, and the inspired universalism of the poetry.

No such notion exists in Johnson's discussion, although there are significant differences in emphasis in his treatment of Milton's prose and poetry – reflected, for example, in the confinement of the prose to the biographical section, and the poetry to the critical. Milton's prose elicits from Johnson a very different kind of critical judgment than *Paradise Lost*, yet there is no sense in Johnson's writing that the prose is a *lesser* rhetorical effort. That Johnson did not *like* Milton's prose and finds his opinions dangerous should not obscure the critical seriousness with which he engaged their arguments about historically and universally important issues, as well as Milton's iconoclastic character.

Johnson's grasp of the effective continuity of Milton's prose and poetry anticipates a modern perspective which highlights the "interaction between textual effects and the world of power,"[73] applying to both prose and poetry. Reading Johnson's remarks on Milton's politics as directly *related to* his texts – as the prefatory nature of the *Lives* requires – adds a logic to his critique that is missing from the assumption that he writes merely in the spirit of conservative detraction. Johnson's language in this life, indeed, reminds the reader of the imperious and sarcastic tone and, above all, the extraordinary level of intellectual confidence of Milton's prose itself: Milton's "warmest advocates must allow that he never spared any asperity of reproach or brutality of insolence" (para. 127). To some extent these characteristics explain commensurate qualities in Johnson's prose here, which are not typical of his prose in other lives. The "sheer conviction," in William Kerrigan's words,[74] of Milton's polemical prose prompts Johnson's incisiveness: what Milton does to Salmasius, Johnson does to Milton. Milton's prose has been described as seeking and implying "strenuous readers," who are "ingenuous, ingenious, acute, intelligent, diligent, attentive, judicious, knowing, learned, elegant, equal, charitable"[75] – all qualities which describe Johnson as a reader.

But this serendipity is uncomfortable. In discussing Milton's ideas on education (paras. 36–44), Johnson commends his social conscientiousness in setting up a school and in instructing his pupils in religion, but he challenges the basis of Milton's system. Thus, Milton is described as trying to do something exceptional yet odd in his curriculum "by reading those authors that treat of physical subjects; such as the Georgick, and astronomical treatises of the ancients" (para. 38). This attempt to "teach something more solid than the common literature of schools" (para. 38) distinguishes Milton's plan from the standard grammar-school curriculum of the early seventeenth century, especially by emphasizing the importance of the trivium – grammar, rhetoric, and logic.[76] Johnson challenges Milton by articulating a broad, humane view of liberal education, emphasizing "the religious and moral knowledge of right and wrong ... an acquaintance with the history of mankind, and with those examples which may be said to embody truth and prove by events the reasonableness of opinions" (para. 39). He concludes his eloquent plea by invoking an affiliation with Socrates' moral position which "turn[s] philosophy from the study of nature to speculations upon life," against such "innovators" as Milton who "are turning off attention from life to nature" (para. 41).

Persuasive as this plea sounds, there is also something paradoxical about it, for Johnson knows very well that Milton's ambitious educational views, at least in "Of Education" (1644), fall squarely *within* the classical–humanist and Christian tradition – of which Johnson otherwise approved.[77] As Milton sought to distinguish his plan from the views of Vives, Comenius, and Hartlib[78] he developed an ideal curriculum that moved *away from* the vocational towards the liberal, because, as he explains, "our understanding cannot in this body found it selfe but on sensible things, nor arrive so cleerly to the knowledge of God and things invisible, as by orderly conning over the visible and inferior creature, the same method is necessarily to be follow'd in all discreet teaching."[79]

Milton's curriculum is squarely based in the study of languages and the theory and practice of poetry, and includes the practical study of virtue across the curriculum – what Milton describes as "a speciall reinforcement of constant and sound endoctrinating to set them [students] right and firm, instructing them more amply in the knowledge of vertue and the hatred of vice."[80] In short, Milton's educational views should be very attractive to Johnson, whose animadversions appear to be an example of the psychological tension that some find to energize his attitude to Milton. For Johnson's misreading of Milton's ideas essentially enables him – in a very Miltonic gesture – to usurp Milton's position, and thus perhaps to repress an identification he feels with the object of his criticism.[81]

This is a different dynamic from the cutting down to size or tragic exposure that many have seen governing Johnson's comments on Milton's activities. Furthermore, one gets the sense that Johnson is trying to understand and to formulate a view of the kind of mind that is the source of Milton's many powerful and confident intellectual positions, many of which seem to Johnson to be "founded in an envious hatred of greatness, and a sullen desire of independence; in petulance impatient of control, and pride disdainful of authority" (para. 169). Self-importance and aloofness were clearly aspects of Milton's perceived character that sharpened Johnson's criticism: "He had accustomed his imagination to unrestrained indulgence, and his conceptions therefore were extensive. The characteristic quality of his poem is sublimity" (para. 230). This concatenation of ideas about Milton's personality and politics, suggests that what starts out as willful distrust of the autonomy of the world issues into a great and beautiful poem. In the plot of Milton's life thus constructed, Johnson's argument is that the qualities of mind exemplified in Milton's political writings cease to be baffling or obnoxious when enlisted in the poetic enterprise that is *Paradise Lost*.

Such transformations characterize Milton's religious opinions, as perceived by Johnson. He emphasizes Milton's distancing himself from all churches, Anglican, Presbyterian, and Catholic, and raises the possibility that by "chang[ing] his party by his humour" and having "determined rather what to condemn than what to approve," he "loves himself rather than truth" (paras. 56, 165). One new illustration, from the *Whole Duty of Man*, added by Johnson to the noun "offender" in the fourth edition of the *Dictionary* (1773) touches on this subject: "He that, without a necessary cause, absents himself from publick prayers, cuts himself off from the church, which hath always been thought so unhappy a thing, that it is the greatest punishment the governors of the church can lay upon the worst *offender*." Thus, by excluding himself from the historical and theological experience represented by the Church, Milton might also be opening himself to a loss of his Christian and essentially human status.

How does a man, Johnson seems to wonder, who has the "profoundest veneration" for the Holy Scriptures, and a "confirmed belief of the immediate and occasional agency of Providence" (para. 166) live without worship? Johnson never directly answers this implied question, but, once he brings Milton's poetry into play, the paradox ceases to be problematic and becomes, instead, expressive of the complexity of Milton's character. So: "That he lived without prayer can hardly be affirmed; [because] his studies and meditations were an habitual prayer" (para. 167). However, Johnson does not extrapolate biographically from the poetry and say that because Milton represents Adam and Eve as praying therefore he himself must have prayed. Instead, he writes as if the intelligence in the poetry is continuous with the consciousness of prayer, and, without making an explicit comparison, Johnson's narrative uses Adamic terms in which to vindicate Milton.[82] Adam and Eve are seen as "praying acceptably in the state of innocence, and efficaciously after their fall" (para. 167), and they "rise again to reverential regard when we find that their prayers were heard" (para. 240).

It is in a "fictional" realm, then, between life and text, in which Johnson creates a representation of Milton's character, implying that it is in this in-between place where character appears, testifying to Henry James's idea that "the deepest quality of a work of art will always be the quality of the mind of the producer."[83] It is in this biographical site, that the discrepancy between Milton's life and text seems to vanish: "That he lived without prayer can hardly be affirmed; his studies and his meditations were an habitual prayer" (para. 176); and "In Milton every line breathes sanctity of thought and purity of manners" (para. 238). All this suggests that the gigantic self-confidence of Milton's resistance to ordinariness is transformed into something extraordinarily beautiful by his greater seriousness when his mind is filled by the "*mens divinior*":

"The heat of Milton's mind might be said to sublimate his learning, to throw off into his work the spirit of science, unmingled with its grosser parts" (para. 229). Appropriating the rich image of Milton's being made pregnant by the Muse, as the "vast abyss" is similarly impregnated by the Holy Spirit (Bk. 1, 17–26),[84] Johnson uses it to describe how Milton's genius transforms received truths – the "few radical positions which the Scriptures afforded him" (para. 249) – into the uniqueness that is *Paradise Lost*:[85] "This Milton has undertaken, and performed with *pregnancy* and vigour of mind peculiar to himself... Here is a full display of the united force of study and genius; of a great accumulation of materials, with judgement to digest and fancy to combine them" (para. 249).

These are qualities that lead Johnson to suggest that "from his book alone the Art of English Poetry might be learned" (para. 272), an art which clearly grows out of a deeply personal engagement with life, society, politics, and letters. Consequently, the narrative movement of the "Life of Milton" from Milton's personal characteristics to the manifestation of qualities of mind in poetry, is marked by the diminishment of personalized and ironic treatment on Johnson's part. It is not that Johnson sees any radical division between Milton's polemical prose and his poetry; it is just that in *Paradise Lost* Milton's mind seems to come free, legitimately encountering no opposition from civil law or social constraint, and is able to expand to the limits of imagination. Repeatedly, Johnson observes Milton's ability to "realize fiction" (para. 208), for it is in that artistic realization that he discovers the poet's sublime character, having left behind the remnants of the personality who engaged in political controversy and insisted on his own separateness:[86]

To display the motives and actions of beings thus superior, so far as human reason can examine them or human imagination represent them, is the task this mighty poet has undertaken *and performed*... He had considered creation in its whole extent, and his descriptions are therefore learned. He had accustomed his imagination to unrestrained indulgence, and his conceptions therefore were extensive. The characteristick quality of his poem is sublimity. (paras. 213, 230)

Such criticism clearly testifies to Johnson's enormous approval of Milton's poetry. If there is tension in the life it is not to be explained in the Bloomian terms of Johnson's psychological constraints under Milton's genius, but by his critical response to the sustained heroic status of Milton's poetic character. The heroic is not a mode of being and writing with which Johnson is most comfortable. It is not the mingled reality he valued in Shakespeare's drama, and of which others variously partake. In contrast to Shakespeare, Milton "knew human nature only in the gross, and had never studied shades of character, nor the combinations of concurring or the perplexity of contending passions" (para. 268). Nonetheless, not only does *Paradise Lost* satisfy the formal and imaginative demands of a Classical epic – the topics discussed by Johnson follow those of Le Bossu's treatise on the epic[87] – but it overrides the moral resistance Johnson has towards most religious verse:[88] "[*Paradise Lost*] contains the history of a miracle, of Creation and Redemption; it displays the power and the mercy of the Supreme Being: the probable therefore is marvellous, and the marvellous is probable" (para. 220).

Johnson's attitude to this poetic vision is thus twofold. Echoing Addison,[89] he affirms the "universally and perpetually interesting" aspect of the poetry: "All mankind will, through all ages, bear the same relation to Adam and to Eve, and must partake of that good and evil which extend to themselves" (para. 221). At the same time, Johnson registers the emotional and imaginative distance of the poetry from the common reader: "The plan of *Paradise Lost* has this inconvenience, that it comprises neither human actions nor human manners" (para. 244). It is from this fundamental aspect of the poem that Johnson's infamous, apparently decisive observation seems to come: "The want of human interest is always felt. *Paradise Lost* is one of the books which the reader admires and lays down, and forgets to take up again. None ever wished it longer than it is. Its perusal is a duty rather than a pleasure" (para. 252).

Such criticism sounds final, but it is much modified when taken in context, representing only one aspect of Johnson's more complex overall understanding in this life. If no one ever wished the poem longer, no one, likewise, wished it shorter, for the very good reason, as Johnson points out, that it is perfectly imagined and artistically finished: "To the *compleatness* or *integrity* of the design nothing can be objected . . . There is perhaps no poem of the same length from which so little can be taken without apparent mutilation" (para. 224);[90] and "he has interwoven the whole system of theology with such propriety that every part appears to be necessary, and scarcely any recital is wished shorter for the sake of quickening the progress of the main action" (para. 210). Furthermore, Milton "chose a subject on which *too much could not be said*, on which he might tire his fancy without censure of extravagance" (my emphasis – para. 231). Indeed, Johnson welcomed as poetically necessary digressions that which Addison considered inappropriate for an epic:[91] "The short digressions at the beginning of the third, seventh, and ninth books might doubtless be spared; but superfluities so beautiful who would take away? . . . Perhaps no passages are more frequently or more attentively read than those extrinsick paragraphs; and, since the end of poetry is pleasure, that cannot be unpoetical with which all are pleased" (para. 224).

Sublimity and pleasure are often thought of as mutually exclusive in Johnson's aesthetic[92] – a dichotomy he himself sometimes upholds, especially when it is the Burkean sublime under discussion – but there is no division between these discourses in Johnson's criticism of a poem which, itself, does not force such divisions. "The probable therefore is marvellous, and the marvellous is therefore probable" (para. 220). The opening digressions of Books 3, 7, and 9 are evidently not the only sections to give Johnson pleasure. He takes pleasure in Abdiel's praise of fortitude (Bk.v, 872f) and the exchange between Raphael and Adam in response to Adam's curiosity about the planets (Bk. VIII, 66–197). Everything about Adam and Eve pleases Johnson in the way excellent poetry pleases, *including their fall*, the introduction of "anguish arising from the consciousness of transgression" which is the only real moment in which the "passions are moved" (para. 241).

Furthermore, Milton provides Johnson with a framework for some of his most characteristic thoughts. The movement of Adam and Eve from Paradise into "our present state" – through transgression, repentance, and forgiveness – could be described as Johnson's master-narrative, structuring all of his moral thought and his thinking about temporality. Indeed, in the heavily revised fourth edition of the *Dictionary* (1773) Johnson incorporates a very large number of new quotations from *Paradise Lost*, as a means of turning his text towards the sacred and the ecclesiastical. According to Allen Reddick, the second part of the alphabet (M–Z) in the *Dictionary* has two-hundred quotations from Milton (as opposed to 139 from Young, 100 from Cowley, 80 from Pope, 33 from Dryden, and 21 from Shakespeare).[93] All of these Miltonic quotations contribute toward the furtherance of a sub-narrative in the *Dictionary*, of transgression, repentance, and redemption, suggesting, in Reddick's words, "that [Johnson] was possessed in a profound way by the poem, as if its lines suggested fresh meanings or significance, linguistic, spiritual, or otherwise, for him at this later stage of his life" (123).[94] Crucially, this is one discourse in *Paradise Lost* in which sublimity and pathos are one, as Johnson recognizes in his comment on the action of the poem in relation to the human actors. While Addison sees the Messiah as the hero of the poem, and John Dennis places Satan in that role,[95] Johnson finds Adam and Eve fulfilling this imaginative function:[96] "Dryden... denies the heroism of Adam because he was overcome; but there is no reason why the hero should not be unfortunate except established practice... However, if success be necessary, Adam... was restored to his Maker's favour, and therefore may resume his human rank" (para. 225).

Johnson takes Dryden to task for upholding Satan's heroic status,[97] but in doing so actually aligns himself *with* Dryden's redefinition of the epic in the Preface to *Fables*, where Dryden argues that the "very definition" of an epic is the "imitation of human life," and that Chaucer's "propriety" and nature – especially in the "noble poem of *Palamon and Arcite*, which is of the epic kind"– left that poem "perhaps not much inferior to the *Ilias* or the *Aeneis*."[98] Equally, Johnson equated Adam and Eve's heroism with their humanity, which, I would suggest, includes not only their contingency under divine law following on their transgression (i.e., Bks. IX–XII), but also their normative experience in Paradise (i.e., Bks. IV–VIII). *That* experience is the subject of "Raphael's reproof of Adam's curiosity... with the answer returned by Adam" (Bk. VIII, 66–197), which Johnson said "may be confidently opposed to any rule of life which any poet has delivered" (para. 228):[99]

> ...not to know at large of things remote
> From use, obscure and subtle, but to know
> That which before us lies in daily life,
> Is the prime wisdom... (Bk. VIII, 191–94)

This association of "daily life" – so evidently continuous with Johnson's thought about the present as the site for memory – with the heroic, effectively redefines the notion of the sublime sustaining those parts of the poem that deal with Adam and Eve. For, although Johnson emphasizes the Burkean sublime[100] of Milton's "gigantick loftiness" and "power to astonish" (para. 230), the Adamic discourse appears to be closer to Boileau's understanding of the sublime in *Traité du Sublime* (1674), his version of Longinus, which Johnson appropriated in the "Life of Cowley" in arguing for the sublime as "that comprehension and expanse of thought which at once fills the whole mind, and of which the first effect is sudden astonishment, and the second rational admiration."[101] Adam and Eve's sublimity and humanity are thus both part of their "daily life," and, although Johnson does not write in detail of their love (as Voltaire does[102]), he conveys a clear sense that this aspect of their existence is central to the overall effect of the poem: "To Adam and Eve are given, during their innocence, such sentiments as innocence can generate and utter. Their love is pure benevolence and mutual veneration: their repasts are without luxury, and their diligence without toil" (para. 218). Johnson actually quotes extensively from Milton's love and pastoral poetry in the *Rambler* essays.[103] He takes the blank verse of *Paradise Lost* (not the heroic couplets of Pope, Dryden, Waller, or Denham) as the finest embodiment of harmony of which English poetry is capable, and which comes closest to Homer's "force of imagination, which gave him full possession of every object."[104] It is as if Johnson *agreed* with Milton's notion that poetry is "less subtile and fine, but more simple, sensuous, and passionate."[105]

Johnson also seemed in qualified agreement with Milton's tendentious proclamation that "rhyme be no necessary adjunct or true ornament of poem or good verse,"[106] although the qualification came especially in regard to Milton's notion that "in longer works especially" rhyme was unnecessary. Johnson's attitude to Milton's blank verse is as multi-layered as is his treatment of other aspects of *Paradise Lost*: in comparison to the ancient, inflected languages, the music of English (where music, again, is more philosophical than mere sound) is faint and easily lost, and so the pleasures of poetical harmony are enhanced by the structure of the heroic couplet (paras. 274–75). Furthermore, certain complex subjects require the formality of rhyme to be made coherent. But Milton was so successful in blank verse – at least in *Paradise Lost, Paradise Regained,* and even *Samson Agonistes*[107] – that Johnson could not "prevail on [himself] to wish that Milton had been a rhymer, for [he] cannot wish his work to be other than it is" (para. 276). Contrary to the views of a mid-century critic such as Young, whose understanding of originality demanded that rhyme be banished from English poetry in favour of blank verse,[108] Johnson thought that others were less capable of the same level of success as Milton, especially eighteenth-century Miltonic imitators who did not have the same learning, strength of mind, and poetic grasp of the language. For example, Johnson found attractive and original things in the writing of Thomson, Akenside, and Young – and the "general fabrication" of Akenside's lines to be "perhaps superior to any other writer of blank verse"[109] – but he also saw the formal challenges of blank verse to be where many eighteenth-century poets lost themselves, and failed in some important imaginative way.

Milton's very success in writing sublimely in blank verse may be traced in Johnson's many-faceted admiration for *Paradise Lost,* yet also in the tension maintained between Johnson and the character of the poet produced within that poem. Although Johnson reads the poem so as to re-align Adamic language with sublimity – thus keeping the reader in touch with the realm of nature (a powerful and important discourse in the poem itself) – Johnson also understands that Milton's "gigantick loftiness" extends *further* than the human. It embraces the non-human agents as well as the ideal and allegorical aspects of the poem, and therefore Milton's "peculiar power [is] to astonish" (para. 230). All in all, Johnson seems to feel that Milton's incredible subject – justifying the ways of God to man – is impossible and yet absolutely necessary, its mysteriousness appreciated as such by the author of a dictionary, also impossible, yet also necessary. There is thus something for Johnson both wonderful and appalling in the fact that "difficulties vanished at [Milton's] touch" (para. 277). In contrast to his human characters, Milton is always distant, inviolable, and self-sufficient: "the poet whatever be done is always great" (para. 240), and therefore apparently not in need of the "desire of fond endearments, and tender officiousness" and the "want of hourly assistance"[110] that is a touchstone of Johnson's humanist poetics, that he himself values even as he denies it in the Preface to the *Dictionary*: "it may gratify curiosity to inform it that the *English Dictionary* was written with little assistance of the learned, and without any patronage of the great; not in the soft obscurities of retirement, or under the shelter of academic bowers, but amidst inconvenience and distraction, in sickness and in sorrow" (*SJ*, 328).

Such a spectacle of heroic solitariness as Johnson momentarily exemplifies and also imagines for Milton would seem to lend itself to satiric treatment, for Johnson is severely critical of Milton's involvement in regicide (e.g., paras. 73, 127) and ironic about his self-involvement (e.g., paras. 94–99). In the spirit of Old Testament justice, Johnson seems hardly to be able to stop himself from turning Milton's blindness against himself when Milton complains, after the Restoration and after having escaped retribution, of being "with darkness and danger compass'd round:" "This darkness, had his eyes been better employ'd, had undoubtedly deserved compassion" (para. 127). But Johnson pointedly does *not* use Milton's blindness as a means of demeaning the poet, or as an outward sign of providential punishment, although once in the life the possibility is entertained and declined in a striking juxtaposition of ideas: "Nothing can be more just than that rebellion should end in slavery: that he, who had justified the murder of his king... should now sell his services and his flatteries to a tyrant [Cromwell], of whom it was evident that he could do nothing lawful. He had now been blind for some years" (paras. 73–74). Unlike the panegyrics addressed to Cromwell by Waller and Dryden,[111] actions which might be said to imply a certain historical and even moral blindness in the writers in question, Milton's justification of King Charles's murder (in *Defence of the People* [1651]) is deeply unnatural to Johnson, and he could easily have done as Salmasius (and L'Estrange) did, "reproach . . . Milton with losing his eyes in the quarrel" (para. 73).

Instead, Milton's blindness, though separating him from others materially, informs his imagination, which issues in a sublime commonality. The enslavement of Milton's political positions, as Johnson sees them, is contrasted with and then subsumed in the greater freedom and beauty of the poem. Johnson found the opening of Book 3 about Milton's blindness to be among the most *pleasing* sections of the poem (para. 224). Moreover the process of articulation represented by the poetry was not so much an effort of self-expression as a process in which writing transforms the substance of life through reinvention and remembrance. This mnemonic and *translational* power in Milton created a permanent memory for himself, a realization that is reflected in the sustained seriousness with which Johnson deals with all aspects of Milton's life and writing.

When we emphasize the *dialectic* or relationship between Johnson and Milton, the structure of the life manifests itself as a *lieu de mémoire* or space in which Milton's life can be known *after* it is over, as a form of memory. Like real relationships, this one involves both attraction and resistance: running through the many acts of criticism and resistance in Johnson's text is the psychological and mnemonic demand for a bond with Milton in order to mitigate the solitariness revealed in and induced by the sublime imagination. This is Milton's solitariness – as imagined by Johnson's unsentimental portrayal of his domestic life – as well as the reader's, when he is prompted to "desert our master, and seek for companions" (para. 252). Notwithstanding Johnson's reputation as a talker for victory, companionship was of sustaining value to him in society and in his reading. A correlative of companionship in Johnson's intellectual world is conversation, a humane, civilized activity, and, as he says in "Rambler" 89, "the most eligible amusement of a rational being . . . where every man speaks with no other restraint than unwillingness to offend, and hears with no other disposition than desire to be pleased."[112] Yet the metaphor applies to the "Life of Milton" in only a qualified way, for "heroic generosity, or philosophical discoveries, may compel veneration and respect, but love always implies some kind of natural or voluntary equality."[113]

MEMORY, CHARACTER, AND THE LAW OF GRACE

Initially, Samuel Butler's relation to the reader seems to be more "equal" than Milton's. Yet opposites meet in the questioning of the norms of the classical epic represented by the innovations of both *Paradise Lost* and *Hudibras*,[114] and also in the respective author's accessibility to history. Milton's poetic accessibility to Johnson is a form of memory, even though Johnson is ambivalent about the *value* of Milton's engagement with the world. However, few writers in the *Lives* are able to achieve Milton's level of articulation. Although Butler is the "great author of *Hudibras*,"[115] his poetic relation to history is crucially weak in one vital respect, thus disrupting the formation of a poetic memory on the part of the writer, and thus also effecting the tone and the tension of Johnson's biographical narrative. This is reflected in the structure of the life. Unlike the "Life of Milton," where Johnson maintains first a polemical, then a creative tension with the poet's "character," "Butler" has an emptiness at its center, because the character with which Johnson expects to engage cannot be supplied either by Butler's biography or his poetry.

Consequently, Johnson devotes the first nineteen paragraphs of the life to the biography, paragraphs 22–52 to the writing (almost exclusively to *Hudibras*), and mediates the two sections with two brief paragraphs (20–21) constituting an *anti*-character in which we learn that from none of Butler's posthumous works "can his life be traced or his character discovered" (para. 20). To compensate, the text memorializes more overtly than the lives of Cowley, Milton, Dryden, Pope, or Addison. In contrast to Milton, of whom much is known and who attracted many contemporary memoirs, very little is known about Butler.[116] Johnson cites Wood, Prior, Grey, Clarendon, Jacobs, Packe, Thayer, the *Biographia Britannica*, Dryden, Oldham, and Granger as sources for his meager account of Butler's life, and what information there is yields an unsatisfactory story and no clear character. Unlike *Paradise Lost*, which entered the world innocuously, the appearance of the first two parts of *Hudibras* (1662–63, 1664) were immediately popular with the Court and the Royalists, a momentary fame rekindled on the publication of Part III in 1678.[117] Yet the biographical part of the life ends with a reflection on the precariousness of our hold on the man: "In this mist of obscurity passed the life of Butler, a man whose name can only perish with his language" (para. 21).

The confidence that Butler's "name" could be made available to the world through his own language is enforced in the critical part of the life, where Johnson writes at length and enjoyably about *Hudibras*, a substantial, unique, yet hybrid performance. As he does with *Paradise Lost*, Johnson discusses a number of formal, stylistic, and historical topics traditionally associated with the epic, but now taking into consideration

Hudibras's satiric form and purpose. Johnson touches on its literary model, its characters, its events or action, its dialogue, and the structure or organization of the whole. He also discusses Butler's wit, learning, and lived experience, the composition of the poem, the manners or historical life of the poem, its immediate moral impact, its burlesque style, and its diction, numbers, and measure.

Although Johnson regards "the poem of *Hudibras* [as] one of those compositions of which a nation may justly boast" (para. 22), the subtext of his discussion continually presses the question formulated by Earl Miner: "it is essential to our understanding of *Hudibras* that we know the kinds of connection to make between it and Butler's experience."[118] But this is a relationship which seems never to come into focus for Johnson. Instead, his narrative brings the poet's strivings up against an essentially perishable element in the poem, and hence against a temporal barrier itself:

Such is the labour of those who write for immortality. But human works are not easily found without a perishable part . . . Of *Hudibras* the manners, being founded on opinions, are temporary and local, and therefore become every day less intelligible and less striking. (paras. 40–41)

If Milton is aloof from his social milieu, and his sublime character exempts itself from relationship with his reader, then Butler fails to form a character because he is so immersed in the life of the moment, and essentially remains beyond the reader's grasp. Of course, Butler's immediate and multifarious knowledge of the political, rural, and social life of the 1650s and 1660s constitutes much of the richness of *Hudibras*. The poem exemplifies detailed awareness of popular diversions and amusements, of the abundant store of proverbial wisdom, and of traditional balladry – in short, of what has come to be called the carnivalesque aspect of life during the Interregnum and the early Restoration.[119] Zachary Grey's notes to the poem[120] indicate the very wide range of popular amusements, games, and customs to which Butler alludes, and the traditional lore and superstition about animals and astrology, witchcraft and will-o'-the-wisps, and the country foods and culinary details that are incorporated into the poem. Johnson appreciates Butler's knowledge of the life of his time, for "Butler has not suffered life to glide beside him unseen or unobserved. He had watched with great diligence the operations of human nature and traced the effects of opinion, humour, interest, and passion" (para. 39). But what Butler makes of that immersion in the manners of the time is problematic.

For some, like Miner, there is "bafflement" and "degrading messiness";[121] for others, like Blanford Parker, Butler's skepticism and relentless mockery of the claims of rationality, imagination, and the heroic, facilitate the fideistic initiation of the Augustan project of Pope and Swift.[122] Dryden and Addison attempted to save Butler from himself by suggesting that his genius would have been better suited to some form other than the burlesque.[123] Johnson, however, appreciates the liveliness of Butler's verse, noting the "gross familiar[ity]" of the diction, that the "numbers [are] purposely neglected" (para. 50), and that "the measure is quick, spritely, and colloquial, suitable to the vulgarity of the words and the levity of the sentiments" (para. 51), but he is unable to emerge from a reading of the poem with any general conception of politics, society, or human nature.

Such manners as depend upon standing relations and general passions are co-extended with the race of man; but those modifications of life and peculiarities of practice which are the progeny of error and perverseness, or at best of some accidental influence or transient persuasion, must perish with their parents.
(para. 41)

This "failure" raises the question of the historical relation of past to present informing the biographical project of the entire *Lives*. That temporal distance is metonymically associated with the difficulty of making our experience real and present to ourselves, afflicting even poets of genius. The metaphoric form for this particular relationship with the past is *perishing with your parents*.

Even though this raises the prospect of Butler's annihilation – the disintegration of his poetic body, so to speak, because *Hudibras* "like all bodies compounded of heterogeneous parts, contains in it a principle of corruption" (para. 52) – that is not what Johnson's narrative actually provides. This is a point at which the fictive, transformative power of Johnson's narrative – informed by Johnson's knowledge of fighting oneself into the present under the pressure of circumstance – is paramount in the presentation of Butler's character, in generating a memory of, and *for* Butler. This is Butler's memorability, where remembering is a reconstitution of the poetic body (re-member-ing), and a making of an embodied image for Butler not yielded either by the "external" facts of his life or the "internal" ones of his poetry. We cannot forget Butler when we read Johnson's text, but what we actually remember is itself highly inflected – the difficulty of knowing the unmediated Butler as he was in life, and even through the imaginative life of his language.

The continuity between life and writing in this life is effected by the memory's redemptive work. Through the acceptance of the impenetrability of the past by memory in any logical way, Johnson detects the barrier beyond which Butler cannot project himself. He *thereby* transforms that impenetrable law – which prevents the poet from reaching that universal present – into an instrument of grace, whereby (as Geoffrey Hill says) "the dead are made alive / to their posthumous fame."[124] In this process, grace is not explicitly invoked, nor does Johnson appeal to a Christian teleology,[125] for the consequences of action are to be borne here and now, in the commemorative present of Johnson's literary text.

COMMEMORABILITY

Commemorativeness has analogues in other structures of thought, pertaining to the authority of the literary self or character as represented in the *Lives*. One is in the Christian practice of interceding for the dead, of which Johnson's letters and Prayers (and Boswell's *Life*) are full. For example, a moving letter to James Elphinston on the death of his mother in 1750 testifies to Johnson's belief that certain linguistic rituals undertaken by Elphinston would "increase [her] happiness," for "surely there is something pleasing in the belief, that our separation from those whom we love is merely corporeal."[126] And a prayer for his wife, on 26 April 1752, reveals Johnson's belief that the spirits of the dead spoke to the living, and influenced their conduct, like guardian angels or pure superegos.[127] Indeed, commemoration invariably had religious overtones for Johnson: he defined it in the *Dictionary* as "solemnization of the memory of anything," and illustrated it from Jeremy Taylor: "That which is daily offered in the church, is a daily *commemoration* of that one sacrifice offered on the cross."[128] But the *Lives* themselves, notwithstanding their gracefulness (and their being full of grace), are conspicuously free of the doctrinal and formally religious. They are among the first biographies in English to have incorporated not only the form but the sentiment of the classical lives by Plutarch and Diogenes Laertius, and to have stripped themselves of medieval hagiographic overtones.[129] Apart from the statements about devotional experience offered by Johnson on the subject of religious verse, the *Lives* internalize a Christian perspective and offer a historiography rather than an eschatology. In other words, they are fictional rather than apocalyptic, and Johnson's life-writing is thus not providential, even though it registers the revelatory power of a person's work with regard to the quality of his life.

Sometimes the moral quality of a writer's life – as is most clearly the case with Addison, Watts, and Blackmore – *is* what animates the memory for Johnson and here the structure of Johnson's text places the focus accordingly. With Addison, for example, Johnson is aware that "to write and to live are very different,"[130] and that a degree of skepticism is necessary in assessing Addison's moral professions. Johnson's reluctance to place Addison in the highest category of *writers*, nonetheless honors Addison's writing as that which "employed wit on the side of virtue and religion," and made it "generally subservient to the cause of reason and of truth." Johnson thus emphasizes the symbolic, moral effect of the writer's life in the writing: "This is an elevation of literary character, 'above all Greek, above all Roman fame'" (II, 125–26). Yet he resists the sentimental ideology of the likes of Edward Young, for whom the moral quality of Addison's character (and especially his pious death) is exemplary and sufficient to place him in the category of sublime poets.[131]

On his deathbed, Addison apparently called for his step-son, the young Lord Warwick, and, according to Young's account: "Forcibly grasping the youth's hand, he softly said, 'See in what peace a Christian can die.' He spoke with difficulty, and soon expired." – an event that starts a long eulogy from Young: "What an inestimable legacy were those *few dying words* to the youth beloved? What a glorious supplement to his own valuable fragment on the truth of Christianity?" (101). Johnson also has an important place for Addison's death, but, without diminishing Addison's virtue, Johnson's tone is altogether more skeptical: "When he [Addison] found his life near its end he directed the young lord to be called, and when he desired with great tenderness to hear his last injunctions, told him, 'I have sent for you that you may see how a Christian can die.' What effect this awful scene had on the earl I know not; he likewise died himself in a short time" (II, 117).

Paula Backscheider remarks that "the biographer carries in his voice the power to define people and their places in history,"[132] and one difference between Young and Johnson here lies in Johnson's focus on Addison's writing. For Young, Addison's "compositions are but a noble preface; the ground work is his death" (104). For Johnson, "Addison is to pass through futurity protected only by his genius" (*Lives*, II, 126), and Johnson's assessment of Addison's contributions to English literature in the form of the familiar essay, not the melodrama of his death, capture the contours of that "genius," which "seeks no ambitious ornaments, and tries no hazardous innovations. His page is always luminous, but never blazes in unexpected splendour" (II, 149).

Thus, while piety and spirituality are recognized by Johnson as formative of the memory of such writers as Addison, Watts, and Blackmore – maintaining his conviction that "contemplative piety, or the intercourse between God and the human soul, cannot be poetic,"[133] suggesting that, ultimately, poetry is a mere diversion – other dimensions ameliorate Johnson's perspective, and even the "Life of Milton" seldom invokes the ultimate perspective. Lying outside nature, grace cannot be willed, yet its very supra-rationality constitutes its efficacy; because, like the forgiveness and charity of the New Testament (e.g. St. Luke v: 21–24), it breaks the concatenation of the historical process, freeing an individual from linear time and the inexorable logic of action, releasing him into an eternal present. "Whatever is fulfilled," as Geoffrey Hill says of the mysterious charity of Charles Peguy, "is now the law / where law is grace, that grace won by inches, / inched years."[134]

The poet's "fulfillment" – the transformation of his ontological status from emptiness and forgetfulness to fullness and remembrance – is conferred by the recollective engagement of the biographer acting as storyteller. Johnson's configuring the life of the poet, his speaking for one (such as Butler) who is incarcerated in his silence, and acknowledging others (such as Milton) who tell the story of their own lives, is done from within the limits of what Johnson called general nature. The relationship between narrativity, historicality, and law in Johnson's biographical narrative "presupposes," as Hayden White remarks, "the existence of a legal system against which or on behalf of which the typical agents of a narrative account militate."[135] Johnson thus assimilates the authority of the legal system – as we have already seen him do in discussing legal matters – which is located in the historical–quotidian world, and applies it to an experiential and moral system, which is then revealed in specific works of literature. The nexus of these two systems – the historical and the universal, the fictive and the truthful – form a *lieu de mémoire* underwritten by Johnson's fictionalized contact with the poetic characters in the *Lives*. He does this through a process of historical narrativizing, which acquires a powerful metaphysical significance, for Johnson sets up a boundary, a humane law *(nomos)*, which is either activated (as in Milton), or not (as in Butler) by the poet's "genius."

This reading of the structure of the *Lives* suggests that Johnson's normative, skeptical view of the discrepancy between a writer's intentions and achievements is not tragic. Death always has its terrors and always comes as a blow; in a temporal sense, it is always final. But actively locating themselves within the fractured nature of human endeavor and the distance between the writer's past and the reader's present, the structure and narrative of the *Lives* enunciate a triumph *in* time not unlike what we find in Shakespeare's comedy – or the best translations of the period. In this respect the *Lives of the Poets* operates like translation, a quintessentially differential mode of discourse located between past and present, partaking of both and yet identified with neither, and turning on the commemorative action of memory. Like all creative translations, Johnson's texts are also political, in the non-partisan, philosophical sense, because they shift the *locus* of authority from the momentary and the *merely* present to the historical and to what I have described as an eternally embodied present. The redemption of time – otherwise known as grace – keeps our consciousness in the *present world*, while discovering in history and human difference a powerful and flexible commonality. Grace reveals itself in the *Lives* (as it does in *Rasselas*) where different discourses and temporal planes meet; where the impermanent, imperfect aspects of life are translated into the potentially permanent, remembered realm of literature. Johnson's art as a biographer – and as a literary critic – bridges the gap between the two.

CHAPTER 5

Translation and memory in the Lives of the Poets

It is a commonplace that Dryden and Pope are the great translators of the English seventeenth and eighteenth centuries, but in the present chapter I wish to argue that Johnson's *Lives* construes them not incidentally but *fundamentally* as literary and historical translators, that Johnson understands their respective literary characters as reflecting a *translational* relationship with language, texts, and the world, and that the narrative of literary history he constructs in the *Lives* sees their formal translations as constituting their most characteristic work. I am also interested in Johnson's rhetorical complicity in this narrative, and how it contributes to the translational nature of the *Lives* themselves. Partly because of the relational and prefatory structure of the *Lives* – in which Johnson's remarks are always pitched at some invisible other, which is the writing under discussion – there is a qualitative difference between the function of memory in the lives of Dryden and Pope and in Johnson's moral essays, making the *Lives* more than exemplifications of a "theoretical" structure discussed in the first three chapters. Attitudes to language, time and history that Johnson encountered in the two poets are developed in his narrative, asking us, I suggest, to see the *Lives* not only as great biographies, literary histories and historiographies, but as translations in the Renaissance vein.[1]

The lives of Dryden and Pope frame the fifty-two *Lives* in important ways. "Dryden" was one of the first to be written (completed August 1778),[2] and offers the portrait of a great and imaginatively appealing poet who expanded Johnson's concepts of the natural in human and historical experience, and whose development of the English language, in both prose and verse, became one of the touchstones for Johnson's critical reading. Johnson understood Dryden's writing as originary in eighteenth-century English culture, yet as having been conspicuously written out of eighteenth-century accounts of its own historical evolution. "Learning," we are told, by way of explanation, "once made popular is no longer learning: it has the appearance of something which we have bestowed upon ourselves, as the dew appears to rise from the field it refreshes"[3] – and consequently Johnson's greater fondness for the "memory" of Dryden[4] is an attempt to recollect those aspects of Dryden that made him that great original.

One of the methods by which Johnson historicizes the relations between Dryden and subsequent writers is by placing him in dialogue with Pope, who works within a similar medium but whose sensibility and poetic character are very different. The "Life of Pope" was the last of the lives to be written (completed March 1781)[5] and offers a highly nuanced portrait of a poet of consummate artistry, intelligence, and self-consciousness, whose poetic output commanded Johnson's admiration and nationalistic pride, but whose very success was, he felt, purchased at significant cost. The comparison between these two poets is explicit at various points in the two lives – especially in "Pope," culminating in the formal comparison of intellectual qualities between the two poets ("Pope," paras. 303–11)[6] – but also implicit, working throughout the larger structure of the *Lives*. As one moves chronologically from "Pope" – dealing with the great recently dead poet, who had made a lasting impact on Johnson as a youth – on to the lives of the more recent but less accomplished writers – such as Akenside, Shenstone, Gray, and Lyttleton – Johnson's retrospective point of view begins to identify "points de repère,"[7] centers of poetic excellence where the past is recollected and translated as part of a living and changing continuum, which also represent ways of moving forward in the 1780s. Mostly, Johnson finds these "points" in Dryden.

The biographical problem Dryden posed for Johnson was in writing about a great writer whose daily life was unusually inaccessible. By comparison, Pope's life was rich in anecdote and detail, not only because more was known about Pope than most other writers, but also because in the "Life of Pope" Johnson traces the emergence of the professional writer as a cultural phenomenon. Johnson structures both narratives so as to focus on the manifestation of poetic mind and intellectual and moral character in writing,[8] especially translations in Dryden's case. The qualities of Dryden's writing enable Johnson to trace the transformation of the world of society, politics, history, and literature into a permanent presence which he called "nature."[9] The "Life of Pope," by contrast, explores the relations between living and writing in more detail and more theoretically. Johnson is especially interested in Pope's translation of personal and social life into poetry, and how he created the status of an author for himself. Pope's dedication to authorship is established early (para. 12) and influences all that follows, for Pope "considered poetry as the business of his life" (para. 296). Contrary to the rather decisive separation of Pope's life and writing that characterizes Pope scholarship since the 1950s, Johnson is interested in the psychological complexity, the intelligence, and the artifice with which Pope's poetry is made out of his life and, indeed, out of his body.

DRYDEN'S COMPREHENSIVENESS

Translation in the broadest sense is central to what Johnson values about Dryden's writing. The paucity of particular information about Dryden's life is set against an abundance of general experience to be found in his writing. The only two existing anecdotes about Dryden deriving from his life-time – "one told me that at the house which he frequented, called Will's Coffee-house, the appeal upon any literary dispute was made to him, and the other related that his armed chair, which in the winter had a settled and prescriptive place by the fire, was in summer placed by the balcony; and that he called the two places his winter and summer seat" (para. 190)[10] – serve to draw attention to the biographer's diminishing access to the past, but thus also to their eloquent exemplariness. But separation of the domestic man from the great poet is not absolute, as it was in Butler, because the openness of Dryden to his material world is abundantly discovered in the writing, where the many intellectual and moral compromises of his character are redeemed (though not excused) by the writing, which somehow keeps his mind inviolate.

For example, Johnson takes issue with Dryden's critical judgments – the notion that Chaucer's *Knight's Tale* is "of the epic kind, and perhaps not much inferior to the *Ilias*, or the *Aeneis*"[11] – yet these are excused for Johnson by the actualizing power of Dryden's mind, enabling Johnson to argue that, though less learned than Milton or Cowley, "it cannot be said that [Dryden's] genius is ever unprovided of matter . . . every page discovers a mind very widely acquainted both with art and nature, and in full possession of great stores of intellectual wealth" (para 211). The collocation of such ideas leads to one of Johnson's structuring critical tropes about the difference between local manners and general nature: "In Dryden's general precepts, which depend upon the nature of things and the structure of the human mind, he may doubtless be safely recommended to the confidence of the reader" (para. 202). It is "the nature of things" that one feels Johnson to be articulating in his comments on

Dryden's prefaces, in which the "airy, animated, and vigorous" manner of writing, where "Every thing is excused by the play of images and the spriteliness of expression' . . . [and] though all is easy, nothing is feeble," makes for a perpetually fresh experience. If read as a representation of Dryden's prose, Johnson's lengthy passage (paras. 214–15) suggests not only a very personal medium of expression, but also a mode of apprehension evoking a sense of a mind at home in the world and a thought partaking of a quite real, even phenomenal quality – an unusual imaginative embrace of the materiality of reality.

At the same time, the notion of Dryden's writing being "always 'another and the same' " is the perfect trope for its *translational* quality, sensitive to the differential ways in which language and mind engage with the world, as well as to the many ways in which the present and the past are in continual negotiation and exchange in a civilized culture. On one level, Dryden's writing has the effect of a sensuous and compelling pleasure ("Works of imagination excell by their allurement and delight; by their power of attracting and detaining the attention . . . He only is the master who keeps the mind in pleasing captivity; whose pages are perused with eagerness, and in hope of new pleasure are perused again"; para. 312).[12] On another, Dryden writes so unusually well that he leaves behind few traces that might be imitated or even remembered, for "being always equable and always varied, [his style] has no prominent or discriminative characters. If this quality is one aspect of Dryden's peculiar invisibility in literary history – for a "writer who obtains his full purpose loses himself in his own lustre" (para. 196) – it bespeaks the translational quality of his writing, for, as Paul Hammond remarks of Dryden's rendition of the past, "complete self-presence would make signification redundant, and it is only some form of displacement in time and space which makes the work of signs necessary and possible."[13] Yet, as we have already seen in his appropriation of Dryden's version of Horace ODES, III. 29, Johnson celebrates Dryden's refiguring of time, space, and human happiness so as to produce the fiction of presence and historical continuity. But such a reading of Johnson's view of Dryden's poetry requires our recognition that the qualities discovered in Dryden's prose are *taken up* and extended in the poetry (para. 216),[14] and that the structure of the central section of the life (paras. 217–23) identifies the "nature and harmony" (para. 217) of mature Augustan verse *not* with Dryden's major political satires or his elegies and odes (although this latter category receives strong if brief praise, and "Alexander's Feast" is "allowed to stand without a rival" [para. 318]), but with translation: "The affluence and comprehension of our language is very illustriously displayed in our poetic translations of ancient writers... It was reserved for Dryden to fix the limits of poetical liberty, and give us just rules *and examples* of translation" (para. 223).

The narrative structure of the "Life of Dryden," therefore, directly associates the articulation of Dryden's poetic character with a "natural" experience, with his "refinement" of the English language – finding it brick and leaving it marble (para. 356) – and with his poetic translations, in the formal philological as well as the broadest tropological sense. This move toward "nature" can then be traced in three related ways in Johnson's text: (1) by Johnson linking Dryden's turning away from dramatic immorality and political temporizing with spiritual sentiment and even religious conversion (para. 171);[15] (2) by his remarking that Dryden "settled his principles of versification in 1676," when he wrote *Aureng-Zebe* (para. 264),[16] and thereafter describing Dryden's distinctive contribution to English poetry by linking technique, versification, and diction with ideas of nature, national culture, and civilization: "To him we owe the improvement, perhaps the completion of our metre, the refinement of our language, and much of the correctness of our sentiments. By him we were taught 'sapere et fari', to think naturally and express forcibly" (para. 356); and (3) by tracing Dryden's move toward "nature," not so much by precept and explicit argument as by Johnson's *own* "power of performance," an increasingly pleasurable and expansive response to Dryden's writing marking Johnson's *own* prose. The quality of Johnson's writing clearly changes as he moves from the relatively academic comments on *Annus Mirabilis* (paras. 247–63) and *Absalom and Achitophel* (paras. 268–73) to the more comprehensive and pleasurable evocation in the central portrait (paras. 193–233) of the general qualities of all of Dryden's writing, and especially his translations.

Paradoxically, except for brief comments on the poetic qualities of the Juvenal and Virgil translations (paras. 299–302, 303–13), there is virtually no discussion of Dryden's large body of translation in anything other than bibliographical terms (the *Fables* are treated briefly thus in paras. 314–17). Yet Dryden's performance as a great cultural translator seems to be Johnson's subject in many general observations, even critical ones. Hence Dryden's temporality and liking for occasional verse (in which "no height of excellence can be expected from any mind" [para.230]), and his aversion to "an unwearied pursuit of unattainable perfection" (para. 201), both of which seem to describe weaknesses, but turn out to be perfect vehicles for the flexibility, fluidity, and readiness of mind necessary for successful translation. Hence, too, the description of Dryden's genius concluding the life, that he had "a mind very comprehensive by nature, and much enriched with acquired knowledge. His compositions are the effect of a vigorous genius operating upon large materials" (para. 321), and the new and expanded definition of poetic genius, invented to distinguish Dryden from Pope, as an "energy that collects, combines, amplifies, and animates" ("Pope," para. 310) – both of which describe translational qualities of Dryden's writing.

POPE'S ARTIFICE

Artifice is a rich and ambiguous value in Johnson's account of Pope, bespeaking the inextricable involvement of linguistic refinement and personal manipulativeness that he sees as characteristic of Pope. Pope's attempt, for example, to pass off his *Narrative of the Frenzy of John Dennis* as an altruistic defence of Addison's play *Cato*, which Dennis had attacked in his *Remarks on Cato*, leads Johnson into an analysis of Pope's "cant of sensibility" (para. 67). Addison "knew the heart of man from the depths of stratagem to the surface of affectation" ("Addison," para. 11), and was only made more suspicious of Pope's efforts, and because he himself had attempted to obstruct Pope's career ("Addison," para. 109). However, the broader context of the exchange suggests a more historically significant narrative to Johnson, moving beyond the disintegrating relationship of the two antagonists, to include the transference of literary power from one to the other: "Addison and he were now at the head of poetry and criticism; and both in such a state of elevation, that, like the two rivals in the Roman state, one could no longer bear an equal, nor the other a superior" ("Pope," para, 103).[17] Declining Ruffhead's intemperate attack on Addison,[18] Johnson offers a more measured and historically cogent narrative of the transformation of cultural power, the psychological measure of which is to be found in Pope's depiction of himself as the *subject* of power, and confirmed by the success of Pope's *Iliad*: "the voice of the publick was not long divided" between Pope's version and Tickell's (supported by Addison), "and the preference was universally given to Pope's performance" (para. 113).

The artistically developed self which Pope takes as the *locus* of power characterizes his whole œuvre, including the letters. His letters raise a significant general point for Johnson with regard to the ideology of self-construction. By the early eighteenth century in England the familiar letter had evolved – through the efforts of Cowley, Sprat, Temple, Osborne, and William Walsh – into a serious sub-genre, governed by two metaphors locating the letter in a domestic realm of intimate sociability: one likened the language of the familiar letter to the spontaneity of conversation; the other licensed an expressive honesty as the appropriate epistolary style, often in the form of undressing the soul or heart.[19] Pope's letters pirated and published by Curll in 1735, as well as the authorized edition of the correspondence published by Pope in 1737, were governed by these metaphors and revealed documents which "are scribbled with all the carelessness and inattention imaginable," by a writer whose "style, like my soul, appears in its natural undress before my friend."[20]

As we know, however, not only were many of Pope's letters constructed after the event of their first sending – effectively forged from originals for publication[21] – but all were written so as to convey an ideal picture of Pope as sociable, conscientious, benevolent, and virtuous. While Pope's nineteenth-century readers found the artifice of his letters manipulative, a shocking confirmation of the inauthenticity of the satirist,[22] modern Pope scholars have striven to exonerate his duplicity by reference to circumstances (e.g., Pope's need to defend himself against Curll, his desire to record for posterity his friendship with Swift), and by emphasizing the literary nature of personal correspondence.[23]

The idea of Pope's artistry, however, has obscured the question of its representativeness and its relation to the truth Pope claimed for his letters. James Winn perhaps too readily identifies truth with an unmediated sense of self-revelation in Pope's prose, and then too easily dissolves those claims in "the complex artistry with which Pope's acts of counterfeiting were carried out."[24] The theoretical implication of such an argument is that a text can either be self-expressive – the self therein *actually* unmediated – or artful, the self therein being *merely* rhetorical. But it is hard to see how such formalism adequately answers the complexity of Pope's correspondence or Johnson's remarks, which acknowledge – with a skepticism applied equally to *Lycidas* and Gray's Odes – the mythic and contradictory terms in which letters were theorized: "It has been so long said as to be commonly believed that the true characters of men may be found in their letters, and that he who writes to his friend lays his heart open before him. But the truth is that such were the simple friendships of the *Golden Age*, and are now the friendships only of children" (para. 273). Thus the rhetorical formalities of the genre (a "calm and deliberate performance in the cool of leisure") tend to be used not only to hide embarrassments but to shape a desirable image of the self.

These observations are not offered as criticisms, for Johnson's aim is to establish the *continuity* between the familiar letter and other kinds of literature, noting, as he puts it in "Rambler" 152, that "as letters are written on all subjects, in all states of mind, they cannot be properly reduced to settled rules, or described by any single characteristic... nothing is to be refused admission [in composing a letter] which would be proper in any other method of treating the same subject."[25] Yet it is revealing that it is apropos of *Pope's* attempt to communicate a semblance of "true character" – rather than Dryden's, Swift's, Cowley's, or even Milton's – that Johnson has recourse to such psychological language of contrivance. To be sure, the ideal self-portrait projected by Pope's letters – they "exhibit a perpetual and unclouded effulgence of general benevolence and particular fondness (para. 273) – is unfounded (though, as scholars point out, not entirely untrue); yet, in showing how the formal qualities of the letter, and the readers' expectations, can be rhetorically manipulated, Johnson is not necessarily denying, as Keymer argues, "the letter its representational claims."[26] Texts do not represent in only one way; or, as Johnson puts it in "Rambler" 152, "a letter has no peculiarity but its form" yet "should be written with strict conformity to nature... because nothing but conformity to nature can make any composition beautiful or just" (v, 45, 46).

Precisely what weight should be given to "nature" in this formulation is difficult to say, but what is clear from Johnson's analysis of Pope's psychological investment in his correspondence is that his letters need to be read with theoretical awareness in order to determine the status of their representativeness. Johnson's own correspondence reveals that he did not think that epistolary artifice *necessarily* militates against the representation of one's true character. In a famous letter to Mrs. Thrale (27 October 1777) he playfully employs the clichés of the familiar letter to make a point:

In a Man's Letters you know, Madam, his soul lies naked, his letters are only the mirrorur of his breast, whatever passes within him is shown undisguised in its natural process. Nothing is inverted, nothing distorted, you see systems in their elements, you discover actions in their motives... Of this great truth sounded by the knowing to the ignorant, and so echoed by the ignorant to the knowing, what evidence have you now before you. Is not my soul laid open in these veracious pages? do not you see me reduced to my first principles? (*Letters*, III, 89–90)

Johnson's tongue is firmly in his cheek here, and the succinctness of his Minim-like parody of the conventional language of undress reminds us of the conventionality of the form, and how easily its substance can be lost. Yet these formulaic qualities can also be its strength. Johnson could rely on Mrs. Thrale to read his letter not only with knowledge of epistolary conventions, but also with sensitivity to Johnson's style, and a lively memory of their friendship. Read thus, Johnson's irony has the effect not of *hiding* himself from Mrs. Thrale, as he says Pope's letters hide *him* from his correspondent, but of bringing Johnson closer to her. Were Mrs. Thrale to take Johnson's words literally – that is, to fail to *read* their humourous inflection – the opaqueness of the medium would indeed hide the author from her, and the pleasure of communication would cease.[27]

However, the rhetorical success of the letter, which is inseparable from its evident warmth and intimacy, does indeed *represent* something true about its author's character – "These are the letters by which souls are united, and by which Minds naturally in unison move each other as they move themselves. I know, dearest Lady, that in the perusal of this such is the consanguinity of our intellects, you will be touched as I am touched" (III, 90) – even though it is not the consequence of a simple expressiveness, nor is the "character" itself unmediated. "Truth" continues to be a significant concept for Johnson, but it is clearly inseparable from the language and style of the letter itself.

In the case of Pope's letters, however, Johnson feels that the artifice *detracts from* rather than enhances the "nature" capable of being realized. Contrary to Ruffhead's enthusiastic acceptance of the letters at their face value (*Life of Pope*, 470), Johnson is willing to enter into the psychology of Pope's method of composition, recognizing how his skill in adopting personae and participating in the feelings of his correspondent lend themselves to a legitimate fantasy – "There is, indeed, no transaction which offers stronger temptations to fallacy and sophistication than epistolary intercourse" in accordance with the disposition of a friend "whose kindness he desires to gain or keep" (para. 273–74). Simultaneously, however, Johnson feels that this writing gives rise to a discrepancy between persona and an emergent self, on the one hand, and the achieved construct on the other: "While such [benevolent] ideas are formed they are felt, and self-love does not suspect the gleam of virtue to be the meteor of fancy" (para. 275). What I am describing, of course, is integral to Pope's satire, a stylistic cornerstone to the personal timbre, and the moral confidence and assertiveness of the Horatian imitations.

Since 1951, Pope's satirical posture has been explained within the terms of Maynard Mack's essay, "The Muse of Satire."[28] Mack clearly distinguishes between the historical and the rhetorical Pope, the measure of which is the "impersonality" of the fictionalised voices of the poetry – not to be equated with Pope's actual sentiments and intentions – which transform the objects of attention into something fictional. Mack is clearly right in drawing attention to the coherence of such lines as the Sporus portrait, but to describe them as being "historically about Hervey, [but] . . . rhetorically about the enemy" (92) is to propose a division between history and rhetoric that cuts off Pope's passage from the context and effectiveness that would give it substance and leverage. For history functions in the portrait in two ways: as an already-existing realm in which we know Hervey to exist and *against which* we measure Pope's fictional portrait; and as a set of engagements which comes into existence as a *result of* Pope's poetry and its impact on the reader. Both of these senses of history are necessary for the effectiveness of Pope's lines as they attack a morally debilitated individual, and offer moral alternatives – otherwise, as Irvin Ehrenpreis argues, we are left with a "flawless piece of ratiocination," fostering only the fantasy of moral and artistic integrity.[29] It is not that Johnson does not understand Pope's rhetorical use of language, for "When Pope murmurs at the world . . . [he] either wilfully disguises his own character, or, what is more likely, invests himself with temporary qualities, and sallies out in the colours of the present moment" (para. 285), and this is as good a description of the satiric "persona" as one will find. But it is one that maintains a lively connection between the rhetoric and the "personal animus" that fuels Pope's art, that Mack underplays. In maintaining the continuity between history and rhetoric in his criticism, Johnson is asking Pope to be fully responsible for his literary creations, and placing a *greater* moral and political burden on his satire than critics do who would want to save Pope from himself.

Commensurate with these attitudes in the correspondence, Johnson sees all of Pope's writing as harboring a consciousness that dichotomizes the world: "Ask you what Provocation I had? / The strong Antipathy of Good to Bad."[30] Though rhetorically dramatic, such opposition also makes for a signifying discreteness of consciousness. Johnson sees the artifice of self-supremacy in the letters as a narcissistic fantasy of control ("He expected that everything should give way to his ease and humour, as a child whose parents will not hear her cry has an unresisted dominion in the nursery" [para. 259]) that plays itself out on two levels in the full biography. On one level it points to a certain disembodied ineffectiveness in Pope's writing. On another, Johnson recognizes that Pope's energy and power as a writer flourish within this psychological site. Pope's affected contempt for his own poetry (para. 277) and for public opinion (para. 280), the professed disregard for political power, hierarchy, and nobility (para. 279, 281), the hostility to "any excellence that has not some affinity with [his] own" (para. 284), might all be psychologically described as narcissistic, yet, artistically, they are largely effective attempts to create a self-sufficient and heroic self-image. In imbricating these sides of Pope's poetic personality, and identifying the process by which Pope becomes a subject, involving his *own* subjectification to a self-initiated discourse, Johnson implicitly names a discourse of power that is usually assumed to be the later province of Foucault and Althusser.[31]

In *Discipline and Punish*, and other works by Foucault, the process of subjectification takes place in and through the body. To a greater degree than in any of the other lives, Johnson's narrative in "Pope" is energized by the various links between the subject's body and his text. Pope's physique and the realities of his physical existence were of great imaginative and emotional importance to himself, who was relentlessly attacked for these aspects of his existence, and who consciously incorporated them into his creations.[32] Johnson probes Pope's crippled body with seriousness yet great tact, as the material basis for Pope's imagination, and as a metaphor for his poetry.[33] As with Milton's blindness, which Johnson invokes as a physical component of the extraordinary inner light of Milton's poetry – as if in psychological compensation *and occasion* for the outer darkness – so Johnson's references to Pope's body are offered with insight into the connectedness of different sides of our being:

He was then so weak as to stand in perpetual need of female attendance; extremely sensible of cold, so that he wore a kind of fur doublet under a shirt of very coarse warm linen with fine sleaves. When he rose he was invested in boddice made of stiff canvas, being scarce able to hold himself erect till they were laced, and he then put on a flannel waistcoat. One side was contracted. His legs were so slender that he enlarged their bulk with three pair of stockings, which were drawn on and off by the maid; for he was not able to dress himself, and neither went to bed nor rose without help. His weakness made it very difficult for him to be clean. (para. 257)[34]

This passage is part of an extended exploration of the place of Pope's body – its pain, materiality, and defectiveness – in his consciousness, and the incorporation, projection, and introjection of Pope's body in his reading and writing of the world.[35] Johnson's description is perhaps deepened by the understanding that comes from long personal experience of the pain and inconvenience brought on by Tourette's syndrome, described by Boswell and other contemporary biographers.[36] At the same time, Johnson conveys restraint and dignity – arising, partly, from the recognition of the possibility of making crushing satire, yet choosing not do to so in the name of a more comprehensive discourse.[37] For close to the surface of the passage above lies a parody along the lines of the *Rape of the Lock*: Pope "invested" in armour by the domestics before going out to do battle with the world. Yet the eloquent power of the passage arises more from Johnson's knowledge of the near impossibility for the subject to *represent* bodily pain: as Elaine Scarry observes, "pain is not 'of' or 'for' anything – it is itself alone. This objectlessness, the complete absence of referential content, almost prevents it from being rendered in language."[38] Bodily pain, therefore, more often than not makes for pathos rather than tragedy or satire, generating situations in which, as Arnold notes, "suffering finds no vent in action . . . everything [is] to be endured, nothing to be done . . . When they occur in actual life, they are painful, not tragic; the representation of them in poetry is painful also."[39]

Johnson's larger discourse, however, recognises how fundamental the memory of the body is in the individual subject's attempts at imagining and organising experience:[40] as Deutsch remarks, he does seem "determined to reanchor Pope's polished art in the writer's aberrant body."[41] Johnson, that is, attempts to map what one might call Pope's textualizing of his body as a strategy of power, a maneuver which recognizes, as Peter Brooks remarks of the advent of the body into modern historiography, that "signing or marking the body signifies its passage into writing, its becoming a literary body, and generally also a narrative body, in that the inscription of the sign depends on and produces a story."[42] What Johnson does, however, is to offer a contrasting narrative whereby he – so to speak – takes Pope's body out of Pope's private, psychological world and places it within the context of the varied and differentiated world of things and experience. Traces of the bodily impact on Pope's writing are everywhere in the life: "he was of a constitution originally feeble and weak, and as bodies of a tender frame are easily distorted his deformity was probably in part the effect of his application" (para. 255).[43] If Brooks is right (5) in suggesting that one of the projects of eighteenth-century novelistic realism is the recuperation of the human body into consciousness – and recent scholarship on the novel supports this claim – then Johnson's life-writing recognizes a parallel exploration in eighteenth-century poetry, while using the critical realism of the *Lives* to propose a counter historiographical understanding of cultural discourse.

In the "Life of Pope" Johnson develops this alternative narrative in two ways: by placing Pope's body in relation to the give-and-take of the world, including the eventual mortality of the body; and by reading the effects of Pope's body *in his texts*. Pope's death eventually releases his texts into the world as a linguistic sign or memory *of* the absent body, a fictional counterpart to the memory *in* the body that, notwithstanding their eloquence in talking about it, both Johnson and Pope know to evade representation. For Walter Benjamin, death is one of the sources of memory, for "not only a man's knowledge or wisdom, but above all his real life – and this is the stuff stories are made of – first assumes transmissible form at the moment of his death."[44]

LANGUAGE, HISTORY, POETIC CHARACTER

Pope's poetic "refinement" is both ideological and aesthetic, transforming language from a style into a cultural and social discourse,[45] and it is used by Johnson as a tool to open the dynamic of Pope's life. In the critical section of the life (paras. 312–82) Johnson examines one of the central (but dead by 1781)[46] metaphors of Augustan poetry, that of language as the dress of thought. The coincidence of sound and sense, of body and dress, was "a precept which Pope is allowed to have observed beyond any other English poet" (para. 330), and though Johnson was not impressed by "representative metre" as a principle – furnishing little more than "sounds of the words considered singly, and the time in which they are pronounced" (para. 331) – he saw it as touching something essential in Pope's poetry.

The *Rambler* essays (numbers 86, 88, 90, 92, and 94) on Milton's versification provide a context in which Johnson approaches this aspect of Pope's versification. These essays reveal how Johnson relates prosody to the general imaginative effects of verse, moving from the right "accents and pauses" to the combination of "musick with reason," and "from the proper disposition of single sounds" to "that harmony that adds force to reason, and gives grace to sublimity; that shackles attention, and governs passion."[47] Johnson's ideal in this harmonic movement is Homer, for "the sound of many of his verses very justly corresponds with the things expressed," and because "the force of his imagination . . . gave him full possession of every object."[48] Johnson thus imagines a mini literary history in which the movement from Homer to Virgil to Vida and Pope is characterized by an increasing linguistic decorousness, in which the "sound should seem an echo to the sense" (*Essay on Criticism*, line 365) while never quite capturing Homer's distinctive "force of imagination, which gave him full possession of every object" (IV, 125).

In contrast to Pope's "imagery of sound" (IV, 129), Milton's "complete compass of sound" (IV, 114) comes closest to Homer's "harmony," and Johnson cites many Miltonic passages which he felt "performed all that our language would admit" (IV, 115).[49] Though the "greatest master of numbers," Pope's "representative metre" was, for Johnson, a decidedly lesser thing than Milton's harmony (para. 333). Yet Pope himself invited scrutiny of his wit by appropriating Timotheus's music as an example of representative metre:

> Hear how Timotheus' vary'd lays surprize,
> And bid alternate passions fall and rise!
> ...
> ...The pow'r of Music all our hearts allow,
> And what Timotheus was, is Dryden now.
> (*Essay*, lines 374–83)

Pope's equation of Dryden with Timotheus, however, falsifies Dryden's poetry, and draws attention to the contrast between Pope's own "Ode for St. Cecilia's Day" and "Alexander's Feast" which is worth pondering for a moment. Pope's ode was considered by Spence as the best instance of "the method of signifying motions, and actions, and all that vast variety of our passions by *Sounds*,"[50] but Johnson compares it to Dryden's poem in order to highlight the limits of Pope's "melody." Notwithstanding Johnson's reputed tone-deafness, his comments on Milton's prosody suggest that he saw music as a powerful metaphor for, and generator of, universal experience. In his Dedication to Charles Burney's *History of Music* (1776) Johnson also remarks that "the science of musical sounds, though it may have been depreciated, as appealing only to the ear, and affording nothing more than a momentary and fugitive delight, may be with justice considered as the art that unites corporeal with intellectual pleasure, by a species of enjoyment which gratifies sense, without weakening reason" (*P&D*, 29).

In various ways "Alexander's Feast" exemplifies these principles for Johnson. The poem's coherent embrace of the extremes of nihilism and human affirmation is part of the process by which Dryden's poem is equated with, yet also *exceeds*, the music of Timotheus, which manipulates the hero Alexander through a diverse range of emotions. Each of the states of mind engendered in Alexander by Timotheus' music – he is a conqueror, a god, a reveller, a lover, a child, a savage warrior – is dramatized absolutely, yet also with cool distance and control, so that, however depraved or sentimental the action becomes, it remains strangely bereft of pain or compromise for the musician Timotheus and for the reader, though not for the fictional Alexander. His claims to greatness and divinity, for example, are qualified by the folly which Timotheus' music reveals as governing his actions. Dryden adapts the myth (as promulgated by such as Plutarch)[51] that Alexander was the son of Jove; yet he is made to seem faintly ridiculous since he is so absolutely consumed by his passion.

At the same time, however, Timotheus' music breaks down the divisions between the realms of humankind, divinity, and nature in the poem, and brings them into relationship with each other, thereby complicating and deepening the tone of Alexander's existence. Of course, mythic as Alexander is, it is only the ironic music that permits us to take him seriously in this poem, that is, to feel both his power and his weakness to be real.[52] These qualities, I suggest, enable Johnson to describe the poem as exemplifying the "highest flight of fancy" and the "exactest nicety of art" ("Dryden," para. 318), and to formulate one of his most suggestive critical *apercu* when comparing "Alexander's Feast" with Pope's "Ode:"

> Dryden's plan is better chosen; history will always take stronger hold of the attention than fable: the passions excited by Dryden are the pleasures and pains of real life, the scene of Pope is laid in imaginary existence. Pope is read with calm acquiescence, Dryden with turbulent delight; Pope hangs upon the ear, and Dryden finds the passes of the mind. ("Life of Pope," para. 320)

Significantly, the "history" that Dryden exemplifies is not *opposed* to poetry, but is rather the *outcome* thereof. It is because Dryden's poem is written with the "exactest nicety of art" that it is more historical and less fabulous than Pope's. Contextualised within standards established by Dryden's poem, Johnson's comments on Pope's ode (para. 320–27) have little to say about its larger effect, but concentrate rather on technique. In all but one stanza Johnson feels that sound and language work in isolation from experience in Pope. That stanza, the third, is "not unworthy the antagonist of Dryden" (para. 324), but even here the grammar of Johnson's compliment implies Dryden's unassailability. While Johnson finds the stanza to offer "numbers, images, harmony, and vigour" (para. 324), its experience is actually as a passive and reported event in comparison to the dramatic "turbulent delight" of Dryden's poem:

> But when our Country's Cause provokes to Arms,
> How martial Musick every Bosom warms!
> So when the first bold Vessel dar'd the Seas,
> High on the Stern the *Thracian* rais'd his Strain.

> While *Argo* saw her kindred Tress
> Descend from *Pelion* to the Main.
> Transported Demi-Gods stood round,
> And Men grew Heroes at the Sound...
>> ("Ode for Musick on St. Cecila's Day,"
>> lines 36–43)

Pope's idea of men being like gods is a fantasy, and points to a decorous aloofness on the part of the poet from the action of the poem, contrasting with Dryden's exemplification *and* containment of Timotheus' musical power.[53] This makes "Alexander's Feast" a particularly attractive illustration of the comprehensiveness that Johnson identified as characteristic of Dryden's writing, for it is "comprehensiveness" that enables the easy flow between the human, the natural, and the irrational in the poem, and between the present political moment and history, taking these large ideas with just the right combination of seriousness and levity to make their coexistence work.

Of Dryden's last stanza Johnson noted that it "has less emotion than the former; but it is not less elegant in the diction," and continued: "The conclusion is vicious; the musick of Timotheus, which 'raised a mortal to the skies,' had only a metaphorical power; that of Cecilia, which 'drew an angel down,' has a real effect; the crown therefore could not reasonably be divided" ("Life of Dryden," para. 320). Scholars have argued that Cecilia's harmony supersedes Timotheus' music.[54] But such historical discreteness gainsays the values Johnson finds in Dryden's comprehensiveness, which seems to *include* both Timotheus and Cecilia as different coexistent aspects of art and human experience over time. The change of tone in the last stanza – less emotional but equally elegant as the rest of the poem – is beautifully marked by the lengthened and swelling rhythms of Dryden's verse, making for a new harmony:

> Thus, long ago
> 'Ere heaving Bellows learn'd to blow,
> While Organs yet were mute;
> *Timotheus*, to his breathing Flute,
> And sounding Lyre,
> Cou'd swell the Soul to rage, or kindle soft Desire.
> At last the Divine *Cecilia* came,
> Inventress of the Vocal Frame;
> The sweet Enthusiast, from her Sacred Store,
> Enlarg'd the former narrow Bounds,
> And added Length to solemn Sounds,

> With Nature's Mother-Wit, and Arts unknown before.
> Let old *Timotheus* yield the Prize,
>   Or both divide the Crown;
> He rais'd a Mortal to the Skies;
>   She drew an Angel down. (lines 155–70)

Johnson was obviously serious about the lasting benefit of Christianity, symbolized by Cecilia's music, yet he surely did not believe that her music *literally* drew an angel down! He thus enacts a double gesture, just as Dryden does: Timotheus is old and past, Cecilia supersedes him – yet the poem itself counteracts such a literalist reading of history, so "Let . . . both divide the crown." Johnson's point about the "metaphoric power" is that *in the poem* it produces the most "real effect," thus equating Dryden's music – which embodies that of *both* Timotheus and Cecilia – with the experience of the poem.[55]

Johnson's distinction between the "passes of the mind" found by Dryden's "art," and the "ear" at which Pope's artifice ends, places him in a long tradition of Renaissance criticism about poetic style and the relations between *res* and *verba*,[56] but it also permeates his consideration of Pope and his poetry. Johnson's observations on the two St. Cecilia odes suggest a significant difference between the two poets in their personal relation to their imaginative construct, brought to a head in the account of Pope's "intellectual character" (paras. 293–302) and then extended and qualified in the famous comparison between his poetic genius and Dryden's (paras. 303–311). This portrait sees Pope's intellectual skills as animated by a commensurate yet contrasting concept of genius. Pope's good sense ("a prompt and intuitive perception of consonance and propriety") – the "constituent and fundamental principle" of his mind (para. 293) – as well as his strong memory and "incessant and unwearied diligence" (paras. 295–96) are animated by a "mind active, ambitious, and adventurous"(para. 294).

In contrast to Joseph Warton's more modest estimate of Pope as a poet who exemplified judgment but never had genius enough to be sublime,[57] Johnson's criticism reflects a very high degree of admiration for a poet whose coherence, creativity, and sheer productivity place him in the very highest category. There is something exemplary for Johnson in Pope's extraordinary diligence, not only by contrast with Johnson's own dilatoriness, but with the different kind of mind he sees at work in Shakespeare and Dryden, writers who "seldom struggled after supreme excellence" ("Dryden," para. 340).

At the same time, Johnson registers Pope's imagination as being problematically unrealized, only *striving toward* a vision that is never quite embodied. Pope's excellence, thus, raises the prospect of a compulsive and dissatisfied mind that is "always investigating, always aspiring; in its widest searches still longing to go forward, in its highest flights still wishing to be higher; always imagining something greater than it knows, always endeavouring more than it can do" (para. 294). But realizing Pope's linguistic finish needed to be contextualised in terms other than itself in order to be fully comprehended – that is, to be translated into different terms – Johnson invokes Dryden as a standard of *difference*, exemplifying a more comprehensive form of genius by which to measure Pope: "Of genius, that power which constitutes a poet; that quality without which judgement is cold and knowledge is inert; that energy which collects, combines, amplifies, and animates – the superiority must, with some hesitation, be allowed to Dryden" (para. 310).

The subject here is the dialogue between two different forms of recollecting and imagining experience, between a "heroic" and a "natural" mind. Consequently, "Dryden knew more of man in his general nature, and Pope in his local manners. The notions of Dryden were formed by comprehensive speculation, and those of Pope by minute attention" (para. 308). So, if Dryden's poetic genius is one that "collects, combines, amplifies, and animates," and whose operation locates the self (however fictive) firmly in the world of differential material experiences, then Pope's is one that strives to transcend the world, although Johnson's critique also registers his sense that, despite himself, Pope could not wholly leave the world behind. Crucially, however, the consequences of Pope's relentlessness take a toll not only on his writing but on his moral being:

With such faculties and such dispositions he excelled every other writer in *poetical prudence*; he wrote in such a manner as might expose him to few hazards . . . Pope was not content to satisfy; he desired to excel, and therefore always endeavoured to do his best: he did not court the candour, but dared the judgement of his reader, and, expecting no indulgence from others, he shewed none to himself. He examined lines and words with minute and punctilious observation, and retouched every part with indefatigable diligence, till he had left nothing to be forgiven. (paras. 300, 305)

Strangely, desire to excel here *diminishes* the poet's engagement with the world ("expose him to few hazards"), and bespeaks both confidence and aloofness ("he did not court the candour . . ."). Given the Augustinian turn of Johnson's life-writing, the notion that Pope "had left nothing to be forgiven" is a telling observation on the state of his heart – one which, seemingly, excludes redemption because it resists the forgiveness that comes with the free acknowledgment of the need for human contact. Pope himself had envisaged just such a sacrifice as the necessary consequence of writing, when, in a letter to Bolingbroke, he imagines authorship as entailing departure from mother and father, and even as a sacrifice of one's soul.[58] This letter, however, also strikes a pose, in its parody of the marriage service, suggesting that frustrated love may have channeled into the creative force of Pope's writing.[59] Pope may be willing to transcend body and sacrifice soul for immortality, laboring his works "first to gain reputation, and afterwards to keep it" (para. 298), but when Johnson reads Pope's poetry we are reminded that memory is actually deeply rooted not only in the soul but also in the body.

SOME VERSIONS OF THE *ILIAD*

Pope's version of the *Iliad* (1715–20) is integral to Johnson's account of Pope – he considered it as Pope's greatest "performance" (para. 382) and saw the poem as one of the most significant events in English literary history – as well as the larger commemorative and historiographical structure he develops in the *Lives*. Contrary to Ruffhead (451–52) and Warton (257), Johnson thought that Pope's comic appropriation of the Homeric machinery in the *Rape of the Lock* contributed to the originality and success of that poem: not only had Pope given the sylphs their "first poetical existence" (para. 337) but he had endowed them with "powers and passions proportionate to their operation" (para. 335).[60] But the challenge of the imaginary world of Homeric gods were entirely different for one attempting to translate rather than parody Homer, and Johnson's critique of the Homer translation recognises their importance in assessing a poem which "may be said to have tuned the English tongue" (para. 348).

Johnson himself does not have a uniform notion of the Homeric deities, nor should he be unequivocally identified with the enlightened distrust thereof.[61] One identifiable attitude of Johnson's to the Greek gods is to be found in his response to them as embodiments of an autonomous religious system. In a conversation of 1776 Johnson argues the notion that the "ancient philosophers" held their beliefs with good humour on the basis of their lack of religious seriousness. Had they been "serious in their belief, we should not have had their Gods exhibited in the manner we find them represented in the Poets;" their good humour, according to Johnson, derives from their lack of interest in the truth of their beliefs. Thus "Lucian, the Epicurean ... keeps his temper," but the "Stoick grows angry... [because] those only who believed in revelation have been angry at having their faith called in question... they only had something upon which they could rest as matter of fact" (*Life*, III, 10–11). Perhaps bearing in mind the attacks of the *philosophes* on Christianity, Johnson is here not concerned to see Epicureanism and Stoicism as evolving stages of humankind's effort to understand the purpose of life. Rather, the momentous spiritual and historical event – the "matter of fact" – of God's intervention in human history through Christ excludes pre-Christian thinkers from the *kind* of truth now available.

If Johnson is roused into opposition by the thought of the Greek gods as theology, he sometimes simply dismissed them as imaginatively obsolete, "still more so," as he said to Samuel Parr, "in the Grecian tragedies, as in that kind of composition a nearer approach to Nature is intended" (*Life*, IV, 16–17). Because "time has tarnished the splendour" of these images,[62] all now depends on their use and the weight they are expected to bear. Classical mythology may be used decoratively, but because it has no vital relation to "common usages," as Johnson puts it in "Rambler" 168, or to the "prevailing customs and fashionable elegance," it fails to engage the eighteenth-century reader.[63] Nothing important can rest on "mythology" which has not undergone the creative adaptation exemplified by such a poem as the *Rape of the Lock*, because its fictitiousness emphasises the distance between the present and the ancient past, and prevents a fiction from being taken as real experience.

At the same time, Johnson had a complex sense of what the "proper" function of machinery might be in a modern poem. For example, in a brief remark on Waller's "Of His Majesty's Receiving the News of the Duke of Buckingham's Death," he notes that Waller has "used the pagan deities with great propriety," and then he quotes: "'Twas want of such a precedent as this / Made the old heathen frame their gods amiss."[64] Waller's poem commends the patience and fortitude of King Charles on hearing of the death of Buckingham, and confirms Charles' virtues by contrasting them with Achilles' passionate indulgence at the death of Patroclus. Johnson noticed Waller's identification of the respective religious systems with the behavior of the two protagonists – Waller arrives at the half-conceit that Homer's gods are ineffective because they did not have Charles, the epitome of patience, as a subject. Johnson's observation – that Waller's reflection on the *limits* of the gods is to depict them *appropriately* – continues the advocacy for the superiority of Christian values. Yet there is a more interesting thought here, for, by suggesting that Christianity enables Charles to face the problems of life (and eventually his death) more successfully, Johnson argues that the pagan gods *could* fulfill a similar function. Johnson's interest is thus not in the gods *in vacuo*, or as metaphysical entities, but in the *effect* they have on actors in a poem, on *how* characters act as a consequence of their relation to the gods. It is the effect – and, indeed, the effectivelessness – of the sylphs in the *Rape* that attract much of Johnson's notice in his criticism of that poem.

Johnson understood that the deities of the ancients "were considered as realities, so far as to be received by the imagination, whatever sober reason might even then deduce."[65] What was and was not accessible to the imagination in the Ancients had been central in the Battle of the Books, but by the mid-eighteenth century the more controversial phase of the quarrel had passed, and Homer – who had been a symbolic figure in that battle between the 1670s and the publication of Swift's *Tale of a Tub* and Pope's Homer[66] – had been assimilated into literate culture as the Ancient who embodied all the ideals of natural genius, even if he was also regarded as less artful than Virgil.[67] There is evidence, however, to suggest that Johnson's Homer – the "prince of poets," as he called him[68] – was something more than the commonplace repository of classical ideals that was so widespread in the eighteenth century, and that – like Pope, Dacier, Dryden, and Boileau before him – Johnson had a serious inward relationship with Homer's texts, drawing upon them as touchstones of vital poetic formulations for different kinds of experience, much as Arnold saw Johnson's own *Lives* operating as *points de repère* for later generations.

The question in the eighteenth century of what was meant by, and what required to translate, Homer's "naturalness" was highly complex, but it is generally agreed that Pope stands in the tradition of Dryden (drawing on the formative examples of Fanshawe, Denham, Rochester, and Oldham) and Boileau in understanding translation as a creative enterprise that approximates self to other and past to present, in the translator's attempt to recreate the spirit of his original rather than the literal meaning of his language. Scholars have vindicated Pope's version of Homer – from accusations against its inaccuracy, such as Bentley made[69] – by placing it in the European heroic tradition originating in Virgil, providing Pope with a linguistic and historical bridge between ancient Greece and Augustan England.[70] Pope also partly conceived his version as a mediating intervention in the *querelle*,[71] thus accounting for the scholarly apparatus (Preface, life of Homer, notes, mini-dissertations, and indexes) appended to the translation, designed to handle critical questions about Homer and his times, and especially to distinguish that which was deemed to be culturally alien and morally objectionable in Homer (i.e. the ancient manners *of which* he wrote), from that which was felt to be universal and natural in his poetry (and which, correspondingly, made him accessible to Pope and his age).

Johnson saw Pope's style as the best way of translating Homer in the 1720s, just as he accepted Dryden's as being the best manner of translating Horace, Virgil, and other writers in the Restoration. In that Pope surpassed his contemporaries as a poet, to that extent was his translation of Homer superior.[72] Johnson may have preferred the first lines of Tickell's[73] version of the first book of the *Iliad*, but he thought that Pope's complete poem clearly surpassed it and other versions:[74] it was "certainly the noblest version of poetry which the world has ever seen" (para. 93), and Pope's capacities had been fully taxed *and more than fully expressed* in translating the *Iliad*. Clearly, Pope's emphasis on the poetic qualities of Homer's text was the right one for Johnson: "It is to the Strength of this amazing Invention," Pope observed, that "we are to attribute that unequal'd Fire and Rapture, which is so forcible in *Homer*, that no Man of a true Poetical Spirit is Master of himself while he reads him."[75] Modern textual criticism has confirmed what eighteenth-century scholars already knew, that Homer's language is as context-specific as that of any poet – Johnson notes the cultural distance between Homer and Virgil and Pope, by citing the greater "demand for elegance" (para. 349) as one moves from one poet to the next. Yet Johnson's understanding of Homer's imagination (which "gave him full possession of every object"), and what it means to translate a poet whose language is highly inflected ("the sound of many of his verses very justly corresponds with the things expressed"),[76] leads him to emphasize the universal experience of the *Iliad* and to de-emphasize considerations of linguistic difference and of historical obscurity: "Minute inquiries into the force of words are less necessary in translating Homer than other poets, because his positions are general, and his representations natural... To this open display of unadulterated nature it must be ascribed, that Homer has fewer passages of doubtful meaning than any other poet either in the learned or in modern languages" (para. 83).

However, Johnson's stance on Pope's style is double. On the one hand, his version "cultivated our language" and "tuned the English tongue" (para. 348), but thereby lost Homer's "original and characteristic manner... his awful simplicity, his artless grandeur, his unaffected majesty" (para. 349). On the other, Pope's choices are justified by the principle "necessitas quod cogit defendit:" "Pope wrote for his own age and his own nation: he knew that it was necessary to colour the images and point the sentiments of his author; he therefore made him graceful, but lost him some of his sublimity" (paras. 349, 352).[77]

This combination of ideas suggests Johnson's understanding of the creative nature of translation, and how the cultural and poetic authority of Homer is partly found and partly invented in translation. Homer's (or Virgil's) texts may be nominally "original," the occasion *for* translation, but they are *not* originary in any final way, and the event of translation surpasses its origin. Not only does the original or source text (as Derrida, for example, argues)[78] reach forward to be translated, by virtue of the commonality it shares with the human nature of later generations, but the original is itself, at the same time, created *by* the translation. While eighteenth-century translators and scholars are more or less schooled in Greek – Johnson observed that Pope was *less* schooled (para. 83)[79] – in a real sense Homer only exists for them through acts of creative memory. It was Pope's conviction (as it was Dryden's before him) that he appreciated something essential about Homer's poetic mind, and that this enabled him confidently to undertake a translation *without* what many considered as the requisite scholarly and linguistic training.

That Pope employed Parnell and Broome to provide most of the scholarship for the edition, and that he drew heavily on the edition of Barnes, the translation of Dacier, and the scholia of Eustathius, was unproblematic for Johnson – although there must have been some sweet irony in the discrepancy between the apparatus of the Homer translations and the contempt for textual scholarship affected by the Scriblerians. But the notion of an elegant Homer problematizes the translation. All of Johnson's definitions of "elegance" hinge on the notion of social propriety and decorum – "Beauty rather soothing than striking ... the beauty of propriety not of greatness; any thing that pleases by its nicety" – and, while these qualities refer to the intellectual pleasures of a sophisticated modern audience,[80] they also suggest a certain superficiality when compared to Homer. "Such a series of lines so elaborately corrected and so sweetly modulated took possession of the publick *ear*" (para. 348), but, apparently, were unable to find the passes of the mind.[81]

Commentators agree that Pope translated Homer so as to bring out the grandeur and humanity in the poem, yet what were the implications of this decision for his conception of the Homeric gods, heroes, and religious framework? While Pope had a fuller understanding of the Homeric gods than Perrault, La Motte, and Terrasson[82] or Kames and Wood[83] – all of whom adopt an untroubled superiority to Homer's "paganism" – his difficulty in finding a poetic equivalent for the simultaneous human and non-human quality of the gods, for aspects of the poem which were deemed to be both primitive and universal, made his version especially revealing. Translating these aspects of Homer necessitated assimilating the ancient theological scheme to Christian teleology.[84]

One of the places in which this happens is Book 1, lines 188–225 in the Greek (Bk. 1, lines 251–94 in Pope's version and Bk. 1, lines 284–331 in Dryden's), in which Athene intervenes to prevent Achilles from killing Agamemnon after Agamemnon had threatened Achilles' honor by depriving him of his consort, Briseis. Both versions evince their rootedness in English Augustan culture, particularly in their interpretation of the rather literal division in Achilles's breast – "his heart was torn between two courses"[85] – as representing a moral struggle between Reason and Passion. Pope, for example, sees Achilles as: "Now fir'd by Wrath, and now by Reason cool'd" (line 254), and, whereas Homer's Achilles is simply told to "hold your hand" (*The Iliad*, trans. Rieu, 28), Pope's is told by the goddess: "To Reason yield the Empire o'er his Mind" (line 277). In general Pope draws out the religious significance of the intervention by the goddess,[86] and exemplifies a moral consciousness that is not there in Homer.

Homer's logic is less strict. Just as Achilles is simply divided between alternatives (that turn out, in the course of the narrative, to be part of an already-determined action), so Hera (whose emissary is Athene) is simply divided between Achilles and Agamemnon: "It was Here [*sic*], goddess of the White Arms, that sent me down, loving the two of you as she does and fretting for you both" (*The Iliad*, trans. Rieu, 28). There are, however, important distinctions to be made between Dryden's and Pope's versions. While both writers place the action in a context of moral conflict, Pope is more uniform than Dryden, his Achilles has great respect for Athene, and is quick to agree with her explicitly reasonable suggestions (lines 276–77): by obeying the will of the gods Achilles yields to Reason.[87] Dryden, for his part, also says that Achilles' passion has extinguished his reason, and that the goddess has come to check his violence and to calm him (lines 311–12), but, unlike Pope's goddess ("Forbear!..."), Dryden's utters no injunctions, and his Achilles is offered a series of alternatives: (1) if Athene calms his mind then reason may return (lines 311–12); (2) Athene is really only doing the bidding of Juno (line 313); and (3) since Juno loves them both, Achilles is asked to respect her wishes (lines 314–15). Dryden's syntax thus creates a looser relationship between Achilles and Hera, suggesting a sense of indifference in the goddess, and the distance that

Achilles has to move to comply with her request. Pope emphasizes the moral imperative of Achilles' consciousness, whereas Dryden stresses the contractual aspect of the encounter.

These differences are maintained in the respective attitudes towards the material realm. Pope's Athene (Minerva) has a physical presence to accompany her moral gravity, and she acts with graceful authority: "Behind she stood, and by the Golden Hair / Achilles seized" (lines 264–65); but Dryden emphasises the physical force used against Achilles: "Her Hand she fasten'd on his Hair behind; / Then backward by his yellow Curls she drew: / ... Tam'd by superiour Force" (lines 301–02, 304). Dryden's goddess – faintly comic as Achilles is "stupid with Surprize" (line 305) – is very physical and entirely external to Achilles, not intellectually assimilated to him or to the point of view of the poet, suggesting that, if Pope's version sees Achilles and the goddess as manifestations of the same moral substance, the common element in Dryden's is the sheer materiality of the world in which man and goddess find themselves.[88] This experiential difference is supported by the difference in the verse. Pope achieves a graceful dignity by making every word, phrase, and rhythm work towards a single point at which Reason triumphs and the goddess wings her way back to the heavens: "The Goddess swift to High *Olympus* flies, / And joins the sacred Senate of the Skies" (lines 293–94). By contrast, Dryden is less obviously harmonious and his passage is awkward by comparison: "Her message done, she mounts the bless'd Abodes, / And mix'd among the Senate of the Gods" (lines 330–31). This slippage, however, suggests that there is some value *in* the goddess which cannot quite be contained in the verse and its dissonant rhyme (Abodes/Gods). Even though Achilles and Athene are seen as sharing a physical substance, heaven and earth cannot easily be assimilated to each other.

Dryden's responsiveness to the amorality of Achilles and the gods grew out of the experience of writing the heroic plays of the 1670s and the translations of the 1680s. Dryden's idea of the heroic had changed considerably since his translation of Virgil (1697), so that, by the time he started translating the *Iliad* in 1699, he expressed the notion that Homer's "fire," "impetuosity," "vehemence," and "invention" were "more according to [his] genius" than Virgil.[89] Neither does his view of Achilles in 1699 betray the moral scruple of the Preface to *Examen Poeticum* (1693), where Homer's heroes are "ungodly man-killers" given to the "destruction of God's images."[90]

Pope was less comfortable with the amorality of both Homer's men and gods, and with the materiality of Homer's world whose "seeming

Defects will be found upon Examination to proceed wholly from the Nature of the Times he liv'd in."[91] Unlike Dacier, however, Pope does not privilege the manners of Homeric Greece,[92] but seeks to accommodate Homer's "representations" to his own sense of universal nature. He consequently translates so as (1) to allegorize or symbolize the gods, as he does in a passage on the gods of the winds in Book XXIII, lines 235–71, where the "person's of the gods" are equated with Homer's "poetical Dress" (*TE*, VIII, 500); (2) to suggest a moral reserve if not disapprobation, as in the episode of Jove's seduction by Juno in Book XIV;[93] and (3) to refine, finish, and make less substantial the physical details of sacrifices, meals, and the material components of similes.

These characteristics are exemplified in Pope's version of the meeting of the gods concluding Book I (lines 531–611 in the Greek, lines 688–781 in Pope's version, and lines 667–815 in Dryden's), in which Vulcan (Hephaestus) mediates between the arguing Jove (Zeus) and Juno (Hera) in order to bring harmony and good cheer to the gods. This was a crucial passage for determining Homer's concept of the heroic, and a traditionally difficult one for the translator, because it required, as H. A. Mason discusses, having to enter "imaginatively into two states of belief which rarely exist at the same time," recognising the gods both as natural forces and as imaginative playthings.[94] Pope recognised that Homer had made his gods very human in this episode, but because "Commentators have taken a License from thence to draw not only moral Observations, but also satyrical Reflections out of this part of the Poet,"[95] Pope follows a strictly allegorical, Longinian line in translating.[96] In deciding thus, he had the support of Addison, who, in "Spectator" 279 (19 January 1712), observed that "Sentiments which raise Laughter, can very seldom be admitted with any Decency into an Heroic Poem, whose Business it is to excite Passions of a much nobler Nature."[97]

Homer depicts Jove and Juno in human contact with each other, maintaining a sense of personal psychology (Jove's stern reasonableness, Juno's perceptive jealousy), while suggesting the absoluteness of their respective positions and the immutability of Jove's action: "'Madam,' replied the Cloud-compeller, 'you think too much, and I can keep no secrets from you. But there is nothing you can *do*, except to turn my heart even more against you, which will be all the worse for yourself'" (*The Iliad*, trans. Rieu, 38). Homer, however, does not relinquish the human particularities of the encounter to generalize its religious significance. Pope does. Jove is made inscrutable and identified with irrevocable Fate and Providence, and Juno's attempt to influence his behaviour is represented not as unbecoming, or tiresome, or simply dangerous, but as hubristic: "Oh restless Fate of Pride / That strives to learn what Heav'n resolves to Hide; / Vain is the Search..." (lines 726–28). Juno hence becomes coy instead of clever (she "Roll'd the large Orbs of her majestic Eyes," line 713), and forgoes her resistance in order to agree with Jove's version of himself: "Thy boundless Will, for me, remains in Force, / And all thy Counsels take the destin'd Course" (lines 716–17).

Dryden, by contrast, develops the human characteristics of the gods: his conversational tone makes the exchange between Jove and Juno in his version sound like a quarrel between a real man and woman.

> My Houshold Curse, my lawful Plague, the Spy
> Of *Jove's* Designs, his other squinting Eye;
> Why this vain prying, and for what avail?
> *Jove* will be Master still and *Juno* fail.
> (lines 752–55)

This is one of the places Pope thought Dryden had overstepped the mark: in his note Pope says that "Mr. *Dryden* has translated all this with the utmost Severity upon the Ladies, and spirited the whole with satyrical Additions of his own" (*TE*, VII, 121). But it is only in the light of a heroic ideal such as Pope and Addison hold that Dryden's version could be thought to be satiric. Dryden is clearly trying to elicit the comedy of the situation: Jove's manner is humanly flawed – he is tetchy, proud, secretive, and not altogether sure of his dominance in this relationship – and Juno is crafty, and does not allow her jealousy to incapacitate her, but first professes innocence and indifference to Jove's machinations, only to follow these up with a sly dig at his duplicity: "But well thou does, to hide from common Sight / Thy close Intrigues, too bad to bear the Light" (lines 745–46).

These tonal innovations indeed sail close to the wind of burlesque, but at the same time they seem to find in Homer certain truths about political power and human relationships which had been evolving in Dryden's own mind, as partly manifested in the states of extreme passion depicted in the heroic plays and in the translations from Lucretius, Ovid, and Boccaccio. But the smile that comes as one is drawn into his Homeric narrative is not that of superiority, but of the recognition of kinship – something like the "admire but not esteemed" response of Johnson to Falstaff[98] – and the confidence with which Dryden occupies the realm of the human when the subject is divinity.[99]

The last forty lines of the book asked translators to find a workable form for Homer's combination of reverence and irreverence towards the deity.

Pope's difficulty here lay in deciding in what Vulcan's humor lay, and to what extent he could exert Vulcan's presence in the scene. In a note on the passage Pope understood that "Homer's introducing *Vulcan*, proceeded not from a want of Choice, but an insight into Nature. He knew that a Friend of Mirth often diverts or stops Quarrels, especially when he contrives to submit himself to the Laugh, and prevails on the angry to part in good Humour or in a Disposition to Friendship" (*TE*, VII, 123). This, however, was a "Nature" into which Pope was unable to follow Homer: the heroic and the divine could not be sullied with laughter. He therefore adds to the Greek text references to the dignity, grace, or spiritual power of the gods,[100] making Vulcan a rather formal young man who places unity over pleasure: "Thou, Goddess–Mother, with our Sire comply, / Not break the Sacred Union of the Sky" (lines 746–47). He complies with Jove's power with more alacrity than the Greek warrants – "What God so daring in your Aid to move, / Or lift his Hand against the Force of *Jove*?" (lines 758–59) – so that the "unextinguish'd Laughter" sounds a little hollow when it comes.

> *Vulcan* with awkward Grace his Office plies,
> And unextinguish'd Laughter shakes the Skies.
> Thus the blest Gods the Genial Day prolong,
> In Feats Ambrosial, and Celestial Song.
> *Apollo* tun'd the Lyre; the *Muses* round
> With Voice alternate aid the silver Sound.
> (lines 771–76)

By asserting the dignity and formality of the gods, Pope excludes the Homeric link between the gods' love of pleasure and their divinity, a facet that seemed to quicken Dryden's imagination. So in translating this scene Dryden *exaggerates* Vulcan's disability – "hopping here and there (himself a Jest)" (line 769) – making it an extension of Vulcan's self-consciousness, and emphasizing his role of mediator as the "lame architect" (line 812). For Vulcan, in this episode, mirth is more important than inexorable principle ("Not only you provoke him to your Cost, / But Mirth is marr'd, and the good Chear is lost," lines 778–79), and in order to restore "good Humour" (line 783) he plies his own good humored manipulativeness by playing several roles, "To *Jove* obsequious, yet his Mother's Friend" (line 771). In dwelling on Vulcan's lameness Pope thought that "Mr. *Dryden* has treated *Vulcan* a little barbarously. He makes his Character perfectly comical, he is the Jest of the Board, and the Gods are very merry upon the Imperfections of his Figure."[101] But does Vulcan's humour make him "the Jest of the Board?" Significantly, Vulcan (and *not* Jove) controls the action in Dryden's version of this episode: he creates even as he submits to the comedy, and while his exaggerated lameness makes him vulnerable, its effect on the other gods is to release in them one of their most characteristically divine attributes, a laughter and pleasure that *exceed* the object of their attention.

Pope's own physical deformity might have made Dryden's rendition of Vulcan especially sensitive for him. Dryden, for his part, seems to have taken a particular pleasure in translating Homer as he did, perhaps also seeing something of himself not only in Homer ("more suitable to my temper") but in Vulcan when, in the Preface to *Fables*, he described himself as "a cripple in my limbs."[102] As with other poems in *Fables*, Dryden's focus on the laughter in Homer's *First Book* is a response to political power, as manifested in the amoral and dangerous power of Jove.[103] All the darker, primitive and violent powers, typical of the pre-Homeric gods, brought into the otherwise ordered lives of people in the tragedies, are still alive as a memory in the activities of the Homeric gods, and these powers seem present to Dryden's imagination. His laughter is a way of containing – of comprehending – Jove's unlimited power by having Vulcan dramatize the contradiction of Homeric divinity. Dryden's way of handling the gods' paradoxical likeness and unlikeness, is to have Vulcan – who *is* a god – offering himself up as a kind of sacrifice by playing on his humanity. Dryden's Vulcan is so intriguing a figure precisely because he wins his way by yielding to the tide, by participating in the "ritual of supplication," as explained by John Gould, of Greek religion, where the "force of the ritual act lies in the self-abasement, the enacted inferiority of the suppliant and that in turn is charged with symbolic meaning precisely because it is a total reversal of normal, face-to-face dealings between unrelated individuals."[104]

This Vulcan is subservient to Jove, making every concession to his power, yet also superior, by virtue of his capacity to stimulate laughter. Marcel Detienne and Jean-Pierre Vernant have argued that Vulcan's intelligence (*metis*) is structurally linked to his deformed feet, and their mythical associations with the ability to move in more than one direction at once.[105] This is an intelligence whose "suppleness and malleability give it the victory in domains where there are no ready-made rules for success" (*Cunning Intelligence*, 21). Dryden's Vulcan seems to work within this understanding of his attributes.[106] The *literary effect* of Vulcan's ploy, like all good jokes (even ones in bad taste), is to generate a certain intimacy and community across time[107] – here it is an intimacy between reader and writer echoing that between the characters in the narrative, as well as the historical continuity felt and embodied by Dryden as he contemplates the great distance between himself and Homer. This benign though by no means simple notion of community is informed by Dryden's skeptical, yet humane experience which has its roots in two different cultural discourses: the religious perception of power in Homer; and the experience of Christian grace which enables the poet to offer *himself* as a mediator between past and present, and which is – in the secularized mode of translation – a form of redeeming the time. If Pope's version of the conclusion of *Iliad* Book 1 envisages a moral unity that coincided with the ideal intellectual aspirations of his age, such as he replicated in the *Essay on Man*, then Dryden aims to capture a more intimate, more humanly recognizable strata of the harmony between humankind, nature, and divinity.

> They drank, they laugh'd, they lov'd, and then 'twas Night.
> Nor wanted tuneful Harp, nor Vocal Quire;
> The Muses sung; *Apollo* touch'd the Lyre.
> Drunken at last, and drowsy they depart,
> Each to his House; Adorn'd with labour'd Art
> Of the lame Architect: (lines 807–12)

This excursus into the Homer translations enables a fuller understanding of what Johnson meant when he identified Dryden as "always 'another and the same,'" and describes him as a writer who "does not exhibit a second time the same elegances in the same form, nor appears to have any art other than that of expressing with clearness what he thinks with vigour" ("Life of Dryden," para. 215). He might also have had in mind the easy movement in Dryden's *Ilias* from anger to laughter to love and harmony, when he ended the life with what looks like a reservation, but is really an appreciative observation about Dryden's comprehensive mind: "With the simple and elemental passions, as they spring separate in the mind, he seems not much acquainted, and seldom describes them but as they are complicated by the various relations of society and confused in the tumults and agitations of life ... He hardly conceived [of love] but in its turbulent effervescence with some other desires; when it was inflamed by rivalry or obstructed by difficulties; when it invigorated ambition or exasperated revenge" (paras. 322, 324).

It is impossible to determine *in detail* what Johnson approved and disapproved of in the two versions of Homer, but it is clear that his views advance on several overlapping fronts. He regarded Pope's version as a greater *overall* achievement than any other comparable work in English, more impressive, far more influential than Dryden's fragment, of which Johnson said that, "considering into what hands Homer was to fall, the reader cannot but rejoice" that Dryden did not fulfill his intention to translate the whole *Iliad* ("Dryden," para. 151). Yet, notwithstanding the imaginative integrity of Pope's version and its appropriateness for its time, he lost some of Homer's "awful simplicity, artless grandeur and unaffected majesty." Many have remarked how much Pope's Achilles resembles Virgil's and Dryden's Aeneis, and Johnson noted that the "chief help of Pope . . . was drawn from the versions of Dryden" (para. 348).[108] The difference between Homer's "elevation and comprehension of thought" and Virgil's "grace and splendour of diction" ("Dryden," para. 304), Johnson sees as being parallel to that between Homer's Greek and Pope's English, and Homer's Greek and the Latin cribs used by Pope to supplement his knowledge of the Greek. But Pope's use of Latin cribs is excused because "among the readers of Homer the number is very small of those who find much in the Greek more than in the Latin, except the musick of the numbers" ("Pope," para. 84). Yet the "harmony" of Homer's verse resonated loudly for the eighteenth century, suggesting everything desirable in Homer that seemed to be unreachable by the later age, but which poets like Pope encoded under the rubric of "nature." Pope praised Dacier's version by saying that it had "lost little [of Homer] besides the Numbers."[109] Knightly Chetwood saw the supremacy of Greek spreading throughout the language: "Latin is but a corrupt dialect of Greek; and the French, Spanish, and Italian, a corruption of the Latine" – but presumably English, or Dryden's English (since Chetwood's words come in his Preface to Dryden's version of Virgil's *Eclogues*), compensates for these disadvantages, enabling Homer and Virgil to enter "our English palace" without "stooping."[110]

Johnson, of course, understood the "harmony" of Homer's verse to extend much further than sound or melody. Homer's musical harmony, like Dryden's comprehensiveness, is a site for Johnson's conception of literary and cultural memory. But his critique of Pope's *Iliad* draws attention to the other meaning attached by Pope to Homer's language, that everything found by Pope to be philosophically and culturally *alien* in Homer he accounted for by the difference of the Greek language. In a note on sacrifices in Book XXI Pope wrote: "It is impossible to render such Passages with any tolerable Beauty. These Ideas can never be made to shine in *English*, some Particularities cannot be preserv'd; but the *Greek* Language gives them lustre, the Words are noble and musical . . ." (*TE*, VIII, 437–38). For all his ingenuity and genius, *this* range of experience in the Greek language represented for Pope a historical distance which poetry could not bridge, but it is precisely such a cultural distance that Johnson's lives of Pope and Dryden measure, and, in their *own* act of translation and memory, fill the temporal and historical aporia that the eighteenth century felt toward the great original.

BIOGRAPHICAL CHARACTER, AUTHORSHIP, AND NOVELISM

The Homeric translations – and the very mode of translation – are central to the lives of Dryden and of Pope. Within eighteenth-century terms, translation was writing that refined the language and shaped the English nation: as Dryden says of his Virgil, echoing Milton on *Paradise Lost*, "what I have done ... will be judged in after ages, and possibly in the present, to be no dishonour to my country, whose language and poetry would be more esteemed abroad, if they were better understood."[111] Translation is also writing that actively shapes the respective minds of Dryden and Pope, and the intellectual qualities detected by Johnson as fundamental to their poetic characters ("Pope," paras. 303–11), most aptly describe their translations (though not exclusively so).

As with Dryden's translation of classical, French, and Italian poets from the 1680s onwards, Pope's encounter with Homer uniquely enabled Pope to become more fully himself as a poet, ready for the Horatian Imitations and Moral Essays, on which his modern reputation rests. In the process, the Homer translations made a significant cultural statement which, to paraphrase Eliot, changed not only the subsequent development of English poetry but also its history,[112] how its origins were imagined to *arise* in Homer and Virgil. Johnson's discussion of Pope suggests that Homer was an appropriate object for "a mind active, ambitious, and adventurous, always investigating, always aspiring" (para. 294). Yet, looked at from the point of view of Pope's whole life of writing, these are overdetermined qualities, describing a never quite realized longing ("still longing ... still wishing ... always imagining ... always endeavouring"), which is also the historical distance between Pope and Homer. Although commonplace in its terminology, Johnson's dialogical conception of Dryden and Pope – "Dryden knew more of man in his general nature, and Pope in his local manners" (para. 308)[113] – speaks to the limits of the "poetical prudence" which Johnson saw as identifying Pope's writing.

"Poetical prudence" is an ambiguous quality for Johnson, for, while it might "expose [Pope] to few hazards" (para. 300), enabling him to exercise an extraordinary degree of control over his manuscripts and published texts,[114] it also suggested a besieged presence in the language that bespoke Pope's relation to the world: "Pope was not content to satisfy ... he did not court the candour, but dared the judgement of his reader, and, expecting no indulgence from others, he shewed none to himself ... He examined lines and words with minute and punctilious observation, and retouched every part with indefatigable diligence, till he had left nothing to be forgiven" (para. 305). The self under construction here is a modern, punitive, disciplined one that is part of the discourse of alienated self-consciousness that John Sitter has identified in the sublimation of history in the poetry of mid-eighteenth-century England and that is the subject of Foucault's archaeologies of the eighteenth century.[115] For Johnson, Pope's intense individuality was not only a sign of his deformed body, and his deformed body a sign of his alienated social existence, but a disruption of the relation between writer and text in the process of literary history.

One needs to emphasize the textual and characterological *mise en abyme* to which Johnson points in recognizing the essential inaccessibility of the self in the artifice that is Pope's couplets. Having taken it upon himself to speak for the best in his world, Pope discovers that the only way he can do so is to cut himself off *from* that world. In presenting powerful images of the death of a civilization, Pope satisfies a civilized need. For the individual, this symbolic movement is represented as the death of the body; yet Pope found this experience most problematic, so that the compensating disembodied refinement never manages to establish the kind of relation between character and world that Johnson's narrative structure proposes as the basis for historical and personal memory.

It is, of course, not only Pope who had a punitive and disciplined attitude toward his own individuality: Johnson himself was known in his own day, and later became notorious, for the severity and the categorical decisiveness with which he controlled his own emotional, psychological, and physical being.[116] He invested enormous energy in constructing a kind of imaginary panopticon within which to organize himself, and in some ways his handling of his own subjectivity – as well as its depiction by his contemporary biographers – exemplifies Foucault's idea in *Discipline and Punish* (1979) that in modernity the individual participates in the construction of the self through the (self-)imposition of institutionally and socially mandated disciplinary and categorical forms. However, Johnson's conception of biographical character allows for greater degrees of freedom and flexibility. Although he values exemplariness, there is nothing – after the *Life of Savage* (1744) and a few biographical sketches in the *Rambler* – overtly didactic in his depiction of the writers in the *Lives of the Poets*.[117] Not even Watts, Rochester, Addison, Gay, or Swift – whose lives would have invited didacticism from one so inclined – are pressed into the service of a moral agenda, though, of course, Johnson has no hesitation in judging particular actions of individual writers.

The prudential value of biographical character, as I argued earlier, is primarily measured not in moral terms, but within a commemorative context constructed through the relationship between will, time, and work. As I hope has become clear in the course of this book, in literary terms prudence asks how completely, and in what manner, a writer transforms his personality into the character of the author he seeks to be and, perhaps, becomes. Experientially and formally, then, character is anchored in human nature and time.

It is on these formal grounds, rather than in some more philosophical or generic way, that Johnson's biographical characters differ from those typically found in eighteenth-century novels. Certainly, the characters of Johnson's poets do not aim to exemplify individual subjectivity characteristic of, say, Clarissa or Tristram Shandy or Fanny Price – what Ralph Rader calls "the focal illusion of characters acting autonomously as if in the world of real experience."[118] The novel, in the course of the eighteenth century, in John Richetti's words, "attempt[ed] to project a new sort of particularized presence,"[119] yet, as projections of their own writing, and of Johnson's imaginative engagement *with* that writing, the authors of the *Lives* embody (or are made by Johnson to embody) the particularized presence that *is* their character. Hayden White's argument, therefore, that "viewed simply as verbal artifacts histories and novels are indistinguishable from one another," is true of Johnson's *Lives*.[120] His characters partake of the same legal status as individuals do in novels, where the law, as represented by narrative authority, fixes the individual into a social context and establishes the expectation (whether realized or not) of happiness for the subject.[121]

Additionally, Johnson's characters are brought into historical focus in ways that are consistent with eighteenth-century fictional methods that blurred the boundary between history, (auto)biography, and novel. Since both novel and history laid claim to the verifiable in eighteenth-century aesthetics, history was placed under pressure because, as Everett Zimmerman remarks of the novel's claim to historicity, "the traces on which history founds itself are often only with difficulty characterizable in terms different from those that the novel putatively assumes."[122] Johnson expressed skeptical wariness at the truth-claims of what passed for history;

he still demonstrated the truth-like impact made on *him* as a reader by not only the dramatized characters of Shakespeare and the allegorical figures of Cervantes, Bunyan, and Milton, but also the "realistic" creations of the eighteenth-century novel. His ambivalence about the power of fiction arises not because he is a prude or afraid of the imagination per se, but because he feels the illusory and ideological force of what came to be known as "realism."

When Johnson thus notes of "familiar histories" that "the power of example is so great, as to take possession of the memory by a kind of violence, and produce effects almost without the intervention of the will," he is responding to the ideological dimension of novelistic realism which both mirrors and shapes the bourgeois social and domestic world to which he himself belonged.[123] Just as verisimilitude and historicity remain separate, tropologically, in the early novelists,[124] so Johnson's characters deliberately resist the attractions of realism, and forgo the psychological inwardness associated with the developing novel. This is so not only for the characters of the *Lives*, but also in Johnson's most humane renditions in the *Rambler*. "Ramblers" 170 and 171, for example, tell the story of Misella, given up by her parents, and then enslaved, seduced, and abandoned by her guardian to prostitution and degradation. While describing the inexorability of the destruction of a young person's innocence and her complete rejection by society, these essays also identify and criticize the functions of the social and legal systems within which male power (of which the family for Johnson is here an instrument) operates with impunity and a woman's character is systematically turned against herself. Felicity Nussbaum's argument that "Women's subjectivity [in the eighteenth century] is not a given that precedes entrance into the social formation or can be defined outside of it,"[125] is true of Johnson's understanding of women's experience in these *Ramblers* and other works.

Johnson's tale of Misella is therefore emotionally and politically powerful, anticipating Wollstonecraft's depiction of marriage and the legal system in *Maria: The Wrongs of Women*.[126] Although not a novel, Johnson's essays nonetheless sustain psychological identification with Misella and give a convincing sense of her subjective experience.[127] Significantly, while Misella speaks in her own person, the narrative voice maintains a scrupulous exteriority, unlike the narrative voice of a novel by Richardson, Haywood, Lennox, or Burney, which submerges the narrator within the character. One might see this reluctance to enter the woman's experience as a lack of imagination, or as Johnson simply "defining" woman as the absence of male qualities, as Nussbaum argues he does in the *Dictionary* (149–50). But his depiction of suffering belies this reading, suggesting instead that Johnson's narrative pitch marks a refusal to *reinscribe* Misella's subjectivity, to simply make her situation an extension of his own narrative.[128] One characteristic of Johnson's construction of character in these "Rambler" essays is his unwillingness to claim a knowledge that he does not possess, however much he might imagine it, and a resistance to the liberal-minded approach that sees the personal experience of others as just so many perspectives on social reality. One might even argue that the substantive *absence* of Misella's voice in these essays itself represents a truth about women in eighteenth-century society, and about the fictional narratives in which they habitually found themselves – and in this Johnson is far more radical than most of the men *and women* novelists of the century. Johnson is thus not tempted to indulge in what Clifford Siskin calls "novelism," "the habitual subordination of writing to the novel" that accompanies the domestication of language and the development of disciplinary and professional categories in Britain in the course of the eighteenth century.[129]

Finally, though played down psychologically, Misella's character does have agency – albeit overpowered by the patriarchal system in which she finds herself – but it is one that is manifested in the public sphere. Such agency characterizes the literary characters in the *Lives of the Poets*, a work which, though instrumental in the formation of the canon and the institution of literature, continually resists disciplinarity, and keeps open the possibility of the historicity and the critical function of writing.

CHAPTER 6

Historiographical implications

Geoffrey Hartman begins an essay on literary history by declaring that "no one has yet written a history from the point of view of the poets – from within their consciousness of the historical vocation of art."[1] It has been my contention in this book that this is exactly what Johnson has done in the *Lives of the Poets*. Not, of course, that he has written with a romantic inwardness or ideology – which are Hartman's subjects – but that, in writing about the ways poets have embodied their memories, Johnson has produced a literary history whose narrative is directly responsive to their "consciousness." But because literary history is an open and malleable genre, and because it has usually been thought that the *Lives of the Poets* participates in a nationalistic enterprise of canon-formation, privileging the classical–humanist Augustan mode at the expense of other kinds of poetic language and vision, my conclusions themselves raise further questions that I wish briefly to consider here.

It is necessary to remind ourselves that the specifically historical consideration of texts – the textual criticism of the Renaissance[2] – was intended to recover lost texts from a distant past, and to make them available to the present in scholarly acts of reconstruction. This tradition was alive in eighteenth-century England in the work of Birch, Oldys, Warburton, Bentley, Barnes, Porson, and others, including the Wartons and Johnson himself, whose Shakespeare work, for example, stands in the Renaissance tradition of textual emendation, informed by the humanist recognition that "it is vain to carry wishes beyond the condition of human things; that which must happen to all, has happened to Shakespeare, by accident and time" (*Shakespeare*, I, 112).

The eighteenth century also saw a proliferation of more fully developed historical considerations of literary tradition. Thomas Warton's *The History of English Poetry* (1764) and *Observations on Spenser* (1754; rev. 1762), and Joseph Warton's *Essay on the Genius and Writings of Alexander Pope* (1756; 1782), were the first systematic attempts at describing and ordering the

Historiographical implications

different traditions of English poetry; but, although Johnson admired and praised their work, his own ran in different channels. By the 1770s, the experience of "general nature" that he found so powerfully embodied in Shakespeare's drama had been fully assimilated into his own thinking about literature. Concomitantly, as life-writing in the course of the eighteenth century began to extend its classical and antiquarian affinities to become a more critical and self-conscious form, Johnson's literary history became more comparative in method and more conversational in tone. Rather than remaining purely recuperative, I have argued that the *Lives* engaged in a comparative discussion whose object, in Jerome McGann's words, is not the recovery of a lost original text or meaning, but "the multiple possibilities for situating what might be understood as the *loci* of presentness and pastness."[3] In bringing together the recuperative and the comparative in the *Lives*, Johnson actually anticipates one of R. S. Crane's principles of all good literary history, discussed at length in his still seminal "Principles of Literary History"; namely, a synthesis of the "philological and dialectical."[4]

Simply summarized, the *Lives* develop a critical interest in memory as a fictive paradigm by which the relationship between life and literature can be understood. Works of "nature" occupy a permanent present through their relationship with history and language; however, works of "manners" (even such acknowledged great works as Butler's *Hudibras* and Pope's *Imitations of Horace*) are felt to have slipped from public consciousness and so have to be recollected. The recuperative and commemorative principles of Johnson's writing inform the comparative, making it possible for him to address the qualities of specific works while also constructing a narrative that compares individual texts with others of a different kind and of a different historical moment. Animating such comparisons is the apprehension of the revelatory relationship of literature to the lives, abilities, and material circumstances of writers, making a triangular structure between writer, text, and writing. This nexus points to Johnson's interest not only in literary character, but also to that in authorship as an evolving social institution in legal history.[5] Yet, as I have argued throughout, the aporetic site of the "present" is what nurtures Johnson's historiographical understanding of time and human effort; and his distinctive way of bringing the dialectical and the philological to bear upon each other makes the *Lives* more reminiscent of a Foucaultian archaeology than a positivistic historiography.

But, if David Perkins is correct that "literary history cannot depict the past as it actually was, [and] objective representation cannot possibly be its function,"[6] whence comes the truth-value of Johnson's writing as literary history? and by what rhetorical and narrative strategies does it continue to command authority? My concluding, general answer to these questions is that the historical mode of the *Lives* is unique in literary history in performing the work of *translation*, by developing two kinds of intersecting narrative discourse, one pertaining to traditional literary history, and one to the hermeneutics of historiography that points to the status of the *Lives* as *lieu de mémoire*. The conversation between and synthesis of these discourses underlie Johnson's distinctive sense of personal and literary memory that I have been discussing in this book.

THE *LIVES* AND LITERARY HISTORY

Johnson presents Pope's refinement as a necessary and intelligent response to modern conditions and to the state of the English language, but thereby raises the question of the advancement and decline of literature – a problem that preoccupied the eighteenth century[7] – and the specific gains and losses in the English literary tradition discussed in the *Lives*. Johnson is not given to bemoaning the state of literature, and there is no systematic narrative of decline governing his literary history, such as one finds in Goldsmith's *Enquiry into the Present State of Polite Learning in Europe* (1759) or Hume's "Of the Rise and Progress of the Arts and Sciences" (1742). But neither does the trajectory of the *Lives* trace an inexorable "improvement" that Johnson's admiration for Pope's versification is easily assumed to imply. Certainly, as Johnson says in his Dedication to Percy's *Reliques of Ancient Poetry* (1765), "It is prompted by natural curiosity to survey the progress of life and manners, and to inquire by what gradations barbarity was civilized, grossness refined, and ignorance instructed";[8] but this anthropological orientation – shared by the likes of Lord Kames[9] – toward the greater sophistication of one's own cultural forms as compared to the Middle Ages, is complicated in the biographical and critical engagements of the *Lives*.

Clearly, "refinement" and "elegance" – key terms describing modern literature – do not have fixed and unequivocal meanings in Johnson's critical lexicon, and the rise of Augustan teleology is repeatedly disrupted by other, sometimes overlapping priorities. The refinement of Pope's Homer is nicely balanced between cultural necessity, personal revelation, and historical obscurity. Not only is the vitality of the translation closely linked to the social values and forms of Pope's age, thus proposing an always existing gap between Pope and Homer, but the logic of "refinement" has repercussions for Johnson's understanding of poetry *after* Pope, for "to attempt any further improvement of versification will be dangerous" (*Lives*, III, 251). Such refinement is dangerous (and not just aesthetically unpleasing), presumably, because it institutionalizes the division between "general converse" (as Johnson puts it in "Rambler" 168 [v, 129]) and attitudes implied by Pope's poetic language. Standing in a position similar to Wordsworth in 1798, conscious of present needs in relation to past achievements, Johnson looked back in 1781 on his completed project, and saw Dryden's comprehensiveness – and not Pope's wit – as founding the "improvement, perhaps the completion of our metre, the refinement of our language, and much of the correctness of our sentiments," and as teaching us, "'sapere et fari,' to think naturally and express forcibly" (*Lives*, I, 469). Pope's project, finished and brilliant as it was, seemed to foreclose an active afterlife for his works. As a young man, Johnson was no doubt proud to have had his poetic capabilities – in the form of a Latin translation of Pope's *Messiah* (1728) and authorship of *London* (1738) – acknowledged by Pope;[10] but the difference in idiom of the *Vanity of Human Wishes* from Pope's major satires may have been due not only to personal temperament, but to Johnson's recognition as early as the 1740s of the impossibility of working successfully in Pope's vein.

While the mid-century poets were reinventing Milton as an alternate source of inspiration to Pope and Dryden, the Wartons, Young, Gray, and others saw the possibilities of poetry in terms of an opposition between Milton and Pope, borne out, indeed, in the eventual alienation of Pope and the triumph of Milton in the Romantic imagination.[11] The *Lives*, however, do not offer one meta-narrative describing the rise or fall or rise-and-fall of wit, but a series of counteracting narratives placing the discourse of origins against that of advancement. But by the time of Pope's *The First Epistle of the Second Book,* Cowley's "language of the Heart" (line 78) could no longer be heard, and though Gray has a prominent place for Dryden in his *Progress of Poesy*, who "Wide o'er the fields of glory, bear / Two coursers of ethereal race, / With necks in thunder clothed, and long-resounding pace" (lines 104–06), neither Gray nor any of his contemporaries could make much of Dryden's achievement.[12]

This recognition is marked not least by Johnson's rueful tone in the lives of Gray, West, Collins, Akenside, Thomson, and Young, all variously describing a narrative of symbolic flight and abacination, characteristic of the enraptured aviator in *Rasselas*, standing on the edge of a cliff, projecting fantastically sublime passions, only to find himself fated to repeatedly fall. Sentimental literary histories by the Wartons, Gray, Hurd, Blair, Duff, and Smith identified literary genius with primitivism, appropriated the authority formerly associated by the Augustans with the Ancients, and argued that: "The customs, institutions, traditions, and religion, of the middle ages, were favourable to poetry... Ignorance and superstition, so opposite to the real interests of human society, are the parents of imagination."[13] Johnson admired the first volume of Joseph Warton's *Essay on Pope* (1756) and Thomas Warton's *Observations on Spenser's Faery Queen* (1754; rev. 1762), remarking of the latter that "You have shown to all who shall hereafter attempt the study of our ancient authours the way to success,"[14] yet he had little patience with the widespread attempt to naturalize a fashionable primitivism. Gray's odes do not work as poems for Johnson, who found them to be vitiated by a false sublimity – "He has a kind of strutting dignity, and is tall by walking on tiptoe" (*Lives*, III, 460) – and fleeing from both history and the present toward a forged future or a sentimentalized past.

Johnson attacks *The Bard* – and the culture-wide mythologization of the primitive image of "the bard" – for a parochial politics of nation-building and cultural identity-making.[15] His resistance to the sacralization of national boundaries in his critiques of Gray and Macpherson point not only to his greater historiographical sophistication and cosmopolitanism, but also to the translational nature of his literary history. Johnson understood the project of nation-building and historiographical forgery engaged in by Macpherson and the Scottish literati, since he is perhaps the first to *name* the Ossianic discourse *as* forgery. His demand for material evidence for Ossian's authenticity – "Why is not the original deposited in some public library, instead of exhibiting attestations of its existence?"[16] – together with his recognition of the textuality of Macpherson's project – "I believe they [the Ossianic poems] never existed in any other form than that which we have seen" (*Journey*, 118) – effectively name not only the invented, but also the forged nature of the national–historical realm under construction. However, what troubles him is not its textuality, but the *kind* of authority claimed by the Ossianic texts.

While Johnson wanted to perpetuate the Gaelic language,[17] like Macpherson he understood its orality as militating against continuity and institutional status. He recognized the historical value, and the contribution made to national identity, of stories of clan warfare, economic hardship, and recent emigration, because "narrations like this, however uncertain... are the only records of a nation that has no historians, and afford the most genuine representation of the life and character of the ancient Highlander" (*Journey*, 50). At the same time, the lack of documented knowledge of ancient Highland cultures piqued Johnson's skepticism of Ossian: "If we know little of the ancient Highlanders, let us not fill the vacuity with Ossian" (*Journey*, 119). Out of that vacuity – a space contested by the Ossianic and Johnsonian texts – Johnson develops an emotionally engaged, commemorative account of Highland life that is more "representational" than Macpherson's pastoral fantasies, *and* that was verified by Boswell and the Highlanders they met on their travels: "There was perhaps never any change of national manners so quick, so great, and so general, as that which has operated in the Highlands, by the last conquest, and the subsequent laws... Of what they [the clans] had before the late conquest of their country, there remain only their language and their poverty" (*Journey*, 57).

THE *LIVES* AS *LIEU DE MÉMOIRE*

It is out of the experience of such loss, or potential loss, that Johnson's historiographical writing turns translational. The commemorative narratives of the *Journey* and the *Lives* mark a move from what Walter Benjamin calls "Messianic time" to "homogenous, empty time," a process which has been associated with imagining the concept of the nation in the eighteenth century.[18] The doubleness of translation – presenting itself as an act of repetition as well as an interpretation inscribing historical difference – is a paradigm for the nation's constant negotiation between the particular and the universal.[19] Because national identity is constructed, and there is no essential link between the individual's daily life and the perceived timelessness of the nation, "national" discourse translates between the two. In similar vein, the authority of Johnson's texts establishes itself in the liminal space between the particular and the general, mediating between the two discourses – the life and the work of the writer, for example – and locating itself by translation in various *lieu de mémoire*.

In a monumental historiography of modern France, Pierre Nora has argued that the development of *les lieux de mémoire* actually marks a decisive break with the past, and a self-conscious historicity.[20] So, indeed, it is with Johnson's *Lives of the Poets*, which develops a kind of Foucaultian archaeology that reflects on the literary history he has constructed with a consciousness of the historicity, fictiveness, of his own efforts. In 1874, F. H. Bradley observed that all history is prefigured, and that "history stands not only for that which has been, but also for that which is." Pivotal in the conjectural, inferential work of the historian is what Bradley calls "the character of our general consciousness" or "human nature," without which "our hold upon tradition is gone, and with it well nigh our only basis for historical judgment."[21] Johnson's claim of accessibility to this consciousness is, as I have argued at length in this book, what underlies his historiography of the "present"; it is everywhere manifest in his writing, and it has been the bane of Johnson scholarship for a hundred years. Yet Johnson's claim to general nature or commonality is not monolithic, but encompasses various experiential differences as well as implying a subtle and synthetic historical understanding. The intelligence of that historical understanding – and what makes the *Lives* a key work in the formation of modern historiography – is Johnson's ability to give an equal and simultaneous weight to two discourses which have been treated as if they cannot belong together: the conviction that writing gives us access to common experience and to general nature, and that therefore people of different cultures can participate to some extent in common historical experiences; and the conviction that the language through which such truths are made available, is relative, and subject to history and to time.

These two discourses find their focus in Johnson's writing in the *present*, which is, as Nora and Bradley also remark, the site of memory. Such an emphasis on the historical present is not, of course, as odd as it might look, since formal eighteenth-century historiography makes similar philosophical claims. But with the social and sentimental broadening of historical horizons in the eighteenth century, genres like memoir, biography, criticism, philosophy, antiquarianism, and novel were recognized as contributing to a revised, bourgeois notion of historical experience. In this vein, Johnson's thinking about biography responds to the neoclassical conception of history as a public discourse about political and military action by blurring the division between public and private, and privileging the personal experience of the ordinary individual: "I have often thought that there has rarely passed a life of which a judicious and faithful narrative would not be useful" (*Rambler* 60, III, 320). In biography and the sentimental histories of the Scottish Enlightenment, the *vita activa*, as Mark Phillips remarks, "could no longer be thought of as an autonomous field of activity... [and] 'action' itself would need to give way to more inclusive categories of experience."[22] As I have argued, however, Johnson's biographical practice retains some link with formal historiography by rethinking "action" in terms of the work of writing, which, in turn, becomes a site for the revelation of character. His biographical practice also retains a political dimension, but no longer understood in terms of the exemplary actions of great men – as it is, for example, in Bolingbroke's *Letters on History* and *Patriot King* – nor necessarily in terms of party allegiance. The *Lives* is political in more expansive, philosophical ways; in what Isaiah Berlin calls the "perfectly ordinary, empirical, and quasi-aesthetic" way in which politically gifted individuals integrate a large body of disparate and changing material, in such a way as to grasp the nature of the event, all the while seeing that event in relation to "symptoms of past and future possibilities."[23]

Thus it is that the *political* engagement of Johnson's vision comes through in his personal and particular witnessing and recollection of individual effort, poignantly in the small and almost forgotten lives. The *Lives* engages politically with experience in the performativity of Johnson's prose and its various narratives. Though Johnson may have believed – as he wrote in Goldsmith's *The Traveller* (1764) – "How small, of all that human hearts endure, / That part which laws or kings can cause or cure" (lines 429–30) – his political awareness in the *Lives* is really inseparable from his ethical engagement informing the textuality of his whole enterprise, and which, as Robert Scholes identifies in writing of an ethic of reading, "require[s] us to connect what is represented in the text with what we see in the world – in a manner that is ethical because it is political, and political because it is textual... The notion of textuality reminds us that we do nothing in insolation from others."[24]

Hayden White's notion of the "ineluctability of figuration in the representation of historical reality"[25] is not one that Johnson would have contested in any but his most argumentative moods, nor does it do violence to his thought. But Roger Chartier's criticism of White's tropological theory of historical discourse – that he "chooses to champion an absolute... relativism that denies all possibility of establishing 'scientific' knowledge concerning the past"[26] – highlights Johnson's resistance to the postmodern compulsion to see facts as tainting discourse and truth as invariably pre- or non-historical. Johnson on Ossian is only one instance in which he insists on the "facts" as a means of determining the truth and the historicity of the documentary claims in question. Yet Johnson has no hardened ideology of the real, such as one finds in nineteenth-century European realist historiography, or in the postmodern insistence on *opposing* truth and discourse. Neither does he have any doubt that language – whatever the form – can provide an experience of plenitude and truth. But this does not mean that Johnson thinks that the truth status of history emerges naturally from the past; he knows, in the words of Chartier, that there is no "epistemology of immediate coincidence or transparency between knowledge and the true, between discourse and the real," and that the truth status of history arises "as the result of establishing relations among data arranged by the operation of knowing."[27] This is why Imlac's words to his companions as they face the cultural and historical impenetrability of the Pyramids has the ring of a paradigmatic utterance: "To know any thing ... we must know its effects ... To judge rightly of the present we must oppose it to the past; for all judgement is comparative, and of the future nothing can be known. The truth is, that no mind is much employed upon the present" (*Rasselas*, 112).

This relational, comparative structure of thought is the framework for Johnson's epistemology, as well as the structure within which he creates his sense of fact and event. In Johnsonian discourse, "fact" often denotes a relation, and one that, because it is inscribed in the structure of the thought, assumes the form of a difference. "Event," likewise, refers to difference, that pause and emptiness between the past and the future, on which no person's mind is much employed. These notions, as I have tried to demonstrate, are everywhere present in Johnson's writing, but one final example will conclude these remarks.

In 1779 Johnson wrote of Dryden's "Essay on Dramatick Poesy" (1669) that: "He who, having formed his opinions in the present age of English literature, turns back to peruse this dialogue, will not perhaps find much increase of knowledge or much novelty of instruction ... A writer who obtains his full purpose loses himself in his own lustre. Of an opinion which is no longer doubted, the evidence ceases to be examined. Of an art universally practised, the first teacher is often forgotten. Learning once made popular is no longer learning: it has the appearance of something which we have bestowed on ourselves, as the dew appears to rise from the field which it refreshes" (*Lives*, I, 411). This passage posits a retrospective view from 1779 to 1669, in the process commending Dryden's critical thought by remarking the impossibility of distinguishing what we know from what he has taught us. But it is impossible to say exactly what the "fact" is here, and what the "event." Although the *kind* of knowledge offered by Dryden's essay is different from that characterizing scholarship in the late eighteenth century, Johnson's commemorative structure establishes its own mini-narrative wherein it is possible, and even natural, to think of Dryden in terms *of* the present. The work of time in this narrative not only suggests the movement of nature (in the surprising image of the dew and the field), and the fantasy of knowledge as *self*-begetting; it also envisages the almost inevitable erasure by history of the trace of even the great and successful writer. The historical event, arising from between the facts of 1779 and 1669, seems to be swallowing Dryden up in his own lustre.

Yet what Johnson's narrative actually gives us is *not* the eclipse of Dryden, for as the dew seems to rise, so does the memory of Dryden. What *results* is a *lieu de mémoire*. In writing of the vital cultural work done by *lieux de mémoire* in France, as certain phenomena repeatedly rise and fall in the popular memory, always changing over time, yet always remaining the same, Pierre Nora wonders: "What is the essence of this quintessential *lieu de mémoire* – its original intention or its return in the cycles of memory? Clearly both: all *lieu de mémoire* are objects *mises en abime*."[28] And so it is with Johnson's *Lives of the Poets*.

Notes

INTRODUCTION: JOHNSON AND AUTHORITY

1 See *Les Lieux de Mémoire,* sous la direction de Pierre Nora, 3 vols. (Paris: Gallimard, 1984–86; 1993) [*Realms of Memory: Rethinking the French Past,* under the direction of Pierre Nora, ed. Lawrence D. Kritzman, trans. Arthur Goldhammer, 3 vols. (New York: Columbia University Press, 1996)].
2 Hamilton's words are quoted by Boswell, *Life,* IV, 420.
3 *Anecdotes of Samuel Johnson, LL.D.,* in *JM,* I, 350.
4 *Life,* IV, 427–28.
5 See Kevin Hart, *Samuel Johnson and the Culture of Property* (Cambridge University Press, 1999), ch. 2.
6 See Greg Clingham, "Resisting Johnson," in *Johnson Re-Visioned: Looking Before and After,* ed. Philip Smallwood (Lewisburg: Bucknell University Press, 2001), ch. 1.
7 Harold Bloom, *The Western Canon: The Books and School of the Ages* (New York: Harcourt Brace and Co., 1994), 192.
8 Bertrand H. Bronson, "The Double Tradition of Dr. Johnson" (1951), in *Johnson Agonistes and Other Essays* (Berkeley: University of California Press, 1965), 156–76.
9 See, e.g., Alvin Kernan, *Samuel Johnson and the Impact of Print* (Princeton University Press, 1987); and Paul Fussell, *Samuel Johnson and the Life of Writing* (London: Chatto & Windus, 1972).
10 *Life,* I, 383–84.
11 Walter Jackson Bate, *The Achievement of Samuel Johnson* (New York: Oxford University Press, 1955), esp. chs. 1–4, and *Samuel Johnson* (London: Chatto & Windus, 1978).
12 See, e.g., Lee Erickson, *The Economy of Literary Form: English Literature and the Industrialization of Publishing* (Baltimore: Johns Hopkins University Press, 1996); and Jonathan Brody Kramnick, *Making the English Canon: Print-Capitalism and the Cultural Past, 1700–1770* (Cambridge University Press, 1998), ch. 1.
13 *Impact of Print,* 108 and chs. 3–4.
14 John Barrell, *English Literature in History 1730–1780: "An Equal, Wide Survey"* (London: Hutchinson, 1983), 144–61.

15 Tim Fulford, *Landscape, Liberty and Authority: Poetry, Criticism and Politics from Thomson to Wordsworth* (Cambridge University Press, 1996), 92, 99, and 73–115.
16 Fredric V. Bogel, *The Dream of My Brother: An Essay on Johnson's Authority*. English Literary Studies No. 47. (University of Victoria, 1990), and "Johnson and the Role of Authority," in *The New Eighteenth Century: Theory, Politics, English Literature*, ed. Felicity Nussbaum and Laura Brown (London: Methuen, 1987); and Martin Wechselblatt, *Bad Behavior: Samuel Johnson and Modern Cultural Authority* (Lewisburg: Bucknell University Press, 1998).
17 Stanley Fish, *Is There a Text in This Class? The Authority of Interpretive Communities* (Cambridge, MA: Harvard University Press, 1980), 318.
18 Peter Brooks notes: "Conviction in the legal sense results from conviction created in those who judge the story." See "The Law as Narrative and Rhetoric," in *Law's Stories: Narrative and Rhetoric in the Law*, ed. Peter Brooks and Paul Gewirtz (New Haven, CT: Yale University Press, 1996), 18.
19 Robert Weisberg, "Proclaiming Trials as Narratives: Premises and Pretenses," in *Law's Stories*, 68.
20 Paul Fussell long ago drew a parallel between Johnson's attitude to language and to legal rhetoric; *Life of Writing*, ch. 2.
21 In addition to the work by Wechselblatt and Bogel, see Charles H. Hinnant, *"Steel for the Mind": Samuel Johnson and Critical Discourse* (Newark, DE: University of Delaware Press, 1994); Steven Lynn, *Samuel Johnson After Deconstruction* (Carbondale: Southern Illinois University Press, 1992); and Raman Selden, "Deconstructing the Ramblers," in *Fresh Reflections on Samuel Johnson*, ed. Prem Nath (Troy, NY: Whiston, 1987), 269–82.
22 See, e.g., John Bender, "A New History of the Enlightenment," *ECL*, 16 (1992), 1–20.
23 John Locke, *An Essay Concerning Human Understanding*, ed. Peter H. Nidditch (Oxford: Clarendon Press, 1975), III. 10. no. 34.
24 See Fulford, *Landscape, Liberty and Authority*, 99.
25 See, e.g., Lawrence Lipking, *The Ordering of the Arts in Eighteenth-Century England* (Princeton University Press, 1970), ch. 13.
26 *Rambler*, 2, III, 14.
27 *Idler*, 44, 137.
28 "Life of Pope," *Lives*, III, 251.
29 Michel Foucault, *The Order of Things: An Archaeology of the Human Sciences* (New York: Vintage Books, 1970).
30 See, e.g., Hans Robert Jauss, *Question and Answer: Forms of Dialogic Understanding*, ed. and trans. Michael Hays (Minneapolis: University of Minnesota Press, 1989), section E.
31 *Poems*, 438.
32 James Boyd White, *Heracles' Bow: Essays on the Rhetoric and Poetics of the Law* (Madison: University of Wisconsin Press, 1985), 95, 98.

1 JOHNSON AND MEMORY

1 See Boswell, *Life*, I, 39; and Hawkins, 8. Hector, Johnson's school fellow, is identified as Hawkins' source by Boswell; see *Boswell's Note Book 1776–1777*, ed. R. B. Adam (London: Humphrey Milford, 1925), 4.
2 See *Life*, I, 39–40, 48, 263–64; IV, 14, and the memoirs by Thomas Tyers, Joseph Towers, and James Harrison, all in *EB*, 78, 220, 252.
3 William Shaw, *Memoirs of the Life and Writings of the Late Samuel Johnson* (1785), in *EB*, 158.
4 William Cooke, *The Life of Samuel Johnson, LL.D* (1785), in *EB*, 130.
5 "Life of Smith," *Lives*, II, 21.
6 *Rambler*, 63, III, 336.
7 *Rambler* 2, III, 10.
8 *Rasselas*, 15, 18.
9 *Rambler* 8, III, 41.
10 *Rambler* 108, IV, 210–11.
11 *Rambler*, 63, III, 334–35.
12 See, e.g., James Engell, *Forming the Critical Mind: Dryden to Coleridge* (Cambridge, MA: Harvard University Press, 1989), 176.
13 Edward Young, *Conjectures on Original Composition* (1759), Facsimile of 1st edition (Leeds: Scolar Press, 1966), 17; see also 25.
14 *On Difficulty and Other Essays* (Oxford University Press, 1978), 1.
15 On Derrida and Johnson, see Steven Lynn, *Samuel Johnson After Deconstruction: Rhetoric and the Rambler* (Carbondale: Southern Illinois University Press, 1992), 72–73.
16 Richard Terdiman, *Present Past: Modernity and the Memory Crisis* (Ithaca: Cornell University Press, 1993), 7.
17 Patrick H. Hutton identifies the "interplay between repetition and recollection as the foundation of any consideration of the memory/history problem." By "memory/history problem" Hutton means the necessary contribution of memory to historiography, specifically to the recollection of images and the modes of their representation. See *History as an Art of Memory* (Hanover, VT: University Press of New England, 1993), xx, xxii, and ch. 1.
18 See, e.g., David Farrell Krell, *On the Verge: Of Memory, Reminiscence, and Writing* (Bloomington: Indiana University Press, 1990), chs. 4 and 7.
19 *Philebus*, 33dff.
20 *De Anima*, 430a 14–25.
21 See Krell, *On the Verge*, ch. 1.
22 *Confessions*, trans. R. S. Pine-Coffin (Harmondsworth: Penguin Books, 1961), Bk. 10: 8, 216.
23 See James Olney, *Memory and Narrative: The Weave of Life-Writing* (University of Chicago Press, 1998), 60–61 and ch. 1 in general.
24 *Confessions*, II: 20, 269.
25 "Of memory, which makes so large a part of the excellence of the human soul, and which has so much influence upon its other powers, but

26 *Confessions*, 10: 6, 211–13; see Olney, *Memory and Narrative*, 3–4,17, 63.
27 See Olney, *Memory and Narrative*, 85–100 and 211–27 (for Vico), and 101–209 (for Rousseau). Vico and Johnson have other things in common: for example, the sense, in the *New Science*, that people can only know what they themselves have made, that human knowledge is mediated by consciousness, especially by speech (a creative rather than a merely reproductive power) that traces the evolution of humankind from savagery to enlightenment. See Hayden White, "The Tropics of History: The Deep Structure of the *New Science*," in *Tropics of Discourse: Essays in Cultural Criticism* (Baltimore: Johns Hopkins University Press, 1978), 197–217.
28 John Sutton, *Philosophy and Memory Traces: Descartes to Connectionism* (Cambridge University Press, 1998), chs. 6 and 7.
29 See Christopher Fox, *Locke and the Scriblerians: Identity and Consciousness in Early Eighteenth-Century Britain* (Berkeley: University of California Press, 1988), chs. 1–4.
30 Locke's journal for Tuesday 5 June 1683; see Sutton, *Philosophy and Memory Traces*, 166.
31 See Sutton, ibid., 167–68, and Fox, *Locke and the Scriblerians*, ch. 1.
32 *An Essay Concerning Human Understanding*, ed. Peter H. Nidditch (Oxford: Clarendon Press, 1975), II: 10, no. 2, 150.
33 For the distinction between mourning and melancholy, where melancholia compulsively repeats a trauma that cannot be closed and consigned to the past, see Dominick LaCapra, *Representing the Holocaust: History, Theory, Trauma* (Ithaca: Cornell University Press, 1994), 213, 246, and Sigmund Freud, "Remembering, Repeating, and Working Through," in *Beyond the Pleasure Principle*, trans. James Strachey (New York: Norton, 1961), ch. 3.
34 Cf. Cathy Caruth's analysis of this passage of Locke in *Empirical Truths and Critical Fictions: Locke, Wordsworth, Kant, Freud* (Baltimore: Johns Hopkins University Press, 1991), 33–42.
35 *Shakespeare*, I, 78.
36 *Idler*, No. 103, 315.
37 "Life of Dryden," *Lives*, I, 458–59.
38 *Memory and Narrative*, 3–4. In the *Dictionary*, Johnson defines "Elegancy" as "Beauty of art; rather soothing than striking; beauty without grandeur," and offers the following quotation from Raleigh's *History of the World* as illustration: "St. Augustine, out of a kind of elegancy in writing, makes some difference."
39 Merleau-Ponty, *Phenomenology*, quoted by Krell, *On the Verge*, 99.
40 *Rambler*, 2, III, 9.
41 *Rambler*, 7, III, 37–38; see also *Sermons*, No. 3, 35–36; No. 8, 90.
42 Claude Rawson, *Order from Confusion Sprung: Studies in Eighteenth-Century Literature from Swift to Cowper* (London: George Allen & Unwin, 1985), 5.
43 *Rambler*, 8, III, 41.
44 *Rambler*, 2, III, 10.

45 Paul de Man, *Blindness and Insight: Essays in the Rhetoric of Contemporary Criticism* (Minneapolis: University of Minnesota Press, 1983), 92.
46 *Adventurer*, No. 107, 445.
47 Preface to the *Dictionary*, *SJ*, 310.
48 *Rambler*, 41, III, 224–25.
49 Dryden, "Horat. Ode 29. Book 3 Paraphras'd in *Pindarique* Verse," lines 69–72; *Poems*, I, 436.
50 "Secret happiness" is Dryden's term for Horace's choice of words in this poem; Preface to *Sylvae*, Watson, II, 31.
51 For this dimension of Dryden's translating practice, see Greg Clingham, "Translating Difference: The Example of Dryden's 'Last Parting of Hector and Andromache,'" *SLI*, 33 (2000), 45–70; and Paul Hammond, *Dryden and the Traces of Classical Rome* (Oxford: Oxford University Press, 1999), 6–21.
52 *The Sense of an Ending: Studies in the Theory of Fiction* (London: Oxford University Press, 1966), 46.
53 Stuart Sherman, *Telling Time: Clocks, Diaries, and English Diurnal Form, 1660–1785* (Chicago: University of Chicago Press, 1996), 9–12. The quotation is from Walter Benjamin, "Theses on the Philosophy of History," in *Illuminations*, ed. Hannah Arendt, trans. Harry Zohn (New York: Shocken Books, 1969), 261, 263.
54 See Melinda Alliker Rabb, " 'Soft Figures' and 'a Paste of Composition Rare': Pope, Swift, and Memory," *SECC*, 19 (1989), 185–95.
55 See Peter Brooks, *Body Work: Objects of Desire in Modern Narrative* (Cambridge, MA: Harvard University Press, 1993), ch. 1.
56 For a telling feminist critique of this pseudo-Freudian conception of narrative structure, see Susan Winnett, "Coming Unstrung: Women, Men, Narrative," *PMLA*, 105 (1990), 505–18.
57 *Idler*, 232, 138.
58 *Letters*, I, 383–85.
59 *Poems*, 181.
60 *Thraliana: The Diary of Mrs Hester Lynch Thrale*, ed. Katherine C. Balderston, 2 vols. (Oxford: Clarendon Press, 1951), 41.
61 In a letter (*TLS*, 2 May 1929), R. W. Chapman assumes that Mrs Thrale had misquoted Johnson. But Nichol Smith and McAdam note that "the variants are too serious to be explained by [Mrs Thrale's] inaccuracy, what she preserved was probably dictated by Johnson on the spur of the moment," *Poems*, 181.
62 Donald Greene prefers (and prints) Mrs Thrale's version because he thinks Johnson's first version is "inferior poetically;" *SJ*, 26, 797.
63 See Boswell, *Life*, I, 145–47; III, 229, n. 3; Hester Thrale Piozzi's *Anecdotes* in *JM*, I, 239–40, and *Thraliana*, 40; James Clifford, *Hester Lynch Piozzi (Mrs Thrale)* (Oxford: Clarendon Press, 1968), 23–24; and Ronald Paulson, *Hogarth: His Life, Art, and Times*, 2 vols. (New Haven, CT: Yale University Press, 1971), II, 291.

64 In dedicating Charles Burney's *History of Music* (1776) to the Queen, Johnson writes: "The science of musical sounds, though it may have been depreciated, as appealing only to the ear, and affording nothing more than a momentary and fugitive delight, may be with justice considered as the art that unites corporeal with intellectual pleasures, by a species of enjoyment which gratifies sense, without weakening reason," *P&D*, 29.
65 *Rambler*, 2, III, 9.
66 *Johnson the Poet: The Poetic Career of Samuel Johnson* (Newark, DE: University of Delaware Press, 1999), 157.
67 *Forms of Attention* (University of Chicago Press, 1985), ch. 3, esp. 88.
68 "Narrative in Contemporary Historical Theory," in *The Content of the Form: Narrative, Discourse and Historical Representation* (Baltimore: Johns Hopkins University Press, 1987), 52.
69 Paul Ricoeur, "Narrative Time," in *On Narrative*, ed. W. J. T. Mitchell (University of Chicago Press, 1981), 174.
70 "Life of Milton," *Lives*, I, 177.
71 *Rambler*, 24, III, 131–32.
72 Preface to the *Dictionary*, *SJ*, 327.
73 *Idler*, No. 103, 315.
74 Cf. Lynn, *Johnson After Deconstruction*, 113.
75 James Boswell, *London Journal, 1762–1763*, ed. Frederick A. Pottle (New York: McGraw-Hill, 1950), 305.
76 See, e.g., *Sermons*, No. 13, 145; and *Sermons*, No. 14, 150.
77 1 January 1757; *DPA*, 62.
78 The quotation is from *Sermons*, No. 2, 21.
79 *Sermons*, No. 2, 24; see also No. 22, 235.
80 Jacques Le Goff, *History and Memory*, trans. Steven Rendall and Elizabeth Claman (New York: Columbia University Press, 1992), 69–71.
81 See, e.g., *Sermons*, No. 9, 100–01.
82 As a young man Johnson committed the Collects of the Prayer Book to memory; *Life*, I, 40.
83 See Charles E. Pierce, *The Religious Life of Samuel Johnson* (Hamden: Archon Books, 1983), 70. Johnson opens Sermon 22 by saying: "The celebration of the sacrament is generally acknowledged, by the Christian church, to be the highest act of devotion, and the most solemn part of positive religion" (229).
84 See Ricoeur on Augustine, *Time and Narrative*, I, trans. Kathleen McLaughlin and David Pellauer (University of Chicago Press, 1984), ch. 1.
85 *Sermons*, No. 10, 113.
86 Philip Davis, *In Mind of Johnson: A Study of Johnson the Rambler* (Athens, GA: University of Georgia Press, 1989), and Paul K. Alkon, *Samuel Johnson and Moral Discipline* (Evanston: Northwestern University Press, 1967), from whom the quotation comes (177).
87 Michael Suarez, "Johnson's Christian Thought," in *Companion*, 192–208; and Blanford Parker, *The Triumph of Augustan Poetics: English Literary Culture*

from Butler to Johnson (Cambridge University Press, 1998), ch. 7, quotation at 275.
88 "Life of Waller," *Lives*, I, 292.
89 Parker, *Augustan Poetics*, 244.
90 Paul Fussell observes that Johnson "learned a style as well as a substance from *The Book of Common Prayer*" (*Life of Writing*, 79), manifested in the letters written to his mother in the week before her death (*Letters*, I, 174–79); see also Fussell, *Life of Writing*, 132–34 and 216–19, and Davis, *In Mind of Johnson*, 198–217.
91 "It is sufficient for Watts to have done better than others what no man has done well;" "Life of Watts," *Lives*, III, 310.
92 Reddick observes that, in the second half of the alphabet (M–Z), Johnson uses 200 quotations from *Paradise Lost* (in contrast to 71 from all books of the Bible) in the 1773 *Dictionary*; *The Making of Johnson's Dictionary 1746–1773* (Cambridge University Press, 1990 and 1992), 122–30.
93 Geoffrey Hill, "Poetry as 'Menace' and 'Atonement,'" in *Lords of Limit: Essays on Literature and Ideas* (New York: Oxford University Press, 1984), 15. The quotation from Barth is also from Hill's essay.
94 For an eloquent consideration of poetic circumstantiality, see Geoffrey Hill, *The Enemy's Country: Words, Contexture, and other Circumstances of Language* (Stanford University Press, 1991), ch. 1.
95 Geoffrey Hill, "Poetry as 'Menace' and 'Atonement,'" 2. Eliot's words are from "The Three Voices of Poetry," and are quoted in Hill's essay. See also Davis: "in both Taylor and Johnson prudence has to do with *language* as an act of weighing the form and distinguishing the circumstance in which the spirit has to make its earthly way;" *In Mind of Johnson*, 196.
96 Christopher Ricks, "Geoffrey Hill 2: At-one-ment," in *The Force of Poetry* (Oxford University Press, 1987), 323.
97 "This is the use of memory: / For liberation – not less of love but expanding / Of love beyond desire, and so liberation / From the future as well as the past." T. S. Eliot, *Little Gidding*, lines 156–59.
98 See Hannah Arendt, *The Human Condition* (University of Chicago Press, 1958), 22–28.
99 See Fussell, *Life of Writing*, 264.

2 JOHNSON AND NATURE

1 Geoffrey H. Hartman, "Literary Commentary as Literature," in *Criticism in the Wilderness: The Study of Literature Today* (New Haven, CT: Yale University Press, 1980), 201.
2 See John M. Ellis, *Against Deconstruction* (Princeton University Press, 1989), 114–15.
3 Stanley Fish, "Rhetoric," in *Doing What Comes Naturally: Change, Rhetoric, and the Practice of Theory in Literary and Legal Studies* (Durham, NC: Duke University Press, 1989), 471–502.

4 See Scott D. Evans, *Samuel Johnson's "General Nature": Tradition and Transition in Eighteenth-Century Discourse* (Newark, DE: University of Delaware Press, 1999), chs. 1–3.
5 René Wellek, e.g., saw Johnson as a great critic who confuses life with art (*A History of Modern Criticism: 1750–1950. The Later Eighteenth Century* [London: Jonathan Cape, 1955], 79); and Jean Hagstrum's view was that Johnson's criticism is "the simple assumptions of common sense" (*Samuel Johnson's Literary Criticism* [Minneapolis: University of Minnesota Press, 1952], 77). The classic account of Johnson on nature in Shakespeare, to which I am indebted, is G. F. Parker, *Johnson's Shakespeare* (Oxford: Clarendon Press, 1989).
6 *Shakespeare*, I, 62.
7 See *Life*, II, 49, 173–75.
8 *Rambler*, 4, III, 20.
9 See Lennard J. Davis, *Resisting Novels: Ideology and Fiction* (London: Methuen, 1987), ch. 1.
10 See, e.g., *Samuel Johnson on Shakespeare*, ed. W. K. Wimsatt (New York: Hill and Wang, 1960), xxi; and R. D. Stock, *Samuel Johnson and Neoclassical Dramatic Theory: The Intellectual Context of the "Preface to Shakespeare"* (Lincoln, NE: University of Nebraska Press, 1973), 28.
11 See, e.g., F. R. Leavis, "Johnson and Augustanism," *The Common Pursuit* (Harmondsworth: Penguin Books, 1969), 109.
12 See Howard D. Weinbrot, "The Reader, the General, and the Particular: Johnson and Imlac in Chapter Ten of *Rasselas*," *ECS*, 5 (1971–72), 80–96, and Parker, *Johnson's Shakespeare*, 24.
13 *Rambler*, 2, III, 9.
14 *Rambler*, 41, III, 223.
15 See W. R. Keast, "The Theoretical Foundations of Johnson's Criticism," in *Critics and Criticism*, ed. R. S. Crane (University of Chicago Press, 1957), 179.
16 Johnson told Boswell, "a desire of knowledge is the natural feeling of mankind; and every human being, whose mind is not debauched, will be willing to give all that he has to get knowledge"; a statement that was prompted by an interaction they had had with the boy rowing them on the Thames: " 'What would you give, my lad, to know about the Argonauts?' 'Sir, (said the boy,) I would give what I have' " (*Life*, I, 458).
17 "Life of Dryden," *Lives*, I, 459.
18 John Dryden, "The Author's Apology for Heroic Poetry and Poetic Licence" (1677), Watson, I, 207.
19 I am indebted to Mr H. A. Mason for this thought.
20 See E. Audra in *TE*, I, 212–22.
21 "Life of Pope," *Lives*, III, 228.
22 See, e.g., Leavis, "Johnson and Augustanism," 109.
23 "Life of Cowley," *Lives*, I, 19.
24 See Parker, *Johnson's Shakespeare*, 28–37.
25 *Essays of Michael Montaigne*, Made English by Charles Cotton, 3 vols. (London, 1700), III, 143.

26 *Shakespeare*, I, 66.
27 "[H]e has taken into the compass of his *Canterbury Tales* the various manners and humours of the whole English nation in his age; not a single character has escaped him;" "Preface to *Fables*," Watson, II, 284.
28 Hawkins, 482 (whence the quotation comes); and William Hazlitt, *Lectures on the English Comic Writers* (London: Oxford University Press, 1920).
29 The final six volumes of the *Prefaces* were published in 1781. In 1781 all the *Prefaces* were published as the *Lives of the Most Eminent English Poets: With Critical Observations on their Works*, followed in 1783 by a new, revised edition of the same title.
30 See Lawrence Lipking, *The Ordering of the Arts in Eighteenth-Century England* (Princeton University Press, 1970), 428–34.
31 "Life of Pope," *Lives*, III, 251.
32 T. S. Eliot, "The Metaphysical Poets," in *Selected Essays* (London: Faber and Faber, 1972), 287.
33 Christopher Ricks, "In Theory," *London Review of Books* (16 April–6 May, 1981), 3.
34 *Rambler*, 125, IV, 301.
35 See *Paradise Lost*, ed. Thomas Newton, 2 vols. (London, 1749), I, lvi; Dryden "An Essay of Dramatic Poesy" (1668), Watson, I, 24; and Pope, "The First Epistle of the Second Book of Horace Imitated," line 78.
36 Thomas Carew, "An Elegie upon the death of the Deane of Pauls, Dr. Iohn Donne," which was among the funeral elegies concluding *Poems, By J.D. With Elegies on the Authors Death* (London: M. F. for John Marriot, 1633), a copy of which Johnson owned; see J. D. Fleeman, *A Preliminary Handlist of Copies of Books Associated with Dr. Samuel Johnson* (Oxford Bibliographical Society, 1984), 16.
37 Frank Kermode, "John Donne," *Shakespeare, Spenser, Donne: Renaissance Essays* (London: Routledge & Kegan Paul, 1971), 128.
38 Eliot, *Selected Essays*, 282–83.
39 See Anthony Low, *The Reinvention of Love: Poetry, Politics and Culture from Sidney to Milton* (Cambridge University Press, 1993), 47.
40 T. S. Eliot, *Selected Essays*, 286. Eliot later changed his mind about Donne, writing, in "Donne in Our Time," that "In Donne, there is a manifest fissure between thought and sensibility . . . His learning is just information suffused with emotion"; *A Garland For John Donne*, ed. Theodore Spencer (Cambridge, MA: Harvard University Press, 1931), 8. However, Eliot's earlier arguments apropos the metaphysicals in "The Metaphysical Poets" (1921) and "Andrew Marvell" (1921) have carried more weight with readers.
41 *The Metaphysical Poets*, ed. Helen Gardner (Harmondsworth: Penguin, 1975), 28.
42 *Shakespeare*, I, 62.
43 "Life of Milton," *Lives*, I, 163.

44 See David Hopkins, "Cowley's Horatian Mice," in *Horace Made New: Horatian Influences on British Writing from the Renaissance to the Twentieth Century*, ed. Charles Martindale and David Hopkins (Cambridge University Press, 1993), 103–26, to whom I am indebted for this brief sketch of epicureanism (109–12).
45 See Tom Mason, "Abraham Cowley and the Wisdom of Anacreon," *CQ*, 19 (1990), 103–37, and *Abraham Cowley: Selected Poems*, ed. David Hopkins and Tom Mason (Manchester: Carcanet, 1994), xiii–xxix.
46 "So it is not only that he sees what we see in the metaphysicals but values it differently"; Damrosch, *Uses*, 21 – a view shared by Keast, "Johnson's Criticism of the Metaphysical Poets," 307.
47 *Johnson's Literary Criticism*, ch. 7.
48 This is not the Burkean sublime, but Boileau's version of Longinus which distinguished the grand neo-classical style from a simpler idea locating the sublime in a thought, figure, or image. See Parker, *Johnson's Shakespeare*, 31–32.
49 When the experience of admiration is effectively organized and structured for Johnson it seems to provide both pleasure and knowledge; in the *Dictionary* the following quotations are supplied to illustrate "admiration:" (1) "The passions always move, and therefore consequently please; for, without motion, there can be no delight, which cannot be considered but as an active passion. When we view those elevated ideas of nature, the result of that view is admiration, which is always the cause of pleasure" (Dryden); (2) "There is a pleasure in admiration, and this is that which properly causeth admiration, when we discover a great deal in an object which we understand to be excellent; and yet we see, we know not how much more, beyond that, which our understanding cannot fully reach and comprehend" (Tillotson).
50 Greene, "Pictures to the Mind," in *Johnson, Boswell and Their Circle: Essays Presented to Lawrence Fitzroy Powell* (Oxford: Clarendon Press, 1965), 153.
51 See also Johnson on Pope's simile of the Alps in the *Essay on Criticism* (lines 219–32), in "Life of Pope," *Lives*, III, 229.
52 Dryden: *Works*, II, 330.
53 *A History of Modern Criticism*, 99. But cf. Charles H. Hinnant, "*Steel for the Mind*": *Samuel Johnson and Critical Discourse* (Newark, DE: University of Delaware Press, 1994), 203–09.
54 Allen Tate, "Johnson on the Metaphysical Poets," *Essays of Four Decades* (Chicago: Swallow Press, 1965).
55 *The Poetical Works of John Denham*, ed. Theodore Howard Banks, Jr. (New Haven, CT: Yale University Press, 1928), 77; quoted in the "Life of Denham," *Lives*, I, 78.
56 Watson, II, 237.
57 See *Works of Denham*, Appendix E; also 52–57 for the poetic influence of Denham's lines on the eighteenth century. Of the topographical poems inaugurated by *Cooper's Hill*, Johnson said that it has "left scarce a corner of the island not dignified either by rhyme or blank verse" ("Life of Denham," *Lives*, I, 78).

58 "Life of Addison," *Lives*, II, 129.
59 "Life of Cowley," *Lives*, I, 20. Eliot notices that "a degree of heterogeneity of material compelled into unity by the operation of the poet's mind is omnipresent in poetry" ("The Metaphysical Poets," 283), but, alas, will not allow Johnson the same insight, who takes for granted the "unlikeness" of the images being compared; it is the "occult" aspect of the resemblances that seem to bear the weight of his criticism.
60 Preface to the *Dictionary*, *SJ*, 315–16.
61 Donald Davidson, "What Metaphors Mean," in *On Metaphor*, ed. Sheldon Sacks (University of Chicago Press, 1981), 30, 45.
62 William Empson, "Metaphor," *The Structure of Complex Words* (London: Hogarth Press, 1951, 1985), 345–46.
63 Hagstrum, *Samuel Johnson's Literary Criticism*, 119; M. H. Abrams, "Dr. Johnson's Spectacles," in *New Light on Dr. Johnson*, ed. Frederick W. Hilles (New Haven: Yale University Press, 1959), 179.
64 *The Second Part of Mr Waller's Poems* (London, 1690).
65 *John Donne: The Critical Heritage*, ed. A.J. Smith (London: Routledge, 1975), 158.
66 "A Discourse Concerning the Original and Progress of Satire," Watson, II, 76.
67 "Life of Dorset," *Lives*, I, 308.
68 "Life of Waller," *Lives*, I, 296.
69 "Life of Dryden," *Lives*, I, 412. Boswell thought that "in drawing Dryden's character, Johnson has given, though I suppose unintentionally, some touches of his own," *Life*, IV, 45.
70 Christopher Ricks, "Donne After Love," *Literature and the Body: Essays on Populations and Persons*, ed. Elaine Scarry (Baltimore and London: Johns Hopkins University Press, 1988), 42.

3 LAW, NARRATIVE, AND MEMORY

1 *Letters*, IV, 148.
2 See John Zomchick, *Family and the Law in Eighteenth-Century Fiction* (Cambridge University Press, 1993), 1–2.
3 Johnson appealed to Dr. William Adams to ask Richard Smallbrooke to help him obtain a position as an advocate in "Doctors' Commons," a court dealing in canon and civil law; see W. J. Bate, *Samuel Johnson* (London: Chatto & Windus, 1978), 232–33. For Walmsley's legal and political influence on Johnson, see ibid., 84–85, and James Clifford, *Young Sam Johnson* (New York: McGraw Hill, 1955), 103–07.
4 See E. L. McAdam, Jr., *Dr. Johnson and the English Law* (Syracuse University Press, 1951) and Arnold Duncan McNair, *Dr. Johnson and the Law* (Cambridge University Press, 1948).

5 See Sir Robert Chambers, *A Course of Lectures on the English Law, 1767–1773*, ed. Thomas M. Curley, 2 vols. (Madison: University of Wisconsin Press, 1986), I, 3–79, Curley's, "Johnson's Secret Collaboration," in *The Unknown Samuel Johnson*, ed. John J. Burke, Jr. and Donald Kay (Madison: University of Wisconsin Press, 1983), 91–112 and "Johnson, Chambers, and the Law," in *Samuel Johnson After Two Hundred Years*, ed. Paul J. Korshin (Philadelphia: University of Pennsylvania Press, 1986), 187–210.
6 This does not deter Donald Greene from attributing to Johnson, without qualification, the entire 1st lecture of Part II, "Of Criminal Law, and First of the General Nature of Punishments;" *SJ*, 570–79 and 820n.
7 See McAdam, *Dr. Johnson and the English Law*, 55–59. Curley is less certain about Johnson's relationship with Hamilton; *Lectures*, I, 16.
8 See McNair, *Dr. Johnson and the Law*, 79.
9 See Howard Erskine-Hill, "The Political Character of Samuel Johnson," in *Samuel Johnson: New Critical Essays*, ed. Isobel Grundy (Totowa: Barnes and Noble, 1984), 107–36; and J. C. D. Clark, *Samuel Johnson: Literature, Religion and English Cultural Politics from the Restoration to Romanticism* (Cambridge University Press, 1994).
10 *Letters*, I, 238.
11 Pt. I, lecture 16, "Of Corporations"; *Lectures*, I, 293.
12 John Locke, *The Second Treatise of Government. An Essay Concerning the True Original, Extent, and End of Civil Government* (1689–90) and David Hume, "Of the Rise and Progress of the Arts and Sciences" (1741).
13 The first quotation is from *The False Alarm*, the second from *Taxation, No Tyranny*; in *Political Writings*, 325, 448.
14 Jacques Derrida, "The 'Mystical Foundations of Authority,'" in *Deconstruction and the Possibility of Justice*, ed. Drucilla Cornell, Michael Rosenfeld, and David Gray Carlson (New York: Routledge, 1992), 6. Johnson defines "force" as "validness, power of law," and "to enforce" as "to prove, to evince, to show beyond contradiction;" and he quotes Hooker as illustration: "Which laws in such case we must obey, unless there be reason shewed, which may necessarily enforce that the law of reason, or of God, doth enjoin the contrary."
15 *Taxation, No Tyranny*, in *Political Writings*, 423. See Curley (ed.), *Lectures*, I, 140: Pt. I, lecture 2, "The Present Constitution of Parliament."
16 To illustrate "parliamentary," Johnson quotes Hale: "Many things, that obtain as common law, had their original by parliamentary acts or constitutions, made in writings by the king, lords, and commons." To illustrate "affirmation," he quotes Hooker: "The learned in the laws of our land observe, that our statutes sometimes are only the affirmation, or ratification, of that which, by common law, was held before."
17 Introduction, lecture 4, "On the General Division of the Laws of England"; *Lectures*, I, 116.
18 Sir Matthew Hale, *The History of the Common Law of England* (1713), ed. Charles M. Gray (University of Chicago Press, 1971), xxxiv.

19 See Benedict Anderson, *Imagined Communities: Reflections on the Origin and Spread of Nationalism* (rev. edn. London: Verso, 1991), ch. 3.
20 See Curley (ed.), *Lectures*, I, 37–38.
21 Pt. I, lecture 7, "Of the House of Commons"; *Lectures*, I, 193.
22 Pt. I, lecture 1, "The Origin and Forms of Parliament"; *Lectures*, I, 133.
23 See Michel Foucault, "Nietzsche, Genealogy, History," in *The Foucault Reader*, ed. Paul Rabinow (New York: Pantheon Books, 1984), 79.
24 See Frank Brady, *James Boswell: The Later Years, 1769–1795* (New York: McGraw-Hill, 1984), 115–27.
25 For Boswell's presentation of the episode, see *Life*, II, 412–23, from which I quote Johnson's analysis. For Boswell's letter of 2 January 1776, see the *Letters of James Boswell*, ed. Chauncey B. Tinker, 2 vols. (Oxford: Clarendon Press, 1924), II, 284.
26 Roy Porter, *English Society in the Eighteenth Century* (London: Penguin, 1986), 151.
27 Locke, *Second Treatise*, in *Two Treatises of Government*, ed. Peter Laslett (Cambridge University Press, 1988), section 124.
28 *Journal*, 73; see also *Life*, II, 428.
29 See Susan Staves, *Married Women's Separate Property in England, 1660–1833* (Cambridge, MA: Harvard University Press, 1990), ch. 4.
30 See Fussell, *Johnson*, 90, and Greg Clingham, *Boswell: The Life of Johnson* (Cambridge University Press, 1992), 50–54.
31 *Family and the Law*, 1–2.
32 See, e.g., Kathleen Nulton Kemmerer, "*A Neutral Being Between the Sexes:*" *Samuel Johnson's Sexual Politics* (Lewisburg: Bucknell University Press, 1998).
33 Johnson's analysis of the case can be found in Boswell's *Life*, III, 200–05. See James Basker, "Samuel Johnson and the African American Reader," *The New Rambler* (1994/95 issue), 47–57.
34 *Truth and Method* (Westport: Continuum, 1975), 275.
35 For Gadamer's hermeneutics as applied to the issues of Enlightenment law, see Fred Dallmayr, "Hermeneutics and the Rule of Law," in *Deconstruction and the Possibility of Justice*, 283–304.
36 Hayden White, "Value of Narrativity," in *Content of the Form*, 13. White is discussing Hegel's *Lectures on the Philosophy of History*, trans. J. Sibree (1956), 60–63.
37 Robert Weisberg, "Proclaiming Trials as Narratives: Premises and Pretenses," in *Law's Stories: Narrative and Rhetoric in the Law*, ed. Peter Brooks and Paul Gewirtz (New Haven, CT: Yale University Press, 1996), 77, 78.
38 See, e.g., Homi K. Bhabha, "The Postcolonial and the Postmodern," and "How Newness Enters the World," in *The Location of Culture* (London: Routledge, 1994).
39 Preface to the *Dictionary*, *SJ*, 310.
40 *Rasselas*, 85. All citations subsequently included in the text.
41 Early critics tend to see disappointment in the tale as evidence of a questionable moral perspective. Hester Chapone, for example, deduces from the

tale "that human life is a scene of unmixt wretchedness, and that all states and conditions of it are equally miserable; a maxim which, if adopted, would extinguish hope, and consequently industry, make prudence ridiculous, and, in short, dispose men to lie down in sloth and despondency," *Posthumous Works* (London, 1807), I, 108–09. Boswell saw the pervasiveness of failure in the tale as a sign of Johnson's "morbid melancholy [which] made life appear to him more insipid and unhappy than it generally is;" *Life*, I, 343. For a survey of these early views, see Edward Tomarken, *Johnson, "Rasselas," and the Choice of Criticism* (Lexington: University of Kentucky Press, 1989), 5–37.

42 See, e.g., Robert E. Stillman, "Assessing the Revolution: Ideology, Language, and Rhetoric in the New Philosophy," *ECTI*, 35 (1994), 99–118.

43 John Richetti, *Philosophical Writing: Locke, Berkeley, Hume* (Cambridge, MA: Harvard University Press, 1983), 98, and 92–102 (for Locke on language). The quotations from Locke's *Essay* are from II.10.34.

44 See Paul De Man, "The Epistemology of Metaphor," *On Metaphor*, ed. Sheldon Sacks (University of Chicago Press, 1978), 11–28, and William Walker, *Locke, Literary Criticism, and Philosophy* (Cambridge University Press, 1994), 131 and ch. 6.

45 Michel Foucault, *The Order of Things: An Archaeology of the Human Sciences* (New York: Vintage Books, 1970), ch. 3, "Representing." The quotation is actually Carlos Fuentes', introducing Cervantes, *The Adventures of Don Quixote*, trans. by Tobias Smollett (New York: Farrar, Straus, Giroux, 1986), xix.

46 *Rambler* 2, III, 11. In her *Anecdotes*, Mrs Thrale records Johnson as saying: "'Was there yet ever any thing written by mere man that was wished longer by its readers, excepting Don Quixote, Robinson Crusoe, and the Pilgrim's Progress?' After Homer's Iliad, Mr Johnson confessed that the work of Cervantes was the greatest in the world, speaking of it I mean as a book of entertainment"; *JM*, I, 332. See Eithne Henson, "*The Fictions of Romantick Chivalry*": *Samuel Johnson and Romance* (Rutherford, NJ: Fairleigh Dickinson University Press,1992), 137, 111–41.

47 Peter Brooks, *Reading for the Plot: Design and Intention in Narrative* (Cambridge, MA: Harvard University Press, 1984), 235.

48 See Robert Markley, *Fallen Languages: Crises of Representation in Newtonian England, 1660–1740* (Ithaca and London: Cornell University Press, 1993), 15.

49 See Earl R. Wasserman, "Johnson's *Rasselas*: Implicit Contexts," *JEGP*, 74 (1975), 9, 11 – also Irvin Ehrenpreis, "*Rasselas* and Some Meanings of 'Structure' in Literary Criticism," *Novel*, 14 (1981), 113.

50 Cf. Charles Hinnant, *Samuel Johnson: An Analysis* (New York: St. Martin's Press, 1988), 93.

51 Hinnant, *Samuel Johnson*, 99.

52 See Srinivas Aravamudan, *Tropicopolitans: Colonialism and Agency, 1688–1804* (Durham: Duke University Press, 1999), 213.

53 *Lives*, I, 20–21.

54 White, *Content of the Form*, 49.
55 See Fox, *Locke and the Scriblerians*, ch. 1.
56 *Essay*, II. 27. 9.
57 Locke's earliest critics were the theologians, William Sherlock and Matthew Tindal; see Fox, *Locke and the Scriblerians*, 22–23.
58 Charles Taylor, *Sources of the Self: The Making of Modern Identity* (Cambridge, MA: Harvard University Press, 1989), 172.
59 See Richetti, *Philosophical Writing*, 110, and Taylor, *Sources*, 175–76.
60 David Hume, *An Enquiry Concerning Human Understanding*, ed. Eric Steinberg (Indianapolis: Hackett Publishing Company, 1987), 78–79.
61 David Hume, *A Treatise of Human Nature*, ed. L. A. Selby-Bigge, 2nd edn, rev. by P. H. Nidditch (Oxford: Clarendon Press, 1980), 234 ("Of the immateriality of the soul," I, iv, no. 5).
62 Johnson defines "soul" as (1) The immaterial and immortal spirit of man; (2) vital principle; (3) spirit, essence, quintessence, principal part; (4) interiour power; (5) a familiar appellation expressing the qualities of the mind; (6) human being; (7) active power; (8) spirit, fire, grandeur of mind; (9) intelligent being in general.
63 See *Life*, I, 342, and, e.g., Robert De Maria, *The Life of Samuel Johnson: A Critical Biography* (Oxford: Blackwell, 1993), 211.
64 Cf. Hinnant, *Samuel Johnson*, 101–02.
65 James Boyd White, *Heracles' Bow: Essays on the Rhetoric and Poetics of the Law* (Madison: University of Wisconsin Press, 1985), 98.
66 Hume, "On the Immortality of the Soul," in *Essays Moral, Political, and Literary* (Oxford University Press, 1963 and 1974), 603, and Johnson, *Rambler* 125, IV, 300.
67 *Rasselas*, 68.
68 *Adventurer* No. 107, 441.
69 *Shakespeare*, I, 60.
70 "To judge rightly of the present we must oppose it to the past; for all judgment is comparative, and of the future nothing can be known;" *Rasselas*, 73.
71 "Of Experience," *Essays of Montaigne*, trans. Charles Cotton, 3 vols. (London, 1700), III, 466.
72 *Rambler*, 41, III, 223.
73 Alexander Welsh, *Strong Representations: Narrative and Circumstantial Evidence in England* (Baltimore: Johns Hopkins University Press, 1992), 8.
74 For the eighteenth-century novel in the context of the relations of law to literature, see John Bender, *Imagining the Penitentiary* (University of Chicago Press, 1987) and Zomchick, *Family and the Law*.
75 *Analogy of Religion* (London, 1736), 399.
76 See Leo Damrosch, *Fictions of Reality in the Age of Hume and Johnson* (Madison: University of Wisconsin Press, 1989), ch. 1.
77 Chapters 1–3 of R. M. Burns, *The Great Debate on Miracles: From Joseph Glanvill to David Hume* (Lewisburg: Bucknell University Press, 1981), deals with the background and the terms of the debate.

78 Hume, *Essay*, ed. Eric Steinberg (Indianapolis: Hackett Publishing Company, 1977), 76.
79 See Damrosch, *Fictions of Reality*, 31–42.
80 See *Life*, I, 443–45; II, 104–07; III, 153–4.
81 James E. Force, "Hume and Johnson on Prophecy and Miracles: Historical Context," *JHI*, 43 (1982), 463–75.
82 See also William Windham's report that "With respect to evidence, Dr. Johnson observed that we had not such evidence that Caesar died in the Capitol, as that Christ died in the manner related;" *JM*, II, 384.
83 David Hume, "Of the Poems of Ossian," in *David Hume: Philosophical Historian*, ed. David Fate Norton and Richard H. Popkin (Indianapolis: Bobbs-Merrill, 1965), 389–400. Although Gibbon was no antiquarian, he uses similar "scientific" standards of evidence in defending his critical view of Christianity in chapters 15 and 16 of the *Decline and Fall*; see Arnoldo Momigliano, "Gibbon's Contribution to Historical Method," in *Studies in Historiography* (New York: Harper & Row, 1966), 40–41.
84 See *Journey*, 117–19; *Life*, II, 296–98. For Macpherson's own critique of issues of evidence, see Matthew Wickman, "The Allure of the Improbable: *Fingal*, Evidence, and the Testimony of the 'Echoing Heath,'" *PMLA*, 115 (2000), 181–94.
85 *Essay*, 98. In the Introduction to the *Treatise* Hume reflects on the claims of earlier philosophers to knowledge of which the mind is simply incapable (xviii).
86 See *Treatise*, I, iv, 5; and the two essays "On the Immortality of the Soul" and "Of Suicide."
87 *Rambler*, 14, III, 75.
88 Boswell's interview with Hume took place on 3 March 1777; see *Boswell in Extremes, 1776–1778*, ed. Charles McC. Weis and Frederick A. Pottle (New York: McGraw Hill Book Company, 1970), 11–15.
89 See also the letter from Adam Smith to William Strahan recounting Hume's attitude towards death in August 1776, a few days before he died, in Hume's *Dialogues Concerning Natural Religion*, ed. N. K. Smith (Oxford: Clarendon Press, 1935), 244–45.
90 *Life*, II, 106; III, 153.
91 By all accounts Johnson met his own death with fortitude and poise; see *Life*, IV, 415–18, and (among many others) Thomas Tyers, "A Biographical Sketch of Dr. Samuel Johnson (1785)," in *EB*, 63.
92 *Rambler*, 78, IV, 47.
93 The tone of the memoir is struck by Hume's closing words: "I cannot say there is no vanity in making this funeral oration of myself, but I hope it is not a misplaced one; and this is a matter of fact which is easily cleared and ascertained;" "Life of the Author By Himself," in *Essays*, 616.
94 Mossner, *The Life of David Hume* (Oxford: Clarendon Press, 1954), 606.
95 *Strong Representations*, 8.
96 *Hebrews* 11:1.

97 Kim Scheppele, "Foreword: Telling Stories," *Michigan Law Review*, 87 (1989), 2073, quoted in Robert Weisberg, "Proclaiming Trials as Narratives: Premises and Pretenses," in *Law's Stories*, 68.
98 See Parker, *Augustan Poetics*, ch. 7. In 1776 Boswell records Johnson distinguishing between the belief typical of the ancient philosophers and of Christianity: "Those only who believed in revelation have been angry at having their faith called in question; because they only had something upon which they could rest as matter of fact;" *Life*, III, 11.
99 Cf. Damrosch, *Fictions of Reality*, 23.
100 *Practicing Enlightenment: Hume and the Formations of a Literary Career* (Madison: University of Wisconsin Press, 1987), 49.
101 Adam Smith, *Theory of Moral Sentiments*, ed. A. L. Macfie and D. D. Raphael (Indianapolis: Liberty Press, 1982), III, 1.3. For spectatorship in Smith's moral theory, see Charles L. Griswold, Jr., *Adam Smith and the Virtues of Enlightenment* (Cambridge University Press, 1999), 104–09, and David Marshall, *The Figure of Theatre: Shaftesbury, Defoe, Adam Smith, and George Eliot* (New York: Columbia University Press, 1986), 167–92.
102 See Susan Manning, *The Puritan–Provincial Vision: Scottish and American Literature in the Nineteenth Century* (Cambridge University Press, 1990), 38–46.
103 Mark Temmer, *Samuel Johnson and Three Infidels* (Athens, GA: University of Georgia Press, 1988), 108.
104 See Terence Penelhum on the "complex and serious reality . . . at work" beneath a "deliberately assumed persona"; "Hume's Moral Psychology," in *The Cambridge Companion to Hume*, ed. David Fate Norton (Cambridge University Press, 1993), 119.
105 See Stanley Fish, *Is There a Text in This Class? The Authority of Interpretive Communities* (Cambridge, MA: Harvard University Press, 1980), 318.
106 Cf. Damrosch, *Fictions of Reality*, 35–38, and Manning, who sees the "sheer riskiness of the wit" of Hume's turn to nature as "reveal[ing] the extent of Hume's self-possession as he accommodates human reasoning to the irrational extremities of experience" (*Puritan–Provincial Vision*, 46).
107 See *Life*, 502–03, *Letters* I, 78–80, Chapin, *Religious Thought*, 84–88, and, for the immediate response to Hume on miracles, Burns, *Great Debate*, ch. 8. Dr. Adams' report that Hume had complimented him on his civil treatment of Hume's *Essay*, stimulates Johnson's retort that, "When a man voluntarily engages in an important controversy, he is to do all he can to lessen his antagonist... **Adams**. 'You would not jostle a chimney-sweeper.' **Johnson**. 'Yes, Sir, if it were necessary to jostle him *down*'" (*Life*, 692).
108 Donald T. Siebert, "Johnson and Hume on Miracles," *JHI*, 36 (1975), 546.
109 For Johnson and Swift, see Paul J. Korshin, "Johnson and Swift: A Study in the Genesis of Literary Opinion," *PQ*, 48 (1969), 464–78; and Isobel Grundy, *Samuel Johnson and the Scale of Greatness* (Leicester University Press, 1986), ch. 3.

4 NARRATIVE, HISTORY, AND MEMORY IN THE *LIVES OF THE POETS*

1 See, e.g., "Ramblers" 2, 8, 17, 24, 29, and 41, and "Idlers" 44, 72, and 74.
2 See, e.g., Peter Brooks, *Psychoanalysis and Storytelling* (Oxford: Blackwell, 1994), esp. ch. 3.
3 See, e.g., Ralph W. Rader, "Literary Form in Factual Narrative: The Example of Boswell's *Johnson*," in *Boswell's "Life of Johnson": New Questions, New Answers*, ed. John Vance (Athens, GA: University of Georgia Press, 1985), 25–52; and, in general, Ira Bruce Nadel, *Biography: Fact, Fiction & Form* (New York: St. Martin's Press, 1984), esp. ch. 5; *Contesting the Subject: Essays in the Postmodern Theory and Practice of Biography and Biographical Criticism*, ed. William H. Epstein (West Lafayette: Purdue University Press, 1991).
4 *Idler*, No. 84, 262.
5 See Isobel Grundy, "Samuel Johnson: A Writer of Lives Looks at Death," *MLR*, 79 (1984), 257–65.
6 See Mark Salber Phillips, *Society and Sentiment: Genres of Historical Writing in Britain, 1740–1820* (Princeton University Press, 2000).
7 Richard Holmes, "Biography: Inventing the Truth," in *The Art of Literary Biography*, ed. John Batchelor (Oxford: Clarendon Press, 1989), 20.
8 See, e.g., Barbara Foley, *Telling the Truth: The Theory and Practice of Documentary Fiction* (Ithaca: Cornell University Press, 1986); Lionel Gossman, "History and Literature: Reproduction or Signification," in *The Writing of History: Literary Form and Historical Understanding*, ed. Robert H. Canary and Henry Kozicki (Madison: University of Wisconsin Press, 1978), 3–39; J. Hillis Miller, "Narrative and History," *ELH*, 41 (1974), 455–73; William B. Warner, "The Elevation of the Novel in England: Hegemony and Literary History," *ELH*, 59 (1992), 577–96; and Everett Zimmerman, *The Boundaries of Fiction: History and the Eighteenth-Century Novel* (Ithaca: Cornell University Press, 1996).
9 See, e.g., J. Paul Hunter, *Before Novels: The Cultural Contexts of Eighteenth-Century English Fiction* (New York: W. W. Norton, 1990), esp. ch. 14.
10 See, e.g., Arnoldo Momigliano, "Gibbon's Contribution to Historical Method," in *Studies in Historiography*, 40–55.
11 See Douglas Lane Patey, *Probability and Literary Form: Philosophic Theory and Literary Practice in the Augustan Age* (Cambridge University Press, 1984), 213.
12 Jules David Law, *The Rhetoric of Empiricism: Language and Perception from Locke to I.A. Richards* (Ithaca: Cornell University Press, 1993), 12.
13 See Joel Weinsheimer, "Fiction and the Force of Example," in *The Idea of the Novel in the Eighteenth Century*, ed. Robert W. Uphaus (East Lansing: Colleagues Press, 1988), 1–20.
14 The quotation is parsed from Joseph Bartolomeo, *A New Species of Criticism: Eighteenth-Century Discourse on the Novel* (Newark, DE: University of Delaware Press, 1994), 78, emphasizing Johnson's "narrowly didactic criteria" (82) in discussing fiction, but it is echoed by others.
15 "Life of Young," *Lives*, II, 16.

16 The attribution was made by Rev. John Mitford in the *Gentleman's Magazine*, n.s. 20 (1843), 132 and n.s. 21 (1844), 42. See Duncan Isles, "Johnson and Charlotte Lennox," *The New Rambler*, 3 (June 1967), 34–48, and his appendix to the edition of the novel, ed. Margaret Dalziel (Oxford University Press, 1988), 419–22; see also Carey McIntosh, *The Choice of Life: Samuel Johnson and the World of Fiction* (New Haven, CT: Yale University Press, 1972), 14–23. Critics use Johnson's possible authorship to attack his supposed patriarchal ideology towards fiction; see, e.g., Margaret Anne Doody's introduction to the edition mentioned above (xi–xxii); and Patricia Meyer Spacks, *Desire and Truth: Functions of Plot in Eighteenth-Century English Novels* (University of Chicago Press, 1990), 20–24.

17 See *Life*, I, 49; III, 2; and Eithne Henson, *"The Fictions of Romantick Chivalry": Samuel Johnson and Romance* (Rutherford: Fairleigh Dickinson University Press, 1992).

18 See Zimmerman, *Boundaries of Fiction*, 44.

19 Henry St. John, Viscount Bolingbroke, "Letters on the Study and Use of History" (1752), in *Miscellaneous Works*, 4 vols. (Edinburgh, 1768), I, 71. See D. J. Womersley, "Lord Bolingbroke and Eighteenth-Century Historiography," *ECTI*, 28 (1987), 217–34.

20 William Godwin, "Of History and Romance" (*c*. 1797), appendix 4 to *Caleb Williams*, ed. Maurice Hindle (New York: Penguin, 1988), 367, 370.

21 See *Life*, I, 268; and "Life of Mallet," *Lives*, III, 407.

22 For the relations of life-writing to history in the seventeenth century, see Robert Mayer, *History and the Early English Novel: Matters of Fact from Bacon to Defoe* (Cambridge University Press, 1997), chs. 4 and 9; and Zimmerman, *Boundaries*, 24–25.

23 See John A. Vance, *Samuel Johnson and the Sense of History* (Athens, GA: University of Georgia Press, 1984).

24 See R. G. Collingwood, *The Idea of History*, ed. Jan Van Der Dussen, rev. edn (Oxford University Press, 1994), 134–204; and Ernst Breisach, *Historiography: Ancient, Medieval, and Modern*, 2nd edn (University of Chicago Press, 1994), chs. 14–16.

25 See Joseph Levine, *Humanism and History: Origins of Modern English Historiography* (Ithaca: Cornell University Press, 1987), 123–54; Momigliano, "Ancient History and the Antiquarian," in *Studies in Historiography*, 1–39; and Mayer, *History and the Early English Novel*, 20–33.

26 See Francis Bacon, *Selected Writings*, ed. Hugh G. Dick (New York: Random House, 1955), 183–84, 234–45.

27 *Rambler*, 137, IV, 362. Johnson paraphrases Bacon's essay "Of Studies."

28 He commends Clarendon for "his knowledge of nature and of policy; the wisdom of his maxims, the justness of his reasonings, and the variety, distinctness, and strength of his characters," IV, 290.

29 See Vance, *Sense of History*, 158–72. Hume's *History of Great Britain* appeared in 1754–61, Robertson's *History of Scotland* in 1759, his *History of Charles V* in 1769, his *History of America* in 1777, Gibbon's *Decline and Fall* in 1776–88, and

David Ramsay's *History of the American Revolution* in 1789. Voltaire's *L'Histoire de Charles XII* was published in 1731, but *Le Siecle de Louis XIV* (1751) and *Essai sur les moeurs* (1754) post-date the *Rambler*. Bolingbroke's *Letters on the Study of History* (written 1735–38) was published in 1752; and Lord Hailes' *Annals of Scotland* in 1776–79.

30 See Mayer, *History and the Early English Novel*, 11.
31 Richard Knolles, *History of the Turks* (1603).
32 *Lives*, I, 170; see Vance, *Sense of History*, 160.
33 See Mayer, *History and the Early English Novel*, chs. 9 and 10.
34 "Joseph Conrad," in *The Craft of Literary Biography*, 72; see also Karl Miller, *Authors* (Oxford: Clarendon Press, 1989), 182.
35 See James Battersby, "Life, Art, and the *Lives of the Poets*," in *Domestick Privacies: Samuel Johnson and the Art of Biography*, ed. David Wheeler (Lexington: University Press of Kentucky, 1987), 32–33.
36 Stanley Fish, "Biography and Intention," in *Contesting the Subject*, ed. Epstein, 9–16.
37 For the function of death and human limitation in the *Lives* see Robert Folkenflik, *Samuel Johnson, Biographer* (Ithaca: Cornell University Press, 1978), ch. 3; and Isobel Grundy, *Samuel Johnson and the Scale of Greatness* (Leicester University Press, 1986), ch. 11, and "Samuel Johnson: A Writer of Lives Looks at Death," ibid.
38 For Johnson's tragic view of life, see Leopold Damrosch, *Samuel Johnson and the Tragic Sense* (Princeton University Press, 1972), ch. 4; and Folkenflik, *Samuel Johnson*, ch. 3.
39 "Life of Dryden," *Lives*, I, 373.
40 "Life of Smith," *Lives*, II, 20–21.
41 "Life of Dryden," *Lives*, I, 408–9.
42 "Life of Pope," *Lives*, III, 189–90.
43 See White, "The Value of Narrativity in the Representation of Reality," in *Content of the Form*, 20.
44 See also Joshua Foa Dienstag, *Dancing in Chains: Narrative and Memory in Political Theory* (Stanford University Press, 1997), Introduction.
45 Lawrence Lipking, *The Life of the Poet: Beginning and Ending Poetic Careers* (University of Chicago Press, 1981), ix.
46 *Rambler*, 14, III, 75, 76.
47 Louis O. Mink, "Narrative Form as a Cognitive Instrument," in *Historical Understanding*, ed. Brian Fay, Eugene O. Golob, and Richard T. Vann (Ithaca: Cornell University Press, 1987), 198.
48 See Alvin Kernan, *Samuel Johnson and the Impact of Print* (Princeton University Press, 1987), ch. 5.
49 See Jonathan Brody Kramnick, "The Making of the English Canon," *PMLA*, 112 (1997), 1087–101, who mistakenly assimilates Johnson to the critics mentioned solely on the basis of his appreciation of Shakespeare's generality.
50 For Johnson on Richardson and Fielding, see, e.g., Robert E. Moore, "Dr. Johnson on Fielding and Richardson," *PMLA*, 66 (1951), 162–81;

McIntosh, *Choice of Life*, 23–29; and Mark Kinkead-Weekes, "Johnson on 'The Rise of the Novel,'" in *Samuel Johnson: New Critical Essays*, ed. Isobel Grundy (London and Totowa: Vision and Barnes & Noble, 1984), 70–85.

51 Boswell's response to Johnson's use of the clock metaphor reverses the application that usually privileges Richardson: "I cannot help being of the opinion, that the neat watches of Fielding are as well constructed as the large clocks of Richardson, and that his dial-plates are brighter. Fielding's characters, though they do not expand themselves so widely in dissertation, are as just pictures of human nature, and I will venture to say, have more striking features, and nicer touches of pencil"; *Life*, II, 49. For a brief history of the metaphor, see Jocelyn Harris, "Samuel Johnson, Samuel Richardson, and the Dial-Plate," *BJECS*, 9 (1986), 157–63.

52 Michael McKeon discusses how the *Life* "captures ... a general cultural type that the novel has been undertaking to represent for the better part of a century"; "Writer as Hero: Novelistic Prefigurations and the Emergence of Literary Biography," in *Contesting the Subject*, ed. Epstein, 33.

53 Ralph W. Rader, "The Emergence of the Novel in England: Genre in History vs. History of Genre," *Narrative*, 1 (1993), 76.

54 "Life of Pomfret," *Lives*, I, 302; "Life of Congreve," *Lives*, II, 230.

55 "Dryden is 'always another and the same'; he does not exhibit a second time the same elegances in the same form, nor appears to have any art other than that of expressing with clearness what he thinks with vigour"; "Life of Dryden," *Lives*, I, 418.

56 *Criticism in the Wilderness*, 201.

57 "Life of Gay," *Lives*, II, 27.

58 See James L. Clifford, *Dictionary Johnson: The Middle Years of Samuel Johnson* (London: Heinemann, 1978), 57–70.

59 See the reviews by Edmund Cartwright, William Cowper, Francis Blackburne, Robert Potter, Anna Seward, Joseph Towers, and Thomas de Quincey, in *Johnson: The Critical Heritage*, ed. James T. Boulton (London: Routledge & Kegan Paul, 1971), 260, 273, 274, 278, 281, 296–97, 311–12, 378, and 313–15.

60 See "Samuel Johnson," in *Macaulay's Essays*, intro. Hugh Trevor-Roper (London: Collins, 1965), 108.

61 See Robert J. Griffin, *Wordsworth's Pope: A Study in Literary Historiography* (Cambridge University Press, 1995), ch. 1 and passim.

62 T. S. Eliot, "Milton I" (1936) and "Milton II" (1947) in *On Poetry and Poets* (London: Faber & Faber, 1957); F. R. Leavis, "Milton's Verse," in *Revaluation: Tradition and Development in English Poetry* (London: Chatto & Windus, 1936).

63 "Life of Milton," *Lives*, I, 172; citations by paragraph number included parenthetically.

64 The quotation comes from Milton's *Areopagitica*, in *Complete Prose Works of John Milton*, ed. Don Wolfe, 10 vols. (New Haven, CT: Yale University Press, 1959–82), II, ed. Ernest Sirluck (1959), 487.

65 *Rambler*, 14, III, 74. On 24 March 1658 Milton wrote to Emeric Bigot that "I will endeavour to seem equal in thought and speech to what I have well written . . . I shall not seem to have borrowed the excellence of my literary compositions from others so much as to have drawn it pure and unmingled from the resources of my own mind and the force of my own conceptions"; *Prose Works of John Milton*, ed. J.A. St. John, 3 vols. (London: Henry Bohn, 1848), 512.
66 For the lives by John Aubrey, John Phillips, Anthony á Wood, Edward Phillips, John Toland, and Jonathan Richardson, see *The Early Lives of Milton*, ed. Helen Darbishire (London: Constable, 1932).
67 See, e.g., Dustin Griffin, *Regaining Paradise: Milton and the Eighteenth Century* (Cambridge University Press, 1986).
68 For the genesis of the *Lives*, see T. F. Bonnell, "John Bell's *Poets of Great Britain*: The 'Little Trifling Edition' Revisited," *MP*, 85 (1987), 128–52.
69 See Lipking, *Ordering*, 434–42; Grundy, *Scale of Greatness*, 206–32; Folkenflik, *Samuel Johnson*, 165–70; and Stephen Fix, "Distant Genius: Johnson and the Art of Milton's Life," *MP*, 81 (1984), 244–64, "Johnson and the 'Duty' of Reading *Paradise Lost*," *ELH*, 52 (1985), 649–71, and "The Contexts and Motives of Johnson's *Life of Milton*" in *Domestick Privacies*, 107–32.
70 See, e.g.: "'Let us not,' says his last ingenious biographer [i.e. Percival Stockdale], 'condemn him with untempered severity, because he was not the poet, the orator, and the hero'"; "Life of Waller," *Lives*, I, 267.
71 The quotation is Warburton's, see *John Milton, 1732–1801: The Critical Heritage*, ed. John T. Shawcross (London: Routledge & Kegan Paul, 1972), 90–92.
72 The quotation is Macaulay's, *Literary Essays Contributed to the Edinburgh Review* (London, 1925), 25.
73 David Loewenstein and James Grantham Turner, "Introduction: 'Labouring in the Word,'" in *Politics, Poetics, and Hermeneutics in Milton's Prose: Essays*, ed. David Loewenstein and James Grantham Turner (Cambridge University Press, 1990), 3.
74 Kerrigan, "Milton's Place in Intellectual History," in *The Cambridge Companion to Milton*, ed. Dennis Danielson, 2nd edn. (Cambridge University Press, 1999), 259.
75 Nicholas von Maltzahn, "Milton's Readers," in *Companion to Milton*, 238.
76 For the common grammar school curriculum of the early seventeenth-century, see Foster Watson, *The English Grammar Schools to 1660* (Cambridge University Press, 1908), and Donald L. Clark, *John Milton at St. Paul's School* (New York: Columbia University Press, 1948).
77 See Johnson's Preface to Robert Dodsley's *Preceptor* (1748), in *P&D*, 171–89.
78 See the introductory remarks to "Of Education" by Donald C. Dorian, *Prose Works*, II, 357–415.
79 *Prose Works*, II, 368–69.
80 *Prose Works*, II, 396. For Milton's curriculum in detail, see II, 195, n58.
81 See Sigmund Freud, "Repression" (1915), in *General Psychological Theory: Papers on Metapsychology*, ed. Philip Rieff (New York: Collier, 1963), 104–15.

82 Johnson once draws attention to the similarity between Milton's long hair and Adam's, as described in *Paradise Lost*, but this is in the section given to a description of Milton's physical appearance (para. 157), and he never goes so far, as does Thomas Newton, as to suggest that Adam and Eve were modelled on Milton and his wife; see Newton's edition of *Paradise Lost*, 4th edn, 2 vols. (1757), I, 281–82, note to Bk. IV, 305.
83 Henry James, "The Art of Fiction," in *The Art of Fiction and Other Essays*, introduction by Morris Roberts (New York: Oxford University Press, 1948), 21–22.
84 Johnson's first illustration of "pregnant" ("teeming, breeding") in the *Dictionary* are these lines from *Paradise Lost*.
85 Johnson may also have been remembering Milton's appropriation of King Charles' use of "pregnant" in *Eikon Basilike*: Charles "*wanted not such probabilities* (for his pregnant is now come to probable) *as were sufficient to raise jealousies in any Kings heart*"; *Prose Works*, III, 379.
86 Cf. Martine Watson Brownley, "Johnson's *Lives of the English Poets* and the Earlier Traditions of the Character Sketch in England," in *Johnson and His Age*, ed. James Engell (Cambridge, MA: Harvard University Press, 1984), 51; and Lipking, *Ordering*, 438.
87 René Le Bossu, *Traité du Poeme Epique* (Paris, 1675).
88 For Johnson's view that "poetical devotion cannot often please," see "Life of Waller," *Lives*, I, 291–92; "Life of Cowley," *Lives*, I, 49–50; and "Life of Watts," *Lives*, III, 310.
89 *The Spectator*, 8 vols. (London, 1733), No. 273, IV, 90–91.
90 Hume thought otherwise, *History of England*, 6 vols. (Indianapolis: Liberty Fund, 1983), VI, 151.
91 *Spectator*, No. 297, IV, 179.
92 A main proposition of Hagstrum's *Johnson's Literary Criticism*, esp. ch. 7.
93 *Johnson's Dictionary*, 121–22. Reddick notes that "Milton overwhelms even Shakespeare as the most imposing presence and most persuasive voice" (123) in the *Dictionary*, and hence disagrees with De Maria that "the Poet of the *Dictionary* is Pope" (223, n. 6).
94 Speaking to Boswell on 30 April 1773, Johnson said that "I think more highly of him [Milton] now than I did at twenty"; *Life*, II, 239.
95 Addison, *Spectator*, No. 297, IV, 178; Dennis, "The Grounds of Criticism in Poetry" (1704), *The Critical Works of John Dennis*, ed. Edward N. Hooker, 2 vols. (Baltimore: Johns Hopkins University Press, 1939–43), I, 333–34.
96 Leslie E. Moore argues that "when the eighteenth century wished to discern the sublimity that made Milton's poem 'divine' in a positive sense, they turned ... to Adam and his world," *Beautiful Sublime: The Making of "Paradise Lost," 1701–1734* (Stanford University Press, 1990), 30–31.
97 Dryden, "To the Most Honourable ... Earl of Mulgrave; Prefixed to the *Aeneis*," Watson, II, 233.
98 Preface to *Fables*, Watson, II, 290.
99 Johnson paraphrases Raphael's speech in *Rambler*, 180 (V, 183), and applies this "angelick counsel" to the social situation of the writer.

100 Burke's thesis is that the "passion caused by the great and the sublime in nature . . . is Astonishment; and astonishment is that state of the soul, in which all its motions are suspended, with some degree of horror. In this case the mind is so entirely filled with its object, that it cannot entertain any other, nor by consequence reason on that object which employs it"; *A Philosophical Enquiry into the Origin of our Ideas of the Sublime and Beautiful* (1759), ed. Adam Phillips (Oxford University Press, 1992), 53. In "The Grounds of Criticism in Poetry" John Dennis also locates the source of the sublime in the fear of the religious.

101 For the sublime in the eighteenth century, see Samuel Holt Monk, *The Sublime: A Study of Critical Theories in XVIII-Century England* (1935; Ann Arbor: University of Michigan Press, 1960).

102 Of Adam's love poetry, Voltaire says that Milton "soars not above human, but above corrupt, nature; and as there is no instance of such love, there is none of such poetry"; *An Essay Upon the Civil Wars of France* (1727), in *Paradise Lost: An Authoritative Text, Backgrounds and Sources Criticism*, ed. Scott Elledge, 2nd edn (New York: W. W. Norton & Co., 1993), 478–79.

103 *Ramblers* 86, 88, 90, 92, and 94. Johnson also quotes Milton strategically in *Ramblers* 3, 8, 36, 78, 110, 121, 135, 170 and 180, in *Idlers* 31, 49, and 61, and *Adventurers* 39 and 102. *Samson Agonistes* is the subject of *Ramblers* 139 and 140.

104 *Rambler*, 92, IV, 124–25. Dennis uses *Paradise Lost*, Bk. 8 to support his notion of ideal poetry in the *Advancement and Reformation of Modern Poetry* (*Critical Works*, I, 215), although Virgil, not Homer, is taken as the Classical standard. Dennis sees Milton as superior to Virgil because of his Christianity (I, 271).

105 "On Education," in *Prose Works*, III, 473.

106 *Poems of John Milton*, ed. John Carey and Alistair Fowler (London: Longman, 1968 and 1980), 456.

107 Johnson's objection to *Samson Agonistes* lies mainly in its failure as a drama, especially as compared with Shakespeare's plays, but he finds that the work has "many particular beauties," and that there are "many just sentiments and striking lines" (paras. 266–68).

108 Edward Young, *Conjectures on Original Composition* (1759). Facsimile of 1st edition (Leeds: Scolar Press, 1966), 84.

109 "Life of Akenside," *Lives*, III, 417.

110 *Rambler*, 138, IV, 364.

111 "Life of Waller," *Lives*, I, 269–70; "Life of Dryden," *Lives*, I, 334.

112 *Rambler*, 89, IV, 108.

113 *Rambler*, 89, IV, 108–09.

114 See, for e.g., Charles Martindale, *John Milton and the Transformation of Ancient Epic* (Totowa, NJ: Barnes and Noble, 1986); Michael Wilding, "The Last of the Epics: The Rejection of the Heroic in *Paradise Lost* and *Hudibras*," in *Restoration Literature: Critical Approaches*, ed. Harold Love (London: Methuen, 1972), 91–120; and Michael Wilding, *The Last of the Epics* (Oxford University Press, 1987).

115 "Life of Butler," *Lives*, I, 201; subsequent references by paragraph number included parenthetically.
116 See *Butler: Hudibras*, ed. John Wilders (Oxford University Press, 1967), Pt. I; Michael Wilding, "Samuel Butler at Barbourne," *NQ*, n.s. 13 (1966), 15–19; and E. S. de Beer, "The Later Life of Samuel Butler," *RES*, 4 (1928), 159–66.
117 The publication date of Part III is problematic; see *Hudibras*, ed. John Wilders, xliv–xlviii.
118 Earl Miner, *The Restoration Mode from Milton to Dryden* (Princeton University Press, 1974), 158.
119 See Peter Stallybrass and Allon White, *The Politics and Poetics of Transgression* (Ithaca: Cornell University Press, 1986), ch. 5.
120 *Hudibras, In Three Parts*, With Annotations etc., by Zachery Grey, 2 vols. (Cambridge, 1744).
121 Miner, *Restoration Mode*, 196 and 158–97 generally.
122 Parker, *Augustan Poetics*, 25–60.
123 Dryden, "A Discourse Concerning... Satire," Watson, II, 147; Addison, *Spectator* 249 (15 December 1711).
124 *The Mystery of the Charity of Charles Peguy*, from Geoffrey Hill, *Collected Poems* (Harmondsworth: Penguin, 1985), 185.
125 See Greg Clingham, "Life and Literature in Johnson's *Lives of the Poets*," *Companion*, 186–89.
126 *Letters*, I, 45–46.
127 *DPA*, 46–47.
128 See Mary Lascelles, "Johnson and Commemorative Writing," in *Samuel Johnson: New Critical Essays*, ed. Isobel Grundy (London and Totowa, NJ: Vision and Barnes & Noble, 1984), 186–202.
129 See Folkenflik, *Samuel Johnson*, 97–99; and Reed Whittemore, *Pure Lives: The Early Biographers* (Baltimore: Johns Hopkins University Press, 1988), chs. 1–2.
130 "Life of Addison," *Lives*, II, 125.
131 Young, *Conjectures*, 99–108.
132 *Reflections on Biography* (Oxford University Press, 1999), 8.
133 "Life of Waller," *Lives*, I, 291.
134 Hill, *Collected Poems*, 196.
135 "Value of Narrativity in the Representation of Reality," in *Content of the Form*, 13.

5 TRANSLATION AND MEMORY IN THE *LIVES OF THE POETS*

1 See H. A. Mason, *Humanism and Poetry in the Early Tudor Period* (London: Routledge & Kegan Paul, 1959), and Greg Clingham, "Johnson, Homeric Scholarship, and 'The Passes of the Mind,'" *AJ*, 3 (1990), 113–70.
2 See *Letters*, III, 124.
3 "Life of Dryden," *Lives*, I, 411, para. 196.
4 "Life of Pope," *Lives*, III, 223, para. 311.

5 See *DPA*, 303–04; however, neither the *Prefaces*, nor the 1781 or 1783 editions of the *Lives* placed "Pope" last.
6 The formal comparison constitutes a mini-genre, including Dryden's comparison of Jonson with Shakespeare in "Of Dramatick Poesy" (1668) and Juvenal with Horace in "A Discourse Concerning... Satire" (1693), and Pope's comparison of Homer with Virgil in the Preface (1715) to his translation of the *Iliad*; see P. J. Smallwood, "Johnson's Life of Pope and Pope's Preface to the *Iliad*," *NQ*, n.s. 225 (1980), 50.
7 The phrase is Matthew Arnold's when introducing the *Six Chief Lives from Johnson's "Lives of the Poets"* (1878); *Selected Criticism of Matthew Arnold*, ed. Christopher Ricks (New York: Signet, 1972), 351.
8 Damrosch (*Uses*, 168–69), Osborn (*John Dryden*, 25, 28), and Lipking (*Ordering*, 443) see Johnson's scholarship on Dryden as derivative, and paucity of information as necessitating his choices. My point, however, is that Johnson would have emphasized the relationship between mind and text as the most appropriate way of understanding Dryden's poetry, no matter how much new biographical information he had; see Clingham, "Another and the Same," in *Literary Transmission and Authority*, 121–60.
9 For which, see Geoffrey Hill, *The Enemy's Country: Words, Contexture, and Other Circumstances of Language* (Stanford University Press, 1991).
10 From Boswell we learn that the two men are Colley Cibber and Owen MacSwinney (*Life*, III, 72). For Dryden at Will's, see James A. Winn, *John Dryden and His World* (New Haven, CT: Yale University Press, 1987), 130–31 and 138–39.
11 Preface to *Fables*, Watson, II, 290. Johnson quotes Joseph Trapp (*Lectures on English Poetry* [1742], 348) on the wrongness of Dryden's point (para. 202); yet even Trapp's observation conveys a sense of Dryden's empathic connection with his material ("What was in hand was generally most in esteem").
12 See also "Life of Dryden," paras. 196, 200, 221, 227, 334, and "Life of Pope," paras. 309.
13 Paul Hammond, *John Dryden and the Traces of Classical Rome* (Oxford University Press, 1999), 19.
14 Dryden himself describes prose and poetry as two manifestations of one "harmony;" Preface to *Fables*, Watson, II, 272.
15 Biographers have written variously of Dryden's change of sensibility in the 1680s, and the paradox that, while he was engaged in the last stages of the reflections which were to lead to his conversion to Catholicism, he was also composing a series of poems [i.e. *Sylvae*] which are unashamedly pagan in inspiration; see Clingham, "Another and the Same," in *Literary Transmission and Authority*, 113 and 144–50.
16 The Dedication to *Aureng-Zebe* is the first time that Montaigne is mentioned by Dryden, as representing a profound attitude towards the porousness and materiality of human nature; Dryden: *Works*, V, 186.
17 Johnson draws on the writing of both Pope and Addison in making his point: Pope's portrait of Addison ("Atticus") in the *Epistle to Dr. Arbuthnot* contains

the lines: "Should such a man, too fond to rule alone, / Bear, like the *Turk*, no brother near the throne" (lines 197–98); and Johnson's "rivals in the Roman state" perhaps has in mind the tragic impasse in which Addison's Cato and Caesar find themselves, in which "Cato / Disdains a life which he has power to offer" (*Cato*, II. ii; *Miscellaneous Works*, 3 vols. (1753), II, 53 [no line numbers]).
18 Owen Ruffhead, *The Life of Alexander Pope* (London, 1769), 186–87.
19 See Tom Keymer, "Johnson and Epistolary Writing," in *Companion*, 225–26.
20 *The Correspondence of Alexander Pope*, ed. George Sherburn, 5 vols. (Oxford: Clarendon Press, 1956), I, 155–56.
21 For Pope's manipulation of the publication of his letters by Curll, see Maynard Mack, *Alexander Pope: A Life* (New Haven, CT: Yale University Press, 1985), 652–71.
22 See *The Works of Alexander Pope*, ed. Rev. Whitwell Elwin and J. C. Courthope, 10 vols. (London: John Murray, 1871–89), VI, xxi–xxxvi.
23 See Dustin H. Griffin, *Alexander Pope: The Poet in the Poems* (Princeton University Press, 1978), 12.
24 "*A Window in the Bosom:*" *The Letters of Alexander Pope* (Hamden: Archon Books, 1977), 40.
25 *Rambler*, 152, V, 45. Johnson is arguing against the prescriptions of William Walsh (*Letters and Poems, Amorous and Gallant*, 1692), and to demonstrate that "precept has generally been posterior to performance" (44).
26 "Johnson and Epistolary Writing," in *Companion*, 228.
27 Fussell sees "sardonic irony" in Johnson's words and believes that he explodes "the common myth that a genre like the letter . . . is thus a vehicle of genuine self-disclosure;" *Life of Writing*, 47.
28 "The Muse of Satire," *Yale Review*, 41 (1951), 80–92.
29 "Personae," in *Literary Meaning and Augustan Values* (Charlottesville: University Press of Virginia, 1974), 49–60.
30 *Epilogue to the Satires*, II, lines 197–98.
31 See, e.g., Judith Butler, *The Psychic Life of Power* (Stanford University Press, 1997), 1–30.
32 See Marjorie Hope Nicolson and George S. Rousseau, "*This Long Disease, My Life*": *Alexander Pope and the Sciences* (Princeton University Press, 1968); and J. V. Guerinot, *Pamphlet Attacks on Alexander Pope, 1711–1744: A Descriptive Bibliography* (London: Methuen, 1969).
33 Certain eighteenth-century texts drew similar attention to the connections of mind with body; to the notion, as Jonathan Richardson expresses it, that "Painting gives us not only the Persons, but the Characters of Great Men" (*An Essay of the Theory of Painting*, 2nd edn [1725], 10). For Johnson's reading of Richardson, see *Life*, I, 128, n. 2. See also Joshua Reynolds' *Discourses on Art*, No. 7 (10 December 1776).
34 Johnson enlarges and transforms a description of Pope in the *Gentleman's Magazine*, 45 (1775), 435.
35 See Helen Deutsch, *Resemblance and Disgrace: Alexander Pope and the Deformation of Culture* (Cambridge, MA: Harvard University Press, 1996), 33–35.

36 See John Wiltshire, *Samuel Johnson in the Medical World* (Cambridge University Press, 1991), esp. 29–32; and Helen Deutsch, "The Author as Monster: The Case of Dr. Johnson," in *"Defects" : Engendering the Modern Body*, ed. Helen Deutsch and Felicity Nussbaum (Ann Arbor: University of Michigan Press, 2000), esp. 192–202.
37 I cannot agree with Deutsch's designation of Johnson's description of Pope's material existence as "merciless;" see "Author as Monster," 178.
38 *The Body in Pain: The Making and Unmaking of the World* (Oxford University Press, 1985), 162.
39 Preface to *Poems* (1853); *Selected Criticism of Matthew Arnold*, ed. Christopher Ricks (New York: Signet, 1972), 28–29. See H. A. Mason, *The Tragic Plane* (Oxford: Clarendon Press, 1985), chs. 6–7.
40 "What is remembered in the body is well remembered"; Scarry, Body in Pain, 110 and 109–11.
41 "Author as Monster," 178; see also Lennard J. Davis, "Dr. Johnson, Amelia, and the Discourse of Disability," in *"Defects,"* 63.
42 Peter Brooks, *Body Work: Objects of Desire in Modern Narrative* (Cambridge, MA: Harvard University Press, 1993), 3.
43 Johnson here relies on Spence's information (*Observations, Anecdotes and Characters*, ed. James M. Osborn, 2 vols. [Oxford: Clarendon Press, 1966], I, 5–6). Johnson would also have known two accounts of Pope's physical being in relation to his sensibility: Reynolds' personal perception of Pope's face, "an appearance about his mouth which is found only in the deformed, and from which [one] could have known him to be deformed" (an anecdote actually collected by Boswell towards a biography of Reynolds; *Portraits by Sir Joshua Reynolds*, ed. F. W. Hilles [New York: McGraw Hill, 1952], 24), and Burke's parody of Bolingbroke in *Vindication of a Natural Society* (1756), entailing the depiction of Pope as one who "cannot bear every truth" for "he has a timidity which hinders the full exertion of his faculties almost as effectively as bigotry cramps those of the general herd of mankind" (*The Works of Edmund Burke*, 6 vols. [Oxford University Press, 1925], I, 38).
44 "The Storyteller," in *Illuminations*, trans. Harry Zohn, intro. Hannah Arendt (London: Fontana, 1979), 94.
45 See Susan Staves, "Pope's Refinement," *ECTI*, 29 (1988), 145–63.
46 See Christopher Ricks, "Samuel Johnson: Dead Metaphors and 'Impending Death,'" in *The Force of Poetry* (Oxford University Press, 1987), 80–88.
47 *Rambler*, 86, IV, 89; and 88, IV, 99.
48 *Rambler*, 92, IV, 124–25.
49 Johnson cites *Paradise Lost*, VII, lines 8–12 as that which he "could never read without some strong emotions of delight and admiration" (*Rambler*, 90, IV, 115).
50 Joseph Spence, *An Essay on Pope's Odyssey* (Oxford, 1726), 148–49.
51 "The Life of Alexander," *Plutarch's Lives, With Notes Historical and Critical from M. Dacier* [Dryden's translation], 8 vols. (London, 1727), VI, 6–7.
52 In writing of the problem of representation in music, Roger Scruton expands on Croce's aesthetics: "Extramusical thoughts certainly occur in the

appreciation of music... These extramusical thoughts have an 'ostensive' character, as though the music were making a gesture towards something that it cannot define... There is a peculiar 'reference without predication' that touches the heart, but numbs the tongue"; *The Aesthetics of Music* (Oxford: Clarendon Press, 1997), 132; see also ch. 6 on "expression."

53 See John Hollander on "Alexander's Feast" as a "true libretto, rather than merely... another in the series of commendatory odes"; "The Odes to Music," in *Dryden: A Collection of Critical Essays*, ed. Bernard N. Schilling (Englewood Cliffs: Prentice-Hall, 1963), 156.
54 See, e.g., Earl Miner, *Dryden's Poetry* (Bloomington: Indiana University Press, 1967), 273, 270.
55 See Hollander, "The Odes to Music," 163.
56 See Greg Clingham, "Johnson, Homeric Criticism, and 'the Passes of the Mind,'" *AJ*, 3 (1990), 113–70.
57 *An Essay on the Genius and Writings of Pope* [vol. 1] (1756).
58 9 April 1724; *Correspondence*, II, 227.
59 Winn suggests that Pope's love of Martha Blount was frustrated by the obstacle of his body; *Window in the Bosom*, 107–08. Cf. Valerie Rumbold, *Women's Place in Pope's World* (Cambridge University Press, 1989), 254–56.
60 See Felicity Rosslyn, "Of Gods and Men," *CQ*, 13 (1984), 1–20.
61 See Joseph Levine, *The Battle of the Books: History and Literature in the Augustan Age* (Ithaca: Cornell University Press, 1991), 121–47.
62 "Life of Waller," *Lives*, I, 295.
63 *Rambler*, 168, V, 128, 129.
64 "Life of Waller," *Lives*, I, 288. Waller has "heathens" and "Gods," *The Works* (Dublin, 1778), 7.
65 "Life of Waller," *Lives*, I, 295.
66 See Levine, *Battle of the Books*, Part I; and Howard D. Weinbrot, *Britannia's Issue: The Rise of British Literature from Dryden to Ossian* (Cambridge University Press, 1993), chs. 1–8.
67 See Kirsti Simonsuuri, *Homer's Original Genius: Eighteenth-Century Notions of Early Greek Epic (1688–1798)* (Cambridge University Press, 1979).
68 *Life*, II, 129.
69 Richard Bentley said to Pope, that: "'Tis a pretty poem Mr Pope, but it is not Homer", *TE*, IV, 346, for which see his nephew Thomas Bentley, *A Letter to Mr. Pope Occasioned by Sober Advice from Horace* (London, 1735), esp. 14. There are other eighteenth-century sources for the story; see Levine, *Battle of the Books*, 222.
70 See, e.g., Douglas Knight, *Pope and the Heroic Tradition: A Critical Study of his "Iliad"* (New Haven, CT: Yale University Press, 1951); Steven Shankman, *Pope's "Iliad:" Homer in the Age of Passion* (Princeton University Press, 1983); and Maynard Mack, Introduction to Pope's *Iliad*, *TE*, VII, xxxv–ccxlix.
71 See Levine, *Battle of the Books*, ch. 6.
72 Penelope Wilson's view that the most important development in eighteenth-century translation was in the move toward *prose*, stimulated by Dacier's

prose version of the *Iliad* (1711), underestimates the Dryden–Pope–Johnson nexus; see "Classical Poetry and the Eighteenth-Century Reader," in *Books and Their Readers in Eighteenth-Century England*, ed. Isobel Rivers (Leicester University Press, 1982), 80. Johnson regarded the French prose translations as mediocre (*Lives* of Pope [III, 237] and Dryden [I, 421–22]), and said to William Robertson: "Sir'... you could not read [the *Iliad*] without the pleasure of verse" (*Life*, III, 333).

73 Ghost-written by Addison; "Life of Tickell," *Lives*, II, 309.
74 For earlier versions, see Mack, *TE*, VII, cvii–clxiii.
75 Preface to the *Iliad*; *TE*, VII, 4.
76 *Rambler*, 92, IV, 124–25.
77 William Turnbull had invited Pope to "Make [Homer] speak good *English*, to dress his admirable characters in your proper, significant, and expressive conceptions, and make his works as useful and instructive to this degenerate age, as he was to our friend *Horace*"; Letter of 9 April 1708, *Correspondence*, I, 45–46.
78 Jacques Derrida, "Des Tour de Babel," trans. Joseph F. Graham, in *Difference in Translation*, ed. Joseph F. Graham (Ithaca: Cornell University Press, 1985), 184, 190–91.
79 See Levine, *Battle of the Books*, 192, 195–96; Norman Callan, *TE*, VII, lxxxiii–lxxxviii; and Knight, *Pope and the Heroic Tradition*, 111–13.
80 Cf. Patricia Ingham's notion of "elegance" as "the literary accuracy of images used in poetry"; "Dr. Johnson's 'Elegance,'" *RES*, n.s. 75 (1968), 271–78.
81 Steven Shankman, the only critic to discuss Johnson's criticism of Pope's *Iliad* at length, identifies the *value* of Pope's version with his linguistic and generic categories, and sees the critique as vitiated because it does not apply the requisite Renaissance and classic stylist principles; *Pope's "Iliad,"* 55–62, 65–66.
82 Charles Perrault, *Parallele des anciens et des modernes en ce qui regarde les arts et les sciences* (Paris, 1688–97); Antoine Houdar de La Motte, *Discours sur Homere* (1714); Abbe Jean Terrasson, *A Discourse of Ancient and Modern Learning*, trans. Francis Brerewood (London, 1716), and *A Critical Dissertation on Homer's Iliad*, trans. Francis Brerewood, 2 vols. (London, 1723–25).
83 Henry Home, *Elements of Criticism*, 2 vols. (1765), II, 386–89; Robert Wood, *An Essay on the Original Genius and Writings of Homer* (1775), 126–29.
84 See H. A. Mason, *To Homer Through Pope: An Introduction to Homer's 'Iliad' and Pope's Translation* (Chatto and Windus, 1972), 51.
85 *The Iliad*, translated E. V. Rieu (Harmondsworth: Penguin Books, 1976), 28.
86 For example, Rieu has Achilles comply by saying, "The man who listens to the gods is listened to by them" (29), while Pope has Achilles declare: "'Tis just, O Goddess! I thy Dictates hear... Those who revere the Gods, the Gods will bless" (lines 289, 291), and Dryden: "The Gods are just, and when subduing Sense, / We serve their Pow'rs, provide the Recompense" (lines 326–27).

87 See Felicity Rosslyn, "'Awed By Reason': Pope on Achilles," *CQ*, 9 (1980), 189–201, which argues that Pope's "Reason" is Homer's *aidos*, "the clarity of vision that understands and co-operates at the same moment" (201).
88 See Robin Sowerby, "The Freedom of Dryden's Homer," *TLS*, 5 (1992), 39.
89 *The Letters of John Dryden*, ed. Charles E. Ward (Durham, NC: Duke University Press, 1942), 121.
90 Watson, II, 166–67; see also the Preface to the *Aeneis* (1697), Watson, II, 228.
91 Preface to the *Iliad*, *TE*, VII, 13.
92 Dacier's opinion was "that those Times and Manners are so much more excellent, as they are the more contrary to ours"; *The Iliad of Homer*, trans. John Ozell, 5 vols. (London, 1712), I, xxv.
93 "I must needs, upon the whole, as far as I can judge, give up the Morality of this Fable; but what Colour of Excuse for it *Homer* might have from ancient Tradition, or what mystical or allegorical Sense might atone for the appearing Impiety, is hard to be ascertain'd at this distant Period of Time;" *TE*, VIII, 165–66.
94 *To Homer*, 56.
95 Note to Bk. I, line 698; *TE*, VII, 120. The combination of reverence and irreverence has led some scholars to see the scene as burlesque; see Mason, *To Homer*, 39, 59; Cedric D. Reverand, *Dryden's Final Poetic Mode: The "Fables"* (Philadelphia: University of Pennsylvania Press, 1988), 12–14, 22.
96 Longinus, *On the Sublime*: "awe-inspiring as these things are ... if they are not taken as allegory, they are altogether ungodly, and do not preserve our sense of what is fitting"; in *Classical Literary Criticism*, trans. T. S. Dorsch (Harmondsworth: Penguin Books, 1970), 111.
97 *The Spectator*, 8 vols. (London, 1733), IV, 113.
98 *Shakespeare*, I, 523.
99 See H. A. Mason, "Fine Comedy in the *Iliad*," *CQ*, 9 (1979), 17–38.
100 "Architect Divine" (line 741), "sacred Union" (line 747), "blest Abodes" (line 748), "gracious Pow'r" (line 751), "Etherial Height" (line 761), "awkward Grace" (line 770), "blest Gods" (line 772), "awful Head" (line 780).
101 Note to Bk. I, 771; *TE*, VII, 12, a view more or less held by Mason, *To Homer*, 39, 55; Sowerby, "Dryden and Homer," 249, 290; and William Frost, *Dryden and the Art of Translation* (New Haven, CT: Yale University Press, 1955), 64–67.
102 Watson, II, 272.
103 See Sowerby, "Freedom of Dryden's Homer," *Translation and Literature*, 5 (1992), 26–50, at 38 – also Miner, *Dryden's Poetry*, 315–16; Reverand, *Dryden's Final Poetic Mode*, ch. 6; Steven N. Zwicker, *Politics and Language in Dryden's Poetry: The Arts of Disguise* (Princeton University Press, 1984), 158–76; and Judith Sloman, *Dryden: The Poetics of Translation*, (University of Toronto Press, 1985), 152–63.
104 John Gould, "On Making Sense of Greek Religion," in *Greek Religion and Society*, ed. P. E. Easterling and J. V. Muir (Cambridge University Press, 1985), 21. See also Walter Burkert, "Greek Tragedy and Sacrificial Ritual," *Greek, Roman and Byzantine Studies*, 7 (1966), esp. 102–13.

105 Marcel Detienne and Jean-Pierre Vernant, *Cunning Intelligence in Greek Culture and Society*, trans. Janet Lloyd (Surrey: Harvester Press, 1974), 270–73.
106 See also *Iliad*, Bk. XXI, lines 335, 367.
107 See, e.g., Ted Cohen, *Jokes: Philosophical Thoughts on Joking Matters* (University of Chicago Press, 2000).
108 See William Frost, *Dryden and the Art of Translation* (New Haven, CT: Yale University Press, 1955), 81–92; William Myers, *Dryden* (London: Hutchinson, 1973), 166–69; and Levine, *Battle of the Books*, 185–86.
109 Observation from Pope's manuscript; B.M. MS. Add. 4807, f.14, quoted in Levine, *Battle of the Books*, 200.
110 Chetwood, "Preface to the Pastorals," *The Works of Virgil*, trans. John Dryden (London, 1697), n.p. "Our English palace" is part of Dryden's vision of his extensive project in translation of which the Virgil was one aspect; "To the Earl of Roscommon, On His Excellent *Essay on Translated Verse*," lines 77–78.
111 "Postscript to the Reader" (of Dryden's *Aeneid*), Watson, II, 258.
112 "Tradition and the Individual Talent" (1919), in *Selected Essays* (London: Faber and Faber, 1972), 13–22.
113 See also *Pope Versus Dryden: A Controversy in Letters to "The Gentleman's Magazine," 1789–1991*, ed. Gretchen M. Foster (University of Victoria English Literary Studies No. 44, 1989).
114 See Julian Ferraro on the "absolute control" Pope aimed to have over both manuscript and text; "From Text to Work: The Presentation and Representation of *Epistles to Several Persons*," in *Alexander Pope: World and Word*, ed. Howard Erskine-Hill (Oxford University Press, 1988), 111–34 (esp. 133). See also Maynard Mack on the unfinished finish of Pope's poems; *The Last and Greatest Art: Some Unpublished Poetical Manuscripts of Alexander Pope* (Newark, DE: University of Delaware Press, 1984), 16–17.
115 John Sitter, *Literary Loneliness in Mid-Eighteenth-Century England* (Ithaca: Cornell University Press, 1982), ch. 3; and, e.g., Michael Foucault, *The Order of Things: An Archaeology of the Human Sciences* (New York: Vintage, 1970).
116 See Katherine C. Balderston, "Johnson's Vile Melancholy," in *The Age of Johnson: Essays Presented to Chauncey Brewster Tinker*, ed. F. W. Hilles (New Haven, CT: Yale University Press, 1949), 3–14; Walter Jackson Bate, *Samuel Johnson* (London: Chatto & Windus, 1978), 115–29, 371–79; and Gloria Sybil Gross, *This Invisible Riot of the Mind: Samuel Johnson's Psychological Theory* (Philadelphia: University of Pennsylvania Press, 1992).
117 Cf. Thomas Reinert on Johnson's biographical didacticism, *Regulating Confusion: Samuel Johnson and the Crowd* (Durham, NC: Duke University Press, 1996), 105.
118 "The Emergence of the Novel in England: Genre vs. History of Genre," *Narrative*, 1 (1993), 72.
119 *The English Novel in History 1700–1780* (London: Routledge, 1999), 1.
120 "The Fictions of Factual Representation," in *Tropics of Discourse: Essays in Cultural Criticism* (Baltimore: Johns Hopkins University Press, 1978), 122.

121 See John Bender, *Imagining the Penitentiary: Fiction and the Architecture of Mind in Eighteenth-Century England* (University of Chicago Press, 1987), 37; and Zomchick, *Family and the Law*, 29.
122 Everett Zimmerman, *The Boundaries of Fiction: History and the Eighteenth-Century British Novel* (Ithaca: Cornell University Press, 1996), 236.
123 *Rambler*, 4, III, 22; see, e.g., Terry Eagleton, *The Rape of Clarissa: Writing, Sexuality and Class Struggle in Samuel Richardson* (Minneapolis: University of Minnesota Press, 1982), esp. "Introduction."
124 See Michael McKeon, *The Origins of the English Novel 1600–1740* (Baltimore: Johns Hopkins University Press, 1987), 45–64.
125 *The Autobiographical Subject: Gender and Ideology in Eighteenth-Century England* (Baltimore: Johns Hopkins University Press, 1989), 134.
126 For Wollstonecraft's interest in Johnson, see James G. Basker, "Radical Affinities: Mary Wollstonecraft and Samuel Johnson," in *Tradition in Transition: Woman Writers, Marginal Texts, and the Eighteenth-Century Canon*, ed. Alvaro Ribeiro, SJ and James G. Basker (Oxford: Clarendon Press, 1996), 41–55.
127 See Lennard Davis, *Resisting Novels: Ideology and Fiction* (London: Methuen, 1987), 127, and ch. 4 generally.
128 See Kathleen Nulton Kemmerer, *"A Neutral Being Between the Sexes:" Samuel Johnson's Sexual Politics* (Lewisburg: Bucknell University Press, 1998), 79.
129 Clifford Siskin, *The Work of Writing: Literature and Social Change in Britain 1700–1830* (Baltimore: Johns Hopkins University Press, 1998), 172.

6 HISTORIOGRAPHICAL IMPLICATIONS

1 "Toward Literary History," in *Beyond Formalism: Literary Essays 1958–1970* (New Haven, CT: Yale University Press, 1970), 356.
2 See Rudolf Pfeiffer, *The History of Classical Scholarship from 1300 to 1850* (Oxford: Clarendon Press, 1976).
3 "Literature, Meaning, and the Discontinuity of Fact," in *The Uses of Literary History*, ed. Marshall Brown (Durham, NC: Duke University Press, 1995), 46.
4 "Critical and Historical Principles of Literary History," in *The Idea of the Humanities and Other Essays*, 2 vols. (University of Chicago Press, 1967), II, 54–55.
5 Roger Chartier observes that "the irreducible singularity of style and sentiment" that came to express authorship in the eighteenth century was used by William Blackstone in 1760 to establish the "inalienability of the author's ownership" of his text; *The Order of Books*, trans. Lydia G. Cochrane (Stanford University Press, 1994), 36. See also Michael Meehan, "Authorship and Imagination in Blackstone's *Commentaries on the Laws of England*," *ECL*, 16 (1992), 113.
6 *Is Literary History Possible?* (Baltimore: Johns Hopkins University Press, 1992), 182.

7 See James Engell, *Forming the Critical Mind: Dryden to Coleridge* (Cambridge, MA: Harvard University Press, 1989), ch. 2.
8 *P&D*, 167.
9 See, e.g., *Sketches of the History of Man*, 2 vols. (Edinburgh, 1788).
10 See James L. Clifford, *Young Sam Johnson* (New York: McGraw-Hill, 1955), 122–23, 191.
11 See Robert J. Griffin, *Wordsworth's Pope: A Study in Literary Historiography* (Cambridge University Press, 1995).
12 See James Beattie, "On Poetry and Music," in *Essays* (Edinburgh, 1776): "the late and much-lamented Mr Gray of Cambridge, modestly declared to me, that if there was in his own numbers any thing that deserved approbation, he had learned it all from Dryden" (360 n).
13 Thomas Warton, *The History of English Poetry*, 3 vols. (1774–81), II, 462.
14 *Letters* (To Thomas Warton, 16 July, 1754), I, 81; see Lipking, *Ordering*, 362–77.
15 See Clement Hawes, "Johnson's Cosmopolitan Nationalism," in *Johnson Re-Visioned*, ch. 2.
16 Boswell, *Journal*, 380.
17 See *Journal*, 186, 368; *Journey*, 43–44, 57–58, 103–04; and *Letters*, I, 268–71, 280–81, II, 149–50, 218–19.
18 Walter Benjamin, "Theses on the Philosophy of History," in *Illuminations*, 261, 263; Benedict Anderson, *Imagined Communities* (1983; rev. edn, London: Verso, 1991), ch. 2.
19 See, e.g., Homi K. Bhabha, "How Newness Enters the World: Postmodern Space, Postcolonial Times, and the Trials of Cultural Translation," in *The Location of Culture* (London: Routledge, 1994), 212–35.
20 *Les Lieux de Mémoire*, sous la direction Pierre Nora, 3 vols. (Paris: Gallimard, 1984–86; 1993) [*Realms of Memory: Rethinking the French Past*, under the direction of Pierre Nora, ed. Lawrence D. Kreitzman, trans. Arthur Goldhammer, 3 vols. (New York: Columbia University Press, 1996)].
21 F. H. Bradley, *The Presuppositions of Critical History*, ed. Lionel Rubinoff (Chicago: Quadrangle Books, 1968), 96, 99.
22 Phillips, *Society and Sentiment*, 17.
23 See, e.g., Berlin's essays, "The Sense of Reality" and "Political Judgement," in *The Sense of Reality: Studies in Ideas and their History*, ed. Henry Hardy, intro. Patrick Gardiner (New York: Farrar, Straus and Giroux, 1996). The brief quotation comes from "Political Judgement," 46.
24 *Protocols of Reading* (New Haven, CT: Yale University Press, 1989), 154.
25 "The Real, the True, and the Figurative in the Human Sciences," *Profession*, 92 (New York: MLA, 1992), 16.
26 Roger Chartier, *On the Edge of the Cliff: History, Language, and Practices*, trans. Lydia G. Cochrane (Baltimore: Johns Hopkins University Press, 1997), 34.
27 Chartier, *Edge of the Cliff*, 45.
28 Pierre Nora, "Between Memory and History: *Les Lieux de Mémoire*," *Representations*, 26 (1989), 20.

Bibliography

PRIMARY WORKS OF SAMUEL JOHNSON

A Dictionary of the English Language, 1st edn (1755) and 4th edn (1773). Ed. Anne McDermott. CD-ROM. Cambridge University Press, 1996.
The Letters. Ed. Bruce Redford. 5 vols. Princeton University Press, 1992–94.
The Letters. Ed. R. W. Chapman. 3 vols. Oxford: Clarendon Press, 1952.
Rasselas and Other Tales. Ed. Gwin J. Kolb. New Haven, CT: Yale University Press, 1990.
A Journey to the Western Islands of Scotland. Ed. J. D. Fleeman. Oxford: Clarendon Press, 1985.
A Journey to the Western Islands of Scotland. Ed. Mary Lascelles. New Haven, CT: Yale University Press, 1971.
Johnson's Preface to Shakespeare: A Facsimile of the 1778 Edition. Ed. P. J. Smallwood. Bristol: Bristol Classical Press, 1985.
Johnson on Shakespeare. Ed. Arthur Sherbo, intro. Bertrand H. Bronson. 2 vols. New Haven, CT: Yale University Press, 1968.
Samuel Johnson on Shakespeare. Ed. W. K. Wimsatt. New York: Hill and Wang, 1960.
Samuel Johnson: The Oxford Authors. Ed. Donald Greene. New York: Oxford University Press, 1984.
Johnson's Juvenal: London and the Vanity of Human Wishes. Ed. Niall Rudd. Bristol: Bristol Classical Press, 1981.
Sermons. Ed. Jean Hagstrum and James Gray. New Haven, CT: Yale University Press, 1978.
Political Writings. Ed. Donald J. Greene. New Haven, CT: Yale University Press, 1977.
The Poems. Ed. David Nichol Smith and Edward L. McAdam. Oxford: Clarendon Press, 1974.
The Complete English Poems. Ed. J. D. Fleeman. New Haven, CT: Yale University Press, 1971.
Prefaces and Dedications. Ed. Allen T. Hazen. 1937; Port Washington, NY: Kennikat Press, 1973.
Early Biographical Writings of Dr Johnson. Ed. J. D. Fleeman. Farnborough: Gregg International, 1973.

The Rambler. Ed. W. J. Bate and Albrecht B. Strauss. 3 vols. New Haven, CT: Yale University Press, 1969.
The Idler and The Adventurer. Ed. W. J. Bate, John M. Bullitt, and L. F. Powell. New Haven, CT: Yale University Press, 1963.
Lives of the English Poets. Ed. G. B. Hill. 3 vols. Oxford: Clarendon Press, 1905.
The Six Chief Lives from Johnson's "Lives of the Poets," With Macaulay's "Life of Johnson." Ed. Matthew Arnold. London: Macmillan, 1878.
The Works of Samuel Johnson, LL.D. Together with his Life, and Notes on his Lives of the Poets. By Sir John Hawkins. 11 vols. London, 1787.
The Works of Samuel Johnson, With An Essay on His Life and Genius, 12 vols. By Arthur Murphy. London, 1792.

PRIMARY WORKS RELATED TO JOHNSON

Boswell, James. *The Life of Samuel Johnson, LL.D., with a Journal of a Tour to the Hebrides.* Ed. G. B. Hill, rev. L. F. Powell, 6 vols. Oxford: Clarendon Press, 1934–64.
Journal of a Tour to the Hebrides with Samuel Johnson 1773. Ed. Frederick A. Pottle and Charles H. Bennett. New York: McGraw-Hill, 1961.
Brack, O M Jr. and Robert E. Kelley, eds. *The Early Biographies of Samuel Johnson.* Iowa City: University of Iowa Press, 1974.
Chambers, Sir Robert. *A Course of Lectures on the English Law, 1767–1773.* Ed. Thomas M. Curley. 2 vols. Madison: University of Wisconsin Press, 1986.
Hawkins, Sir John. *The Life of Samuel Johnson, LL.D.* 2nd edn. London, 1787.
Johnson: The Critical Heritage. Ed. James T. Boulton. London: Routledge and Kegan Paul, 1971.
Johnsonian Miscellanies. Ed. G. B. Hill, 2 vols. Oxford: Clarendon Press, 1897.
Piozzi, Hester Thrale. *Thraliana.* Ed. Katherine C. Balderston. 2 vols. Oxford: Clarendon Press, 1951.
Dr Johnson by Mrs Thrale: The 'Anecdotes' of Mrs Piozzi in their Original Form. Ed. Richard Ingrams. London: Hogarth Press, 1984.
Potter, Robert. *An Inquiry into Some Passages of Dr Johnson's Lives of the Poets.* London, 1783.
"Remarks on Dr Johnson's Lives of the Poets." *Gentleman's Magazine,* 21 (Oct. 1781), 463–67.

OTHER SELECTED PRIMARY TEXTS

Addison, Joseph and Richard Steele. *The Spectator.* 8 vols. London, 1733.
Augustine. *Confessions.* Trans. R. S. Pine-Coffin. Harmondsworth: Penguin Books, 1961.
Boileau, Nicolas Despreaux. *The Works of Monsieur Boileau Made English.* 2 vols. London, 1712.
Bolingbroke, Henry St. John, Viscount. "Letters on the Study and Use of History." In *Miscellaneous Works.* 4 vols. Edinburgh: 1768.

Burke, Edmund. *A Philosophical Enquiry into the Origin of our Ideas of the Sublime and Beautiful.* Ed. Adam Phillips. Oxford University Press, 1992.

Butler, Joseph. *The Analogy of Religion, Natural and Revealed, to the Constitution and Course of Nature.* London, 1736.

Butler, Samuel. *Hudibras.* Ed. John Wilders. Oxford University Press, 1967.

Denham, Sir John. *The Poetical Works.* Ed. Theodore Howard Banks, Jr. New Haven, CT: Yale University Press, 1928.

Dennis, John. *The Critical Works.* Ed. Edward N. Hooker. 2 vols. Baltimore: Johns Hopkins University Press, 1955.

Donne, John. *Poems . . . With Elegies on the Author's Death.* London, 1633.

Poetical Works. 3 vols. London, 1779.

Dryden, John. *The Poems of John Dryden.* Ed. Paul Hammond. 2 vols. London: Longman, 1995.

The Poems of John Dryden. Ed. James Kinsley, 4 vols. Oxford: Clarendon Press, 1970.

"Of Dramatick Poesy" and Other Critical Essays. Ed. George Watson, 2 vols. London: Dent, 1962.

The Letters of John Dryden. Ed. Charles E. Ward. Durham, NC: Duke University Press, 1942.

The Works. With Notes and a Life of the Author by Walter Scott. 18 vols. London, 1808.

Miscellany Poems. 5th edn. 6 vols. London, 1727.

Godwin, William. "Of History and Romance." In *Caleb Williams.* Ed. Maurice Hindle. London: Penguin, 1988. Pp. 359–73.

Hale, Sir Matthew. *The History of the Common Law of England.* Ed. Charles M. Gray. University of Chicago Press, 1971.

Hazlitt, William. *Lectures on the English Comic Writers.* London: Oxford University Press, 1920.

Hume, David. *The History of England From the Invasion of Julius Caesar to the Revolution in 1688.* 6 vols. Indianapolis: Liberty Fund, 1983.

A Treatise of Human Nature. 2nd edn. Ed. P.H. Nidditch. Oxford: Clarendon Press, 1980.

An Essay Concerning Human Understanding. Ed. Eric Steinberg. Indianapolis: Hackett Publishing Company, 1977.

Dialogues Concerning Natural Religion. Ed. N. K. Smith. Oxford: Clarendon Press, 1935.

"My Own Life" (1777). In *Cambridge Companion to Hume.* Ed. David Fate Norton. Cambridge University Press, 1993.

"Of the Poems of Ossian." In *David Hume: Philosophical Historian.* Ed. David Fate Norton and Richard H. Popkin. Indianapolis: Bobbs-Merrill, 1965.

"Of the Rise and Progress of the Arts and Sciences." In *Essays Moral, Political, Literary.* Oxford: Oxford University Press, 1963.

Le Bossu, René. *Traité du Poeme Epique.* Paris, 1675.

Locke, John. *Two Treatises of Government.* Ed. Peter Laslett. Cambridge University Press, 1988.

An Essay Concerning Human Understanding. Ed. Peter H. Nidditch. Oxford: Clarendon Press, 1975.

Milton, John. *Complete Prose Works.* Ed. Don Wolfe. 10 vols. New Haven, CT: Yale University Press, 1959–82.

The Poems. Ed. John Carey and Alistair Fowler. London: Longman, 1968 and 1980.

John Milton, 1732–1801: The Critical Heritage. Ed. John T. Shawcross. London: Routledge & Kegan Paul, 1972.

The Early Lives of Milton. Ed. Helen Darbishire. London: Constable, 1932.

The Prose Works. Ed. J. A. St. John. 3 vols. London: Henry Bohn, 1848.

Paradise Lost. With Notes By Thomas Newton. 4th edn. 2 vols. London, 1757.

Montaigne, Michael. *Essays, Made English by Charles Cotton.* 3 vols. London, 1700.

Pope, Alexander. *The Twickenham Edition of the Works of Alexander Pope.* General Editor, John Butt. 10 vols. London: Methuen, 1951–67.

The Works. Ed. Rev. Whitwell Elwin and J. C. Courthope. 10 vols. London, 1871–89.

The Works. With Notes by Joseph Warton and Others. London, 1797.

The Works. With Notes by William Warburton. 6 vols. London, 1770.

The Works. With Notes by William Warburton. 9 vols. London, 1751.

The Correspondence of Alexander Pope. Ed. George Sherburn. 5 vols. Oxford: Clarendon Press, 1956.

Reynolds, Joshua. *Discourses on Art.* Ed. Robert R. Wark. New Haven, CT: Yale University Press, 1997.

Smith, David Nicol, ed. *Characters from the Histories and Memoirs of the Seventeenth Century.* Oxford: Clarendon Press, 1918.

Spence, Joseph. *Observations, Anecdotes and Characters of Books and Men.* 2 vols. Ed. James M. Osborn. Oxford: Clarendon Press, 1966.

An Essay on Pope's Odyssey. Oxford, 1726.

Spingarn, J. E., Ed. *Critical Essays of the Seventeenth Century.* 3 vols. Oxford: Clarendon Press, 1908.

Stockdale, Percival. *An Inquiry into the Nature and Genuine Laws of Poetry.* London, 1778.

Waller, Edmund. *Works In Verse and Prose.* Published by Mr Fenton. London, 1729.

The Works. The Second Part [Published by Atterbury]. London, 1690.

Warton, Joseph. *An Essay on the Genius and Writings of Alexander Pope.* 2 vols. London, 1756–84.

Warton, Thomas. *The History of English Poetry.* 3 vols. London, 1774–81.

Wood, Robert. *An Essay on the Original Genius and Writings of Homer.* London, 1775.

Young, Edward. *Conjectures on Original Composition.* Fac.1st edn (1759). Leeds: Scholar Press, 1966.

BIBLIOGRAPHIES

Clifford, James and Donald J. Greene, *Samuel Johnson: A Survey and Bibliography of Critical Studies.* Minneapolis: University of Minnesota Press, 1970.

Fleeman, J. D. *A Bibliography of the Works of Samuel Johnson, 1731–1784: Treating His Published Works from the Beginning to 1984*. 2 vols. Oxford University Press, 2000.
Greene, Donald and John Vance. *A Bibliography of Johnsonian Studies, 1970–1985*. Victoria, BC: University of Victoria Monograph Series, 1987.
Lynch, Jack. *A Bibliography of Johnsonian Studies, 1986–1998*. New York: AMS, 2000.

SELECTED BIOGRAPHICAL AND CRITICAL STUDIES OF JOHNSON

Alkon, Paul K. *Samuel Johnson and Moral Discipline*. Evanston: Northwestern University Press, 1967.
Basker, James G. "Samuel Johnson and the African American Reader." *The New Rambler* (1994/95), 47–57.
  "Radical Affinities: Mary Wollstonecraft and Samuel Johnson." In *Tradition in Transition: Woman Writers, Marginal Texts, and the Eighteenth-Century Canon*. Ed. Alvaro Ribeiro, SJ, and James G. Basker. Oxford: Clarendon Press, 1996.
Bate, Walter Jackson. *The Achievement of Samuel Johnson*. New York: Oxford University Press, 1955.
  Samuel Johnson. London: Chatto and Windus, 1978.
Battersby, James. "Life, Art, and the *Lives of the Poets*." In *Domestick Privacies: Samuel Johnson and the Art of Biography*. Ed. David Wheeler. Lexington: University of Kentucky Press, 1987.
Bogel, Fredric V. *The Dream of My Brother: An Essay on Johnson's Authority*. Victoria, BC: University of Victoria, English Literary Studies, 1990.
Bronson, Bertrand H. *Johnson Agonistes and Other Essays*. Berkeley: University of California Press, 1965.
Chapin, Chester F. *The Religious Thought of Samuel Johnson*. Ann Arbor: University of Michigan Press, 1968.
Clifford, James. *Dictionary Johnson: The Middle Years of Samuel Johnson*. London: Heinemann, 1978.
  Young Sam Johnson. New York: McGraw-Hill, 1955.
Clingham, Greg. *Boswell: The Life of Johnson*. Cambridge University Press, 1992.
  "Resisting Johnson." In *Johnson Re-Visioned*. Ed. Smallwood.
  "Another and the Same: Johnson's Dryden." In *Literary Transmission and Authority: Dryden and Other Writers*. Ed. Earl Miner and Jennifer Brady. Cambridge University Press, 1993.
  "Johnson, Homeric Scholarship, and 'the Passes of the Mind.'" *AJ*, 3 (1990), 113–70.
  "'Himself That Great Sublime:' Johnson's Critical Thinking." *Études Anglaises*, 41 (1988), 165–78.
  "Johnson's Criticism of Dryden's Odes in Praise of St. Cecilia." *MLS*, 18 (1988), 165–80.

"'The Inequalities of Memory:' Johnson's Epitaphs on Hogarth." *English*, 35 (1986), 221–32.

"Johnson *In Memoriam?*" *CQ*, 15 (1986), 78–79.

Clingham, Greg, ed. *The Cambridge Companion to Samuel Johnson*. Cambridge University Press, 1997.

Curley, Thomas M. "Johnson, Chambers, and the Law." In *Samuel Johnson After Two Hundred Years*. Ed. Paul J. Korshin. Philadelphia: University of Pennsylvania Press, 1986.

"Johnson's Secret Collaboration." In *The Unknown Samuel Johnson*. Ed. John J. Burke, Jr. and Donald Kay. Madison: University of Wisconsin Press, 1983.

Damrosch, Leo. *Fictions of Reality in the Age of Hume and Johnson*. Madison: University of Wisconsin Press, 1989.

The Uses of Johnson's Criticism. Charlottesville: University Press of Virginia, 1976.

Samuel Johnson and the Tragic Sense. Princeton University Press, 1972.

"Samuel Johnson and Reader-Response Criticism." *ECTI*, 21 (1980), 98–108.

Davis, Phillip. *In Mind of Johnson: A Study of Johnson the Rambler*. Athens, GA: University of Georgia Press, 1989.

De Maria, Robert, Jr. *Johnson's Dictionary and the Language of Learning*. Chapel Hill: University of North Carolina Press, 1986.

Deutsch, Helen. "The Author as Monster: The Case of Dr. Johnson." In *"Defects": Engendering the Modern Body*. Ed. Helen Deutsch and Felicity Nussbaum. Ann Arbor: University of Michigan Press, 2000.

Eliot, T. S. "Johnson as Critic and Poet." In *On Poetry and Poets*. London: Faber & Faber, 1959.

Erskine-Hill, Howard. "The Poet and the Affairs of State in Johnson's *Lives of the Poets*." *Man and Nature*, 6 (1987), 93–113.

"The Political Character of Samuel Johnson." In *Samuel Johnson*. Ed. Grundy.

Fix, Stephen. "The Contexts and Motives of Johnson's *Life of Milton*." In *Domestick Privacies: Samuel Johnson and the Art of Biography*. Ed. David Wheeler. Lexington: UP Kentucky, 1987.

"Johnson and the 'Duty' of Reading *Paradise Lost*." *ELH*, 52 (1985), 649–71.

"Distant Genius: Johnson and the Art of Milton's Life." *MP*, 81 (1984), 244–64.

Folkenflik, Robert. *Samuel Johnson, Biographer*. Ithaca: Cornell University Press, 1978.

Fussell, Paul. *Samuel Johnson and the Life of Writing*. London: Chatto & Windus, 1972.

Grundy, Isobel. *Samuel Johnson and the Scale of Greatness*. Leicester University Press, 1986.

"Samuel Johnson: A Writer of Lives Looks at Death." *MLR*, 79 (1984), 257–65.

Grundy, Isobel, ed. *Samuel Johnson: New Critical Essays*. London: Vision, 1984.

Hagstrum, Jean. *Samuel Johnson's Literary Criticism*. Minneapolis: University of Minnesota Press, 1952.

"Johnson and the *Concordia Discors* of Human Relationships." In *The Unknown Samuel Johnson*. Ed. John J. Burke, Jr. and Donald Kay. Madison: University of Wisconsin Press, 1983.

Hawes, Clement. "Johnson's Cosmopolitan Nationalism." In *Johnson Re-Visioned*. Ed. Smallwood.

"Johnson and Imperialism." In *Companion to Johnson*. Ed. Clingham.

Henson, Eithne. *"The Fictions of Romantick Chivalry:" Samuel Johnson and the Romance*. Rutherford: Fairleigh Dickinson University Press, 1992.

Hinnant, Charles H. *Samuel Johnson: An Analysis*. New York: St. Martin's Press, 1988.

Hudson, Nicholas. *Samuel Johnson and Eighteenth-Century Thought*. Oxford: Clarendon Press, 1990.

Keast, W. K. "Johnson's Criticism of the Metaphysical Poets." In *Eighteenth-Century English Literature: Modern Essays in Criticism*. Ed. James L. Clifford. New York: Oxford University Press, 1959.

"The Theoretical Foundations of Johnson's Criticism." In *Critics and Criticism*. Ed. R. S. Crane. University of Chicago Press, 1957.

Kemmerer, Kathleen Nulton. *"A Neutral Being Between the Sexes": Samuel Johnson's Sexual Politics*. Lewisburg: Bucknell University Press, 1998.

Kernan, Alvin. *Samuel Johnson and the Impact of Print*. Princeton University Press, 1987.

Keymer, Tom. "'Letters About Nothing:' Johnson and Epistolary Writing." In *Companion to Johnson*. Ed. Clingham.

Kinkead-Weekes, Mark. "Johnson on 'The Rise of the Novel.'" In *Samuel Johnson*. Ed. Grundy.

Kirkley, Harriet. *A Biographer at Work: Samuel Johnson's Notes for the "Life of Pope."* Lewisburg: Bucknell University Press, 2002.

Klinkenborg, Verlyn, "Johnson and the Analogy of Judicial Authority." *ECTI*, 28 (1987), 47–61.

F. R. Leavis, "Johnson and Augustanism." In *The Common Pursuit*. Harmondsworth: Penguin Books, 1969.

"Johnson as Critic." In *"Anna Karenina" and Other Essays*. London: Chatto & Windus, 1973.

Lipking, Lawrence. *Samuel Johnson: The Life of an Author*. Cambridge, MA: Harvard University Press, 1998.

The Ordering of the Arts in Eighteenth-Century England. Princeton University Press, 1970.

Lynn, Steven. *Samuel Johnson After Deconstruction: Rhetoric and the Rambler*. Carbondale: Southern Illinois University Press, 1992.

McGilchrist, Iain. "Johnson." In *Against Criticism*. London: Faber and Faber, 1982.

Morris, John. "Samuel Johnson and the Artist's Work." *The Hudson Review*, 26 (1973), 441–61.

Parke, Catherine N. *Samuel Johnson and Biographical Thinking*. Columbia, MO: University of Missouri Press, 1991.

Parker, Blanford. *The Triumph of Augustan Poetics: English Literary Culture from Butler to Johnson*. Cambridge University Press, 1998.
Parker, G. F. *Johnson's Shakespeare*. Oxford: Clarendon Press, 1989.
"The Skepticism of *Rasselas*." In *Companion to Johnson*. Ed. Clingham.
Reddick, Allen. *The Making of Johnson's Dictionary*. Cambridge University Press, 1990.
Sachs, Arieh. *Passionate Intelligence: Imagination and Reason in the Work of Samuel Johnson*. Baltimore: Johns Hopkins University Press, 1967.
Selden, Raman. "Deconstructing the Ramblers." In *Fresh Reflections on Samuel Johnson*. Ed. Prem Nath. Troy, NY: Whiston, 1987.
Smallwood, Philip. "Shakespeare: Johnson's Poet of Nature." In *Companion to Johnson*. Ed. Clingham.
Smallwood, Philip, ed. *Johnson Re-Visioned: Looking Before and After*. Lewisburg: Bucknell University Press, 2001.
Tate, Allen. "Johnson on the Metaphysical Poets." In *Essays of Four Decades*. Chicago: Swallow Press, 1965.
Tomarken, Edward. *Johnson, "Rasselas," and the Choice of Criticism*. Lexington: University of Kentucky Press, 1989.
Vance, John. "Johnson and Hume: Of Like Historical Minds." *SECC*, 15 (1986), 241–56.
Samuel Johnson and the Sense of History. Athens: University of Georgia Press, 1984.
Venturo, David. *Johnson the Poet: The Poetic Career of Samuel Johnson*. Newark, DE: University of Delaware Press, 1999.
Wain, John. *Samuel Johnson*. New York: McGraw-Hill, 1974.
Wechselblatt, Martin. *Bad Behavior: Samuel Johnson and Modern Cultural Authority*. Lewisburg: Bucknell University Press, 1998.
Weinbrot, Howard D. "The Reader, the General, and the Particular: Johnson and Imlac in Chapter Ten of *Rasselas*." *ECS*, 5 (1971–72), 80–96.
Wiltshire, John. *Samuel Johnson in the Medical World*. Cambridge University Press, 1991.
"Johnson in the Traveled World." In *Companion to Johnson*. Ed. Clingham.

SELECTED GENERAL CRITICAL STUDIES

Anderson, Benedict. *Imagined Communities: Reflections on the Origin and Spread of Nationalism*. Rev. edn. London: Verso, 1991.
Anderson, Howard, Philip B. Daghlian, and Irvin Ehrenpreis, eds. *The Familiar Letter in the Eighteenth Century*. Lawrence: University Press of Kansas, 1966.
Aravamudan, Srinivas. *Tropicopolitans: Colonialism and Agency, 1688–1804*. Durham, NC: Duke University Press, 1999.
Arendt, Hannah. *The Human Condition*. University of Chicago Press, 1958.
Ashfield, Andrew and Peter de Bolla, eds. *The Sublime: A Reader in British Eighteenth-Century Aesthetic Theory*. Cambridge University Press, 1996.
Baines, Paul. *The House of Forgery in Eighteenth-Century Britain*. Aldershot: Ashgate, 1999.

Barrell, John: *English Literature In History 1730–1780: "An Equal, Wide Survey."* London: Hutchinson, 1983.
Bender, John. "A New History of the Enlightenment." In *The Profession of Eighteenth-Century Literature.* Ed. Damrosch.
Benjamin, Walter. *Illuminations.* Ed. Hannah Arendt. Trans. Harry Zohn. New York: Shocken Books, 1969.
Berkhofer, Robert F. *Beyond the Great Story: History as Text and Discourse.* Cambridge, MA: Harvard University Press, 1995.
Bhabha, Homi K. *The Location of Culture.* London: Routledge, 1994.
Bogel, Fredric V. *Literature and Insubstantiality in Later Eighteenth-Century England.* Princeton University Press, 1984.
Bradley, F. H. *The Presuppositions of Critical History.* Ed. Lionel Rubinoff. Chicago: Quadrangle Books, 1968.
Brooks, Peter. *Body Work: Objects of Desire in Modern Narrative.* Cambridge, MA: Harvard University Press, 1993.
  "The Law as Narrative and Rhetoric." In *Law's Stories.* Ed. Brooks and Gewirtz.
Brooks, Peter and Paul Gewirtz, eds. *Law's Stories: Narrative and Rhetoric in the Law.* New Haven, CT: Yale University Press, 1996.
Burns, R. M. *The Great Debate on Miracles: From Joseph Glanvill to David Hume.* Lewisburg: Bucknell University Press, 1981.
Butler, Judith. *The Psychic Life of Power.* Stanford University Press, 1997.
Caruth, Cathy. *Empirical Truths and Critical Fictions: Locke, Wordsworth, Kant, Freud.* Baltimore: Johns Hopkins University Press, 1991.
Chartier, Roger. *On the Edge of the Cliff: History, Language, and Practices.* Trans. Lydia G. Cochrane. Baltimore: Johns Hopkins University Press, 1997.
  The Order of Books. Trans. Lydia G. Cochrane. Stanford University Press, 1994.
Clingham, Greg, ed. *Questioning History: The Postmodern Turn to the Eighteenth Century.* Lewisburg: Bucknell University Press, 1998.
  Making History: Textuality and the Forms of Eighteenth-Century Culture. Lewisburg: Bucknell University Press, 1998.
Collingwood, R. G. *The Idea of History.* Rev. edn. Ed. Jan Van Der Dussen. Oxford University Press, 1994.
Cornell, Drucilla, Michael Rosenfeld, and David Gray Carlson, eds. *Deconstruction and the Possibility of Justice.* New York: Routledge, 1992.
Crane, R. S. *The Idea of the Humanities and Other Essays.* 2 vols. University of Chicago Press, 1967.
Dallmayr, Fred. "Hermeneutics and the Rule of Law." In *Deconstruction and the Possibility of Justice.* Ed. Cornell, Rosenfeld, and Carlson.
Damrosch, Leo. Ed. *The Profession of Eighteenth-Century Literature: Reflections on an Institution.* Madison: University of Wisconsin Press, 1992.
Davidson, Donald. "What Metaphors Mean." In *On Metaphors.* Ed. Sheldon Sacks. University of Chicago Press, 1981.
Davis, Leigh. *Acts of Union: Scotland and the Literary Negotiation of the British Nation 1707–1830.* Stanford University Press, 1998.

Davis, Lennard J. *Resisting Novels: Ideology and Fiction*. London: Methuen, 1987.
de Certeau, Michael. *The Writing of History*. Trans. Tom Conley. New York: Columbia University Press, 1988.
de Man, Paul. "The Epistemology of Metaphor." In *On Metaphor*. Ed. Sheldon Sacks. University of Chicago Press, 1978.
Derrida, Jacques. "The 'Mystical Foundations of Authority.'" In *Deconstruction and the Possibility of Justice*. Ed. Cornell, Rosenfeld, and Carlson.
  "Mnemosyne." In *Memoires for Paul de Man*. Trans. Cecile Lindsay. New York: Columbia University Press, 1989.
Detienne, Marcel and Jean-Pierre Vernant. *Cunning Intelligence in Greek Culture and Society*. Trans. Janet Lloyd. Surrey: Harvester, 1974.
Dienstag, Joshua Foa. *Dancing in Chains: Narrative and Memory in Political Theory*. Ithaca: Cornell University Press, 1997.
Dowling, William C. "Ideology and the Flight from History in Eighteenth-Century Poetry." In *The Profession of Eighteenth-Century Literature*. Ed. Damrosch.
Dworkin, Ronald. *A Matter of Principle*. Cambridge, MA: Harvard University Press, 1985.
Eliot, T. S. "The Metaphysical Poets." In *Selected Essays*. London: Faber and Faber, 1972.
  "Donne in Our Time." In *A Garland for John Donne*. Ed. Theodore Spenser. Cambridge, MA: Harvard University Press, 1931.
Ellis, John M. *Against Deconstruction*. Princeton University Press, 1989.
Empson, William. "Metaphor." In *The Structure of Complex Words*. London: Hogarth Press, 1951.
Engell, James. *Forming the Critical Mind: Dryden to Coleridge*. Cambridge, MA: Harvard University Press, 1989.
Epstein, William H., ed. *Contesting the Subject: Essays in the Postmodern Theory and Practice of Biography and Biographical Criticism*. West Lafayette: Purdue University Press, 1991.
Erickson, Lee. *The Economy of Literary Form: English Literature and the Industrialization of Publishing*. Baltimore: Johns Hopkins University Press, 1996.
Erskine-Hill, Howard. *Poetry of Opposition and Revolution: Dryden to Wordsworth*. Oxford: Clarendon Press, 1996.
Fish, Stanley. *Doing What Comes Naturally: Change, Rhetoric, and the Practice of Theory in Literary and Legal Studies*. Durham, NC: Duke University Press, 1989.
  Is There a Text in This Class? The Authority of Interpretive Communities. Cambridge, MA: Harvard University Press, 1980.
Foley, Barbara. *Telling the Truth: The Theory and Practice of Documentary Fiction*. Ithaca: Cornell University Press, 1986.
Foucault, Michel. *Discipline and Punish: The Birth of the Prison*. Trans. Alan Sheridan. New York: Vintage, 1979.
  The Order of Things: An Archaeology of the Human Sciences. New York: Vintage Books, 1970.

"Nietzsche, Genealogy, History." In *The Foucault Reader*. Ed. Paul Rabinow. New York: Pantheon Books, 1984.

Fox, Christopher. *Locke and the Scriblerians: Identity and Consciousness in Early Eighteenth-Century Britain*. Berkeley: University of California Press, 1988.

Freud, Sigmund. "Repression." In *General Psychological Theory: Papers on Metapsychology*. Ed. Philip Rieff. New York: Collier, 1963.

"Remembering, Repeating, and Working Through." In *Beyond the Pleasure Principle*. Trans. James Strachey. New York: Norton, 1961.

Fulford, Tim. *Landscape, Liberty and Authority: Poetry, Criticism and Politics from Thomson to Wordsworth*. Cambridge University Press, 1996.

Gadamer, Hans-George. *Truth and Method*. Westport: Continuum, 1975.

Griffin, Robert J. *Wordsworth's Pope: A Study in Literary Historiography*. Cambridge University Press, 1995.

Grossman, Lionel. "History and Literature: Reproduction or Signification." In *The Writing of History: Literary Form and Historical Understanding*. Ed. Robert H. Canary and Henry Kozicki. Madison: University of Wisconsin Press, 1978.

Guillory, John. *Cultural Capital: The Problem of Literary Canon Formation*. University of Chicago Press, 1993.

Hartman, Geoffrey H. "Literary Commentary as Literature." In *Criticism in the Wilderness: The Study of Literature Today*. New Haven, CT: Yale University Press, 1980.

"Toward Literary History." In *Beyond Formalism: Literary Essays 1958–1970*. New Haven, CT: Yale University Press, 1970.

Hill, Geoffrey. *The Enemy's Country: Words, Contexture, and Other Circumstances of Language*. Stanford University Press, 1991.

"Poetry as 'Menace' and 'Atonement.'" In *Lords of Limit: Essays on Literature and Ideas*. New York: Oxford University Press, 1984.

Holmes, Richard. "Biography: Inventing the Truth." In *The Art of Literary Biography*. Ed. John Batchelor. Oxford: Clarendon Press, 1989.

Hunter, J. Paul. *Before Novels: The Cultural Contexts of Eighteenth-Century English Fiction*. New York: W. W. Norton, 1990.

Hutton, Patrick H. *History as an Art of Memory*. Hanover, VT: University Press of New England, 1993.

Jacobus, Mary. *Psychoanalysis and the Scene of Reading*. Oxford University Press, 1999.

Jauss, Hans Robert. *Question and Answer: Forms of Dialogic Understanding*. Ed. and trans. Michael Hays. Minneapolis: University of Minnesota Press, 1989.

Kermode, Frank. *The Sense of an Ending: Studies in the Theory of Fiction*. London: Oxford University Press, 1966.

Kramnick, Jonathan Brody. *Making the English Canon: Print-Capitalism and the Cultural Past, 1700–1770*. Cambridge University Press, 1998.

Krell, David Farrell. *On the Verge: Of Memory, Reminiscence, and Writing*. Bloomington: Indiana University Press, 1990.

Krieger, Murray. "The Arts and the Idea of Progress." In *Progress and Its Discontents*. Ed. Gabriel A. Almond, Marvin Chodorow, and Roy Harvey Pearce. Berkeley: University of California Press, 1982.

Kroll, Richard W. F. *The Material Word: Literate Culture in the Restoration and Early Eighteenth Century*. Baltimore: Johns Hopkins University Press, 1991.
Law, Jules David. *The Rhetoric of Empiricism: Language and Perception from Locke to I.A. Richards*. Ithaca: Cornell University Press, 1993.
Le Goff, Jacques. *History and Memory*. Trans. Steven Rendall and Elizabeth Claman. New York: Columbia University Press, 1992.
Lear, Jonathan. *Happiness, Death, and the Remainder of Life*. University of Chicago Press, 2000.
Levine, Joseph. *The Autonomy of History: Truth and Method from Erasmus to Gibbon*. University of Chicago Press, 1999.
 The Battle of the Books: History and Literature in the Augustan Age. Ithaca: Cornell University Press, 1991.
 Humanism and History: Origins of Modern English Historiography. Ithaca: Cornell University Press, 1987.
Lipking, Lawrence. *The Life of the Poet: Beginning and Ending Poetic Careers*. University of Chicago Press, 1981.
Manning, Susan. *The Puritan–Provincial Vision: Scottish and American Literature in the Nineteenth Century*. Cambridge University Press, 1990.
Markley, Robert. *Fallen Languages: Crises of Representation in Newtonian England, 1660–1740*. Ithaca: Cornell University Press, 1993.
Mason, H. A. *To Homer Through Pope: An Introduction to Homer's Iliad and Pope's Translation*. London: Chatto and Windus, 1972.
 Humanism and Poetry in the Early Tudor Period. London: Routledge & Kegan Paul, 1959.
Mayer, Robert. *History and the Early English Novel: Matters of Fact from Bacon to Defoe*. Cambridge University Press, 1997.
McGann, Jerome. "Literature, Meaning, and the Discontinuity of Fact." In *The Uses of Literary History*. Ed. Marshall Brown. Durham, NC: Duke University Press, 1995.
McIntosh, Carey. *The Evolution of English Prose, 1700–1800: Style, Politeness, and Print Culture*. Cambridge University Press, 1998.
McKeon, Michael. *The Origins of the English Novel, 1600–1740*. Baltimore: Johns Hopkins University Press, 1987.
 "Writer as Hero: Novelistic Prefigurations and the Emergence of Literary Biography." In *Contesting the Subject: Essays in the Postmodern Theory and Practice of Biographical Criticism*. Ed. William H. Epstein. West Lafayette: Purdue University Press, 1991.
Meehan, Michael. "Authorship and Imagination in Blackstone's *Commentaries on the Laws of England*." *ECL*, 16 (1992), 111–26.
Meyers, Jeffrey, ed. *The Craft of Literary Biography*. London: Macmillan, 1985.
Miller, J Hillis. "Narrative and History." *ELH*, 41 (1974), 455–73.
Mink, Louis O. *Historical Understanding*. Ed. Brian Fay, Eugene O. Golob, and Richard T. Vann. Ithaca: Cornell University Press, 1987.
Momigliano, Arnoldo. *Studies in Historiography*. New York: Harper & Row, 1966.
Moore, Leslie E. *Beautiful Sublime: The Making of "Paradise Lost," 1701–1734*. Stanford University Press, 1990.

Nadel, Ira Bruce. *Biography: Fact, Fiction and Form.* New York: St. Martin's Press, 1984.
Nora, Pierre. *Realms of Memory: Rethinking the French Past.* Ed. Lawrence D. Kritzman, trans. Arthur Goldhammer. 3 vols. New York: Columbia University Press, 1996.
  "Between Memory and History: *Les Lieux de Memoire.*" *Representations* 26 (1989), 7–25.
O'Brien, Karen. *Narratives of Enlightenment: Cosmopolitan History from Voltaire to Gibbon.* Cambridge University Press, 1997.
Olney, James. *Memory and Narrative: The Weave of Life-Writing.* University of Chicago Press, 1998.
Patey, Douglas Lane. *Probability and Literary Form: Philosophic Theory and Literary Practice in the Augustan Age.* Cambridge University Press, 1984.
Perkins, David. *Is Literary History Possible?* Baltimore: Johns Hopkins University Press, 1992.
Phillips, Mark Salber. *Society and Sentiment: Genres of Historical Writing in Britain, 1740–1820.* Princeton University Press, 2000.
Pocock, J. G. A. *Barbarism and Religion.* 2 vols. Cambridge University Press, 1999.
Popkin, Richard H. *The High Road to Pyrrhonism.* San Diego: Austin Hill Press, 1980.
  "Divine Causality: Newton, the Newtonians, and Hume." In *Greene Centennial Studies: Essays Presented to Donald Greene in the Centennial Year of the University of Southern California.* Ed. Paul J. Korshin and Robert R. Allen. Charlottesville: University Press Virginia, 1984.
Posner, Richard. *Law and Literature.* Cambridge, MA: Harvard University Press, 1998.
Rader, Ralph W. "The Emergence of the Novel in England: Genre in History vs. History of Genre." *Narrative,* 1 (1993), 69–83.
Redford, Bruce. *The Converse of the Pen: Acts of Intimacy in the Eighteenth-Century Familiar Letter.* University of Chicago Press, 1986.
Richetti, John. *The English Novel in History 1700–1780.* London: Routledge, 1999.
  Philosophical Writing: Locke, Berkeley, Hume. Cambridge, MA: Harvard University Press, 1983.
Ricks, Christopher. "Geoffrey Hill 2: At-one-ment." In *The Force of Poetry.* Oxford University Press, 1987.
  "In Theory." *London Review of Books* (16 April–6 May 1981), 3.
Ricoeur, Paul. *Time and Narrative.* 3 vols. Trans. Kathleen McLaughlin and David Pellauer (vol. 1) and Kathleen Blamey and David Pellauer (vols. 2–3). University of Chicago Press, 1984–88.
Rosslyn, Felicity. "Of Gods and Men." *CQ,* 13 (1984), 1–20.
Scarry, Elaine. *The Body in Pain: The Making and Unmaking of the World.* Oxford University Press, 1985.
Scholes, Robert. *Protocols of Reading.* New Haven, CT: Yale University Press, 1989.
Sherman, Stuart. *Telling Time: Clocks, Diaries, and English Diurnal Form, 1660–1785.* University of Chicago Press, 1996.

Siskin, Clifford. *The Work of Writing: Literature and Social Change in Britain 1700–1830*. Baltimore: Johns Hopkins University Press, 1998.
Sitter, John. *Arguments of Augustan Wit*. Cambridge University Press, 1991.
  Literary Loneliness in Mid-Eighteenth-Century England. Ithaca: Cornell University Press, 1982.
Stallybrass, Peter and Allon White. *The Politics and Poetics of Transgression*. Ithaca: Cornell University Press, 1986.
Sutton, John. *Philosophy and Memory Traces: Descartes to Connectionism*. Cambridge University Press, 1998.
Terdiman, Richard. *Present Past: Modernity and the Memory Crisis*. Ithaca: Cornell University Press, 1993.
Trumpener, Katie. *Bardic Nationalism: The Romantic Novel and the British Empire*. Princeton University Press, 1997.
Vernant, Jean-Pierre. *Myth and Thought Among the Greeks*. Trans. Janet Lloyd. London: Routledge, 1983.
Walker, William. *Locke, Literary Criticism, and Philosophy*. Cambridge University Press, 1994.
Warner, William B. "The Elevation of the Novel in England: Hegemony and Literary History." *ELH*, 59 (1992), 577–96.
Weinbrot, Howard D. *Britannia's Issue: The Rise of British Literature from Dryden to Ossian*. Cambridge University Press, 1993.
Weinsheimer, Joel. "Fiction and the Force of Example." In *The Idea of the Novel in the Eighteenth Century*., Ed. Robert W. Uphaus. East Lansing: Colleagues Press, 1988.
Weisberg, Robert. "Proclaiming Trials as Narratives: Premises and Pretenses." In *Law's Stories*. Ed. Brooks and Gewirtz.
Wellek, René. *A History of Modern Criticism: 1750–1950: The Later Eighteenth Century*. London: Jonathan Cape, 1955.
Welsh, Alexander. *Strong Representations: Narrative and Circumstantial Evidence in England*. Baltimore: Johns Hopkins University Press, 1992.
West, Robin. *Narrative, Authority, and Law*. Ann Arbor: University of Michigan Press, 1993.
White, Hayden. *The Content of the Form: Narrative, Discourse and Historical Representation*. Baltimore: Johns Hopkins University Press, 1987.
  Tropics of Discourse: Essays in Cultural Criticism. Baltimore: Johns Hopkins University Press, 1978.
White, James Boyd. *Heracles' Bow: Essays on the Rhetoric and Poetics of the Law*. Madison: University of Wisconsin Press, 1985.
Zimmerman, Everett. *The Boundaries of Fiction: History and the Eighteenth-Century Novel*. Ithaca: Cornell University Press, 1996.
Zomchick, John. *Family and the Law in Eighteenth-Century Fiction*. Cambridge University Press, 1993.

Index

Abrams, M. H., 55
Adams, William, 88
Addison, Joseph, 34, 39, 59, 92, 104, 115, 117, 119, 120, 127, 147, 148, 155
   The Campaign, 53
   on Milton, 109, 110
admiration, 47, 50, 177 n. 49
Akenside, Mark, 46, 112, 123
Althusser, Louis, 132
Anderson, Benedict, 26, 64
Alkon, Paul, 32
aporia, 18–23, 26, 36, 76, 153, 157, 167
Aristotle, 11, 19, 20, 22, 41, 43, 45
Arnold, Matthew, 142
atonement, 31, 34–35
attentiveness, 26, 27–29, 33, 36, 48
Atterbury, Francis, 56
Auchinleck, 65–66
Augustine, 11, 19, 20, 22, 31, 32, 84, 139, 171 n. 38

Backscheider, Paula, 119
Bacon, Francis, 39, 94–95, 96
Barnes, Joshua, 144, 158
Barth, Karl, 34
Battle of the Books, 142–43
Baxter, Richard, 96
Beattie, James, 88
Benjamin, Walter, 26, 134, 163
Bentley, Richard, 158
Berlin, Isaiah, 165
Bhabha, Homi, 69
biography, 1, 12, 28–29, 89–91, 155–57, 159, 164
   and poetic character, 99–101, 103, 107–08, 112–13, 115, 117, 119, 139–40, 155–56, 164–65
   and fiction, 91–92, 97–102, 107, 118, 120
   and history, 96–97, 117
Birch, Thomas, 158
Blackmore, Richard, 119, 120

Blackstone, Sir William, 64
Blair, Hugh, 82, 162
Blake, Admiral Robert, 104
Bloom, Harold, 108
Boerhaave, Herman, 34
Bogel, Fredric V., 4–5, 7
Boileau, Nicolas Despreaux, 41, 42, 111, 142
Bolingbroke, Henry St. John, Viscount, 94, 165
Book of Common Prayer, 32, 33, 174 n. 90
Boswell, James, 1–2, 3, 6–7, 14, 15, 18, 30, 34, 43, 61, 78, 79, 81, 91, 100, 118
   and Hume, 80, 83–84
   and inheritance, 65–68
   and slavery, 68–69
Bouhours, Dominique, 42
Bradley, F. H., 94, 163–64
Brooks, Peter, 72, 133, 169 n. 18
Broome, William, 144
Bunyan, John, 156
Burke, Edmund, 61, 110, 111
Burkhardt, Jacob, 94
Burnet, James, Lord Monboddo, 53
Burney, Frances, 156
Butler, Joseph, 78
Butler, Samuel, 100, 114–18, 120, 124
   Hudibras, 115–18, 159

canon, the, 9–10, 12
   see also nation-building
Carew, Thomas, 45
Carlyle, Thomas, 94
Cervantes, Miguel de, 72, 156
Chambers, Robert, 61–64, 68
Charles I, 113
Charlton, Walter, 48
Chartier, Roger, 165–66
Chaucer, Geoffrey, 42, 124
Chetwood, Knightly, 152
Cheynel, Francis, 104
Christensen, Jerome, 86

Clarendon, Edward Hyde, Earl of, 94, 95, 96, 97
Cleveland, John, 56
Coke, Sir Edward, 64
Comenius, 106
commemoration, 15, 16, 29, 50, 99, 118–21
comprehensiveness, 42, 50, 124–27, 137–39, 150, 151, 161
Congreve, William, 101
Cooke, William, 15
Cowley, Abraham, 43–44, 46, 51, 55, 56–59, 101, 110, 115, 124, 127, 129, 161
  Anacreontiques, 49
  Davideis, The, 34, 43, 48
  Essays in Verse and Prose, 49, 56
  Miscellanies, The, 43, 56
  Pindaric Odes, 56
Crane, R. S., 159
criticism, 12–13, 36, 37–39, 43–55, 57–58
Cromwell, Oliver, 113
Cudworth, Ralph, 75
curiosity, 29

Dacier, Anne Lefevre, Madame, 142, 144, 146, 152
Davidson, Donald, 54–55
Davis, Philip, 32
death, 27–28, 31, 32
Defoe, Daniel, 91–92
De Man, Paul, 11, 24
Denham, Sir John, 112, 142
  Cooper's Hill, 52–55
Dennis, John, 17, 110
Derrida, Jacques, 11, 13, 37, 57, 63, 144
Descartes, René, 20, 75
Detienne, Marcel, 150
difference, 30, 70–71, 72, 73, 74, 76, 88, 121, 125, 166–67
  see also Johnson, and difference
Digby, Kenelm, 20
Diogenes Laertius, 118
Donne, John, 43, 44, 45–52, 55, 56–58, 101
  "Valediction: Of Weeping," 46–47
  "A Nocturnal upon S. Lucies day," 47–48, 50
Dorset, Charles Sackville, Earl of, 56
Drayton, Michael, 45
Dryden, John, 12, 24–26, 29, 34, 39, 40, 41, 42, 44, 46, 54, 57, 59, 100, 101, 110, 111, 112, 113, 115, 117, 122–27, 129, 142, 143, 144, 153, 161
  "Alexander's Feast," 135–38
  "Essay on Dramatick Poesy," 166–67
  "The First Book of Homer's *Ilias*," 145–53
  Heroic plays, 146, 148
  Horace *Odes III.29*, 24–26, 29, 35, 125

Indian Emperor, 51–52
Preface to *Examen Poeticum*, 146
Preface to *Fables*, 111, 150
Preface to Virgil's *Pastorals*, 53
Prose, 124–25
Translations, 125–27, 146, 148
at Will's Coffee House, 98
  see also Johnson, "Life of Dryden"
Duff, William, 162

Ehrenpreis, Irvin, 131
Eliot, T. S., 35, 39, 43, 46, 47, 102, 153
Elphinston, James, 25, 118
Empson, William, 55
Enlightenment, 13
Eustathius, 144
evidence, 70–77
  and Christian miracles, 80–83, 85
  and circumstance, 78, 80
  and death, 84
  and narrative, 91–92, 96
  see also Johnson, on law
experience, 29–30, 31–33, 35, 39–40, 41, 45, 57–58, 70–88, 98, 117, 125, 132–33, 138, 155, 164, 165

familiar letter, 127–30
Fanshawe, Sir Richard, 142
Fielding, Henry, 37, 38, 91–92, 100
Fish, Stanley, 5–6, 37, 87, 97
Foucault, Michel, 12, 13, 26, 72, 99, 132, 154, 159, 163
Francis, Philip, 25
Fulford, Tim, 4, 169 n. 24

Gadamer, Hans-Georg, 69
Gardner, Helen, 48
Garrick, David, 16, 27
Gay, John, 155
generality, 50–51, 55
Gibbon, Edward, 81, 94, 95
Glanvill, Joseph, 20
Godwin, William, 94
Goldsmith, Oliver, 13, 160, 165
Gray, Thomas, 123, 128, 161, 162
Greene, Donald, 51
Grey, Zachary, 116
Grotius, Hugo, 63

Hagstrum, Jean, 50, 55, 175 n. 5
Hale, Matthew, 63–64, 67, 90
Halifax, Charles Montague, Marquess of, 100
Hamilton, William, 1, 61, 62
Hammond, Paul, 125
happiness, 70, 73, 76

Hartlib, Samuel, 106
Hartman, Geoffrey, 11, 36, 57, 101, 158
Hawkins, Sir John, 42, 61
Haywood, Eliza, 156
Hazlitt, William, 42
Hector, Edmund, 14
Herbert, George, 33
Hill, Christopher, 102
Hill, Geoffrey, 34, 118, 120
Hinnant, Charles H, 73
history, 1, 11, 12, 16, 18–27, 31, 32, 33, 44, 66–67, 68–69, 76, 77, 80–81, 85, 115, 120, 131, 136, 138, 155–56
  and biography, 94, 96–98, 164
  and forgery, 162–63
  and historiographical discourse, 7, 90, 118, 133, 159–63, 164, 165–67
  and novel, 91, 94
  and translation, 163–67
Hogarth, William, 27–29
Holmes, Richard, 91
Homer, 12, 77, 112, 124, 134–35, 142, 144–52, 153
Hooke, Robert, 20
Hooker, Richard, 28
Hopkins, Gerard Manley, 33
Horace, 17, 18, 24–26, 29, 41, 143
Hughes, John, 53
Hume, David, 11, 16, 19, 21, 63, 76, 77, 78–88, 94, 95, 160
  Essay Concerning Human Understanding, 79
  "Of Miracles," 75, 79–82, 85–86
  on *Ossian* and evidence, 82
  Treatise of Human Nature, 75, 80, 86–88
Hurd, Richard, 99, 162
Hutchinson, Lucy, 96

Jacobitism, 62
James, Henry, 107
Johnson, Samuel
  "An Account of the Harleian Library," 62
  Dictionary of the English Language, 9, 10, 22, 40, 42, 48, 54, 62, 63, 67, 70, 71, 75, 82, 107, 110, 113, 118, 157, 171 n. 38
  "Epitaph for Hogarth," 27–29
  Idler, 10–11, 30, 31, 32
  "Idler," No. 84, 90
  Journey to the Western Islands of Scotland, 62, 65, 70, 162–63
  Letters, 118, 129–30
  Life of Savage, 96, 154
  Lives of the English Poets, 9, 11, 12, 16, 35, 36, 38, 41, 43, 46, 59, 62, 89–91, 96, 97, 98, 99, 100, 101, 102, 105, 115, 118, 120–21, 122–57, 158, 159, 160–67
  "Life of Addison," 53, 90, 96, 99, 127
  "Life of Akenside," 161
  "Life of Butler," 11, 90, 114–18
  "Life of Collins," 161
  "Life of Congreve," 90
  "Life of Cowley," 40, 43, 49, 52, 58, 90, 99, 111
  "Life of Denham," 52–55
  "Life of Dorset," 56
  "Life of Dryden," 12, 51–52, 90, 99, 101, 122–27, 145–54, 166–67
  "Life of Gay," 90, 102
  "Life of Gray," 90, 99, 161–63
  "Life of Milton," 11, 30, 48, 90, 96, 99, 101, 102–14, 120
  "Life of Otway," 90
  "Life of Pope," 12, 42, 90, 99, 101, 122–24, 127–34, 138, 140–54, 161
  "Life of Rochester," 90
  "Life of Shenstone," 90
  "Life of Smith," 15, 98
  "Life of Thomson," 90, 161
  "Life of Waller," 33, 56, 90, 141
  "Life of West," 161
  "Life of Young," 161
  London, 9, 161
  "On the Death of Dr. Robert Levet," 16
  Parliamentary Debates, 62
  Prayers, 31–33, 118
  Preface to the *Dictionary*, 8, 14–15, 16, 21–22, 38, 39, 113
  Preface to Dodsley's *The Preceptor*, 62
  Preface to Shakespeare, 48, 49, 58, 77, 97
  Rambler, 10, 18, 23, 24–26, 39, 62, 102, 156
  "Rambler" No. 2, 23, 72
  "Rambler" No. 4, 37, 92–93, 156
  "Rambler" No. 5, 23
  "Rambler" No. 41, 18, 24–26, 29, 32, 33, 35, 67
  "Rambler" No. 60, 89–90, 96, 164
  "Rambler" No. 122, 95–96
  "Rambler" No. 152, 129
  "Rambler" No. 168, 141, 161
  "Rambler" No. 170, 156–57
  "Rambler" No. 171, 156–57
  Rasselas, 17, 70–77, 86–87, 101, 121, 161–62, 166
  Review of Jenyns' *A Free Inquiry into the Nature and Origin of Evil*, 49
  Sermons, 31–33, 173 n. 83
  The Vanity of Human Wishes, 35, 97–98, 161
  and anecdote, 98, 124
  and aporia, 36, 76, 153, 157, 167
  and authority, 1–13, 15, 34, 57–58, 60–61, 69, 118, 162–63

and authorship, 2–4, 11, 90, 123–24, 159
  see also Johnson, and character
and the body, 26, 34, 35, 53–54, 60, 132–34, 154
and blank verse, 112
and character, 12, 58–59, 97, 98, 99–101, 103, 104, 106, 107–08, 112–13, 114–18, 119, 120, 123, 129, 132, 138–40, 153, 159, 164–65
  see also Johnson, and authorship
and Christianity, 31–34, 76, 78, 79–81, 85, 140–41
and comedy, 57, 60, 67–68, 121, 149–51
and consciousness, 16–18, 20, 22, 26, 30–34, 35
and conversation, 114
and death, 22, 27–28, 30–31, 60–61, 83–84, 90, 97, 119, 121
and difference, 13, 16, 53–55
  see also difference
and double reading, 24
and epicureanism, 48–49, 141
and the erotic, 25–26
on Falstaff, 148
and genius, 138–39
and the *Gentleman's Magazine*, 62
and God, 60–61, 75
and the heroic, 82, 108, 111, 113
on historical narrative, 94–97
  see also narrative/narratology
on Homer, 140–42, 143–44, 151–54
on Hume, 77–88
  see also Hume
and language, 8–9, 12, 16, 33, 34, 37, 41–42, 45–55, 57–58, 64–65, 69–70, 71–72, 74, 75, 88, 99, 112, 115–16, 125, 126, 134, 151–54, 157, 161–63, 164, 165, 174 n. 95
and law, 6–7, 13, 34–35, 60–70
  see also law
and limits, 13, 17–19, 25, 30, 31, 34, 42–43, 60, 64, 67, 70–88, 97, 117–18, 120, 153–54
and melancholia, 21, 35, 171 n. 33
on the *mens divinior*, 101–02, 107–08
and metaphor, 43–59, 73, 100
on music, 135–36
on the novel, 92–95
  see also novel
and origins, 66
and performativity, 6–8, 34, 101, 126, 165
and political engagement, 164–65
and the present, 11, 17, 18–26, 29–30, 31–32, 34–37, 76, 98, 111, 118, 121, 125, 159–60, 164, 166–67
on religious verse, 33, 109, 119–20

and rhetoric, 6–9, 37, 66–70, 85, 122, 129–31
and sexual difference, 8
and speech, 60–61
and the sublime, 108, 110–111
and textuality, 36, 37, 57–58, 60–61, 69, 162–63, 165
and translation, 12, 24–26, 29, 53–54, 58, 143–44, 159–60, 163
and women's experience, 67–68, 156–57
Jonson, Ben, 50–51
  "On my first Sonne," 50–51

Kames, Henry Home, Lord, 144, 160
Karl, Frederick, 97
Kermode, Frank, 25, 26, 29, 45
Kernan, Alvin, 9–10
Kerrigan, William, 105
Keymer, Tom, 129
Knight, Joseph, 68
Knolles, Richard, 95–96

La Motte, Antoine Houdar de, 144
Langton, Bennet, 67
Lauder, William, 102
law, 60–77, 113–14
  Common Law, 63–64
  and the constitution, 64, 67
  and narrative, 62, 69, 78, 85, 120, 155, 159
  and enforceability, 63
  and evidence, 74, 78
  and experience, 78, 85
  and grace, 114–18
  and inheritance, 65–68
  and rhetoric, 66, 68
  and slavery, 68–69
  Vinerian lectures, 61–64
  see also Johnson, and law
Law, Jules, 92
Law, William, 31
Leavis, F. R., 39, 102
Le Bossu, René, 109
Le Goff, Jacques, 32
Lennox, Charlotte, 93, 156
les lieux de mémoire, 1, 11, 12, 114, 120, 160, 163–67
L'Estrange, Roger, 114
Lipking, Lawrence, 98
literary history, 122, 125, 140, 158–63
Locke, John, 8, 11, 14, 16, 19, 20, 21, 22, 23, 30, 39, 40, 54, 63, 64, 70, 71, 74–75
  Essay Concerning Human Understanding, 20, 74, 76
  Second Treatise of Government, 65
  and personal identity, 74–75

Longinus, 41, 111
Lucretius, 42
Lyttleton, George, 123

Macaulay, Thomas Babington, Lord, 94, 102, 104
Machiavelli, Nicolo, 94
Mack, Maynard, 130–31
Macpherson, James, 82, 162–63, 165
Marvell, Andrew, 42
Mason, H. A., 147
Mason, John, 53
McGann, Jerome, 159
memory, 1, 9–11, 12, 14–27, 31–36, 40, 58–59, 61, 67, 74, 77, 88, 95, 98, 111, 122, 164, 167
   and anecdote, 98
   and the body, 133–34, 140, 154
   and commemoration, 120–21
   and Common Law, 63–64
   and death, 134
   as engrammatology, 20, 21, 22, 89
   and history, 96, 158
   as moral reasoning, 77
   and personal identity, 74–75, 80
   and poetic character, 99, 100, 102–08, 114, 115, 117–18, 120, 154, 155
   see also Johnson, and character
   as story-telling, 19, 120, 159
   and translation, 144, 152–53
Merleau-Ponty, Maurice, 23
Milton, John, 15, 30, 44, 46, 50, 59, 100, 101, 102–14, 115, 116, 120, 124, 129, 153, 156, 161
   Defence of the People, 113
   "Lycidas," 48, 128
   Paradise Lost, 29, 30, 33–34, 102–03, 104, 106, 107–114, 115
   Paradise Regained, 112
   Samson Agonistes, 112
   and blindness, 113–14
   and education, 105–06
   and politics, 103–05, 113–14
   and religion, 106–07
   and versification, 134–35
Miner, Earl, 116, 117
Mink, Louis, 99
Montaigne, Michael, 16, 29, 33, 42, 77
More, Henry, 20
Mossner, Ernest, 84
mourning, 21

narrrative/narratology, 1, 12, 19–27, 29, 30, 32, 35, 69, 70–77, 85, 91, 92–99, 100, 101, 104, 110, 115, 120, 126, 133, 151, 155, 159, 161–63, 164, 166–67

nation-building, 99, 153, 158, 162, 163
   see also the canon
nature, 11, 12, 22, 26, 36–42, 44, 45, 50–52, 57–58, 79–88, 100, 111–14, 115, 117, 120, 123, 124–26, 129, 143, 148, 152–53, 155, 159, 161, 164, 166–67
New Criticism, 39
New Testament, 120
Nora, Pierre, 1, 163, 164, 167
novel, 11, 37–39, 78, 133
   and biography, 96, 97, 155–56
   and characterization, 100–01, 156
   and history, 91–94, 97
   see also Johnson, on the novel
Nussbaum, Felicity, 156, 157

Oldham, John, 142
Oldys, William, 158
Olney, James, 19, 22
Osborne, Sir William, 127

Parker, Blanford, 33, 117
Parker, G. F., 175 n. 5
Parnell, Thomas, 59, 101, 144
Parr, Samuel, 141
Pascal, Blaise, 84
pathos, 50, 110
Paulson, Ronald, 28
Peacham, Henry, 90
Percy, Thomas, 160
Perkins, David, 159–60
Perrault, Charles, 144
Phillips, Edward, 104
Phillips, Mark, 164
Plato, 19, 22, 29
pleasure, 39–40, 42, 47, 49, 109–110, 112, 114, 125
Plutarch, 118, 136
Pomfret, John, 101
Pope, Alexander, 12, 39, 41–42, 44, 46, 50, 54, 59, 100, 101, 110, 112, 115, 117, 122–24, 127–34, 138–40, 161
   correspondence, 127–31
   Essay on Criticism, 41–42, 134–35
   Essay on Man, 151
   Iliad translation, 127, 140, 142, 143, 144–53, 160
   Imitations of Horace, 159, 161
   "Ode for Musick on St. Cecilia's Day," 136–38
   Rape of the Lock, 133, 140, 141, 142
   Sporus portrait, 131
   and the body, 132–34
   and artifice, 127–32, 154
   and Martha Blount, 98

and refinement, 42, 134–35, 138, 147, 160–61
and satire, 130
see also Johnson, and "Life of Pope"
Porson, Richard, 158
Porter, Roy, 65
postmodernity, 12–13
power, 127, 131–33, 153–54, 156
psychoanalysis, 16, 89
Pufendorf, Samuel von, 63

Quine, Willard, 11

Rader, Ralph, 100, 155
Raleigh, Walter, 83, 95
Ramsay, Allan, 95
Rawson, Claude, 23
recollection, 28–29, 30, 32, 40, 166–67
    and biography, 98, 165
    and poetry, 123, 138
    and psychoanalysis, 89
    see also repetition
Reddick, Allen, 34, 110
remembrance, 21, 22, 27, 40, 120
    see also memory; recollection
repetition, 28–29, 30, 32, 71, 75–77, 99
    see also memory; recollection
Richardson, Samuel, 37, 38, 91–92, 93, 100, 156
Richetti, John, 155
Ricks, Christopher, 34–35, 43–44, 58, 102
Ricoeur, Paul, 29
Robertson, William, 95
Rochester, John Wilmot, Earl of, 142, 155
romance, 92–93, 96
Rousseau, J-J, 20
Ruffhead, Owen, 127, 130, 140
Ryle, Gilbert, 11

sacrament, 32–32
Salmasius, 105, 114
Say, Samuel, 53
Scarry, Elaine, 133
Scholes, Robert, 165
Shakespeare, William, 12, 22, 28, 37, 38, 39–40, 42, 44, 50, 51–52, 69, 77, 99 101, 108–09, 110, 121, 138, 156, 158–59
Shaw, William, 14–15
Shenstone, William, 123
Sherman, Stuart, 25–26
Sidney, Sir Philip, 45
Siebert, Donald, 88
sin, 34
Siskin, Clifford, 157
Sitter, John, 154

Smith, Adam, 86, 162
Socrates, 29, 30, 105
Spence, Joseph, 135
Spenser, Edmund, 44, 45
Sprat, Thomas, 43, 127
Stanley, Thomas, 48
Steiner, George, 18
Stoicism, 141
Suarez, Michael, 33
sublime, the, 50, 73–74, 108, 110, 111, 112, 114, 116
Sutton, John, 20
Swift, Jonathan, 23, 88, 117, 129, 155

Tate, Allen, 52–53
Taylor, Charles, 75
Taylor, Jeremy, 31, 118
Temmer, Mark, 87
Temple, Sir William, 10, 127
Terdiman, Richard, 18
Terrasson, Abbé Jean, 144
Thompson, E. P., 26
Thomson, James, 46, 112
Thrale, Hester, 60, 129–30
Tickell, Thomas, 127, 143
time/temporality, 1, 9, 11, 17, 19, 20, 21, 23, 24, 25, 26, 27, 29, 31, 32, 35, 66–67, 68–70, 76, 90, 95, 98, 99, 110, 116, 117, 120, 121, 125, 137, 150–51, 155, 159–60
Toland, John, 104
tragedy, 35, 98–99, 120
translation, 12, 24–26, 58, 114, 121, 122–23, 142–53, 160–63
truth, 6, 7, 24, 36–37, 39–41, 42–43

Upton, John, 99

Venturo, David, 28
Vernant, Jean-Pierre, 150
Vico, Giambattista, 20, 171 n. 27
Vida, Marco Girolamo, 134
Virgil, 42, 124, 134, 142, 143, 144, 152, 153
Vives, Juan Luis, 106
Voltaire, Françoise-Marie Arouet, 111

Waller, Edmund, 33, 56, 104, 112, 113, 141
Walmsley, Gilbert, 15–16, 61, 98
Walsh, William, 41, 127
Warburton, William, 104, 158
Warton, Joseph, 17, 99, 138, 140, 158, 161–62
Warton, Thomas, 17, 99, 158, 161–62
Watts, Isaac, 22, 34, 59, 119, 120, 155
Wechselblatt, Martin, 4–5
Wedderburn, John, 68
Weisberg, Robert, 7, 69

Wellek, René, 52–53, 175 n. 5
Welsh, Alexander, 78, 85
White, Hayden, 29, 69, 74, 120, 155, 165
White, James Boyd, 13, 77
Winn, James, 128
wit, 26, 36, 41–52, 57–58, 161
Wollstonecraft, Mary, 156

Wood, Robert, 144
Wordsworth, William, 12, 21, 26, 58

Young, Edward, 17–18, 110, 112, 119, 161

Zimmerman, Everett, 155
Zomchick, John, 68

OHIO UNIVERSITY LIBRARY

Please return this book as soon as you have finished with it. In order to avoid a fine it must be returned by the latest date stamped below. All books are subject to recall after two weeks or immediately if needed for reserve.

JUN 1 5 2009

RECEIVED
DEC 1 5 2009

CF